EARLY COLD WAR SPIES

Communism was never a popular ideology in America, but the vehemence of American anticommunism varied from passive disdain in the 1920s to fervent hostility in the early years of the Cold War. Nothing so stimulated the white-hot anticommunism of the late 1940s and 1950s more than a series of spy trials that revealed that American Communists had cooperated with Soviet espionage against the United States and had assisted in stealing the technical secrets of the atomic bomb as well as penetrating the U.S. State Department, the Treasury Department, and the White House itself. This book reviews the major spy cases of the early Cold War (Hiss-Chambers, Rosenberg, Bentley, Gouzenko, Coplon, *Amerasia*, and others) and the often-frustrating clashes between the exacting rules of the American criminal justice system and the requirements of effective counterespionage.

John Earl Haynes is a 20th-Century Political Historian in the Manuscript Division of the Library of Congress, Washington, D.C. He received his Ph.D. from the University of Minnesota. He is the author or editor of four books: *Calvin Coolidge and the Coolidge Era: Essays on the History of the 1920s* (editor, 1998); *Red Scare or Red Menace? American Communism and Anticommunism in the Cold War Era* (1996); *Communism and Anti-Communism in the United States: An Annotated Guide to Historical Writings* (1987); and *Dubious Alliance: The Making of Minnesota's DFL Party* (1984).

Harvey Klehr is the Andrew W. Mellon Professor of Politics and History at Emory University in Atlanta. He received his Ph.D. from the University of North Carolina, Chapel Hill. He is the author of five books, *Communist Cadre: The Social Background of the American Communist Party Elite* (1978); *The Heyday of American Communism: The Depression Decade* (1984); *Biographical Dictionary of the American Left* (1986); *Far Left of Center: The American Radical Left Today* (1988); and *The Amerasia Spy Case: Prelude to McCarthyism* (1996). He was honored with the Emory Williams Distinguished Teaching Award from Emory College in 1983.

Haynes and Klehr have jointly coauthored five books: *In Denial: Historians, Communism and Espionage* (2002); *Venona: Decoding Soviet Espionage in America* (1999); *The Soviet World of American Communism* (1998); *The Secret World of American Communism* (1995); and *The American Communist Movement: Storming Heaven Itself* (1992). In addition, their articles have appeared in scholarly journals including *International Newsletter of Communist Studies*, *Film History*, *American Communist History*, *Journal of Cold War Studies*, *Labor History*, *Labour History Review*, and *Problems of Post-Communism*, as well as in such journals of opinion as *Commentary*, the *New Republic*, *New York Review of Books*, *Wall Street Journal*, *American Spectator*, and the *Weekly Standard*.

CAMBRIDGE ESSENTIAL HISTORIES

Series Editor
Donald Critchlow, Saint Louis University

Cambridge Essential Histories is devoted to introducing critical events, periods, or individuals in history to students. Volumes in this series emphasize narrative as a means of familiarizing students with historical analysis. In this series leading scholars focus on topics in European, American, Asian, Latin American, Middle Eastern, African, and world history through thesis-driven, concise volumes designed for survey and upper-division undergraduate history courses. The books contain an introduction that acquaints readers with the historical event and reveals the book's thesis; narrative chapters that cover the chronology of the event or problem; and a concluding summary that provides the historical interpretation and analysis. Volumes also include a bibliographic essay.

Early Cold War Spies

The Espionage Trials That Shaped American Politics

JOHN EARL HAYNES

Washington, D.C.

HARVEY KLEHR

Emory University

CAMBRIDGE
UNIVERSITY PRESS

CAMBRIDGE UNIVERSITY PRESS

Cambridge, New York, Melbourne, Madrid, Cape Town, Singapore, São Paulo

Cambridge University Press
32 Avenue of the Americas, New York, NY 10013-2473, USA

www.cambridge.org
Information on this title: www.cambridge.org/9780521857383

© John Earl Haynes and Harvey Klehr 2006

First published 2006

Printed in the United States of America

A catalog record for this publication is available from the British Library.

Library of Congress Cataloging in Publication Data

Haynes, John Earl.
Early Cold War spies : the espionage trials that shaped American politics / John Earl Haynes,
Harvey Klehr.
p.   cm. – (Cambridge essential histories)
Includes bibliographical references and index.
ISBN 0-521-85738-4 (hardback) – ISBN 0-521-67407-7 (pbk.)
1. Spies – Soviet Union – History – 20th century.   2. Espionage, Soviet – History – 20th
century.   3. Trials (Espionage) – United States – History – 20th century.
4. Communism – Soviet Union – History – 20th century.   5. Anti-communist movements – United
States – History – 20th century.   6. United States – Politics and government – 1945–1953.
I. Klehr, Harvey.   II. Title.   III. Series.
UB271.R9H388   2006
364.1′31–dc22   2006002127

ISBN-13   978-0-521-85738-3 hardback
ISBN-10   0-521-85738-4 hardback

ISBN-13   978-0-521-67407-2 paperback
ISBN-10   0-521-67407-7 paperback

John Earl Haynes

To my son Joshua

Harvey Klehr

To Mickey and Marilyn Steinberg, my father-in-law and mother-in-law,
with love, admiration, and gratitude

Contents

Series Editor's Foreword

In the late 1940s, the shock waves that followed the sensational news of Communist spy rings operating deep inside the government in Washington, D.C., affected American politics, culture, and society for the next decade. The first reverberations of spy activities began in the summer of 1945 when six people, including a high-ranking State Department official, were arrested for passing classified government documents to the left-leaning journal, *Amerasia*, edited by Philip Jaffe, a friend of Communist Party chieftain Earl Browder. Shortly afterward, the American public learned of other spy operations through the revelations of Elizabeth Bentley, a former Communist and courier for a Soviet spy network; Igor Gouzenko, an intelligence officer working in the Soviet embassy in Canada; and Whittaker Chambers, a former underground Communist agent in the 1930s.

These reports revealed the existence of an atomic spy ring headed by Julius and Ethel Rosenberg; two spy rings operating in Washington, D.C., that implicated high officials in the Roosevelt administration, including White House aide Lauchlin Currie, Assistant Secretary of the Treasury Harry Dexter White, and Alger Hiss, a former State Department official in the Roosevelt and Truman administrations. Other cases followed.

Fears of widespread Communist infiltration into American institutions intensified as U.S. relations with the Soviet Union deteriorated, China fell to the Communists in 1949, and the Korean War began in 1950. Republicans used the spy cases to attack Roosevelt's New Deal government and its successor, the Truman administration, for having ignored the insidious nature of Soviet communism. The Truman administration responded by pursuing policies to root out disloyal employees in government. At the same time, liberal anti-Communists, through groups such as the Americans for Democratic Action (ADA), joined efforts to regain control of unions, political organizations, and student groups in which Communists had gained control. In Hollywood, studio executives blacklisted Communist screenwriters and actors who refused to swear loyalty oaths to the United States.

The issue of Soviet espionage raised important issues for a democratic system founded on the rule of law and the protection of civil liberties. The legal cases of American citizens accused of Soviet espionage revealed the precarious balance between protecting national security and preserving individual civil liberties. Government officials seeking legal prosecution of those accused of Soviet espionage found that their cases were often made difficult because their evidence of guilt was based on classified intelligence that, if revealed, would be of use to Soviet spies. As a result, catching one spy meant providing active Soviet espionage agents with detailed information about American intelligence operations. In some cases, federal officials decided it was not worth it. As a consequence, a number of American agents working for the Soviet Union went scot-free.

John Earl Haynes and Harvey Klehr tell a dramatic story that readers will find hard to tear themselves away from. The authors present a complex story in a coherent and engaging manner. Readers interested in Soviet espionage will appreciate the authors' clear organization, readability, and judicious approach. In telling the history of Soviet espionage and the legal cases that followed, Haynes and Klehr raise profound questions for American democracy, foremost among them, Can a balance be struck between the security interests of a nation and the rights of citizens enjoying the liberties of a democratic nation? Such questions are not easily resolved, but they remain fundamental to a democracy such as ours.

Donald T. Critchlow
General Editor
Cambridge Essential Histories

1

Introduction

EARLY COLD WAR SPY CASES

A T THE HEIGHT OF THE EARLY COLD WAR, IN THE LATE 1940S and early 1950s, newspaper headlines repeatedly trumpeted the exposure of yet another nest of Communist spies or saboteurs who had infiltrated American laboratories or labor unions or government agencies. Many Americans worried that a Communist "fifth column," more loyal to the Soviet Union than to the United States, had burrowed into their institutions and had to be exposed and removed.

The issue of Soviet espionage became a U.S. obsession, and domestic security dominated public discourse. Legislative committees vied with one another to expose Communists. The executive branch labored to root out disloyal government employees. The courts wrestled with the balance between constitutional rights and societal self-protection. The trade-union movement expelled from its ranks those unions with hidden Communist leadership. Liberalism, the dominant political movement of the era, fought an internal civil war over whether Communists were legitimate participants in the New Deal coalition, a struggle that ended with the triumph of anti-Communist liberalism and the assignment of Communists and their allies to the fringes of politics.

There was a widespread consensus that Soviet espionage was a serious problem, American Communists assisted the Soviets, and some high officials had betrayed the United States. But in the 1960s this consensus disintegrated. The use of anticommunism for partisan purposes by Senator Joseph McCarthy in the 1950s produced a backlash of incredulity about the extent of the domestic Communist problem. The once-significant presence of the Communist Party, USA (CPUSA) in mainstream politics in some states and the trade-union movement was a fading memory, the hundreds of secret Communists who had worked for the U.S. government were long gone from federal service, and Soviet espionage was only a fraction of

1

what it had been in its heyday in the early 1940s. In retrospect, some wondered if the entire threat had been imagined or drastically exaggerated. Obsessive anticommunism was blamed for foreign policy disasters like the Vietnam War and violations of civil liberties. Revisionist historians challenged the idea that internal security had been a serious problem and accused government officials of cynically and deliberately orchestrating public fear about the issue to advance narrow political and ideological interests and to justify a war economy. In the "New Left" movement of the late 1960s and 1970s and the militant wing of the anti–Vietnam War campaign there were radicals who defined themselves as Marxist revolutionaries of some sort or who were "pro-Communist" in some fashion. But while the CPUSA found a small role in those campaigns, for the most part the student New Left activists of that era operated independently of the small and ineffectual CPUSA and without direct ties to the intelligence services of a hostile foreign power.

In the early years of the twenty-first century, in an age when communism has virtually disappeared from domestic political life and is in eclipse around the world, it is difficult to recall just how formidable it once appeared to be or why serious people were able to justify devoting so many resources to combating it. There are in 2006 probably fewer than two thousand increasingly elderly members of the American Communist Party.

The end of the Cold War in the late 1980s marked the beginning of a major reassessment of twentieth-century history. Such a dramatic and portentous event threw new light on a whole epoch and demanded a rethinking of how and why it happened. Just as important was the limited but dramatic opening of some key archives containing long-buried secrets of the Cold War, which enabled historians to see some major controversies for the first time in more complete detail. Long-contested issues could now be settled with dramatic new evidence.

No branch of history was so affected as the one studying American communism and its relationship with Soviet espionage. After decades of acrimonious debate, hard evidence emerged to end arguments about the guilt or innocence of some of the iconic figures of the McCarthy era. While debate and controversy about some issues remain among historians, the main contours of the story of Soviet espionage against the United States are now largely understood.

The availability of new evidence offers opportunities to look at old problems through clearer lenses. Just as we now know in considerable detail the story of Soviet espionage, we also can look back at the ways in which the American public learned about the problem and how the American government dealt with it. In particular, we can return to the occasions when the executive branch attempted to prosecute those involved in espionage and evaluate not only its successes and failures but also the limitations and difficulties imposed on it by the American legal system. New information about specific cases permits us to assess the stratagems employed by government prosecutors and defense attorneys. One of the most striking facts, and to many people likely disturbing, is that hundreds of Americans spied for the Soviet Union but only a few were ever prosecuted. One possible conclusion is that the Soviet intelligence service was extraordinarily successful and American counterintelligence inept. While there is some truth to this argument, it is not the whole story.

The issue of Soviet espionage can help illuminate something about the American legal system and the role of trials in shaping the public perception of historical events. Trials are inherently dramatic events. They are public occasions during which individuals are confronted with charges that they have violated the norms and rules of the society in which they live. In federal criminal trials, the United States government is arrayed against the accused. The American system of jurisprudence – with its insistence on public trials, an adversarial system with contending lawyers representing the state and the accused, a neutral judge deciding on questions of law and presiding over the contest, and a jury of peers listening to the evidence and then rendering a verdict on guilt or innocence – is particularly well suited to turning these events into spectacles.

Early Cold War Spy Trials

Each of the following six chapters examines one or more of the early Cold War spy cases that shaped public attitudes toward the nature of the Soviet threat, the complicity of American Communists in espionage and betrayal, and the adequacy of the American government's response. Although courtroom trials will be the center of most chapters, the "cases" are broader than just the particulars that were introduced into a specific prosecution. In 1948 Elizabeth Bentley, for example, identified dozens of government officials as Soviet spies, including an assistant secretary of the Treasury and a senior White House adviser, but only three minor prosecutions stemmed from her testimony. Nonetheless, the Bentley "case" had as major an impact on public opinion as the more elaborate trials of Alger Hiss in 1949 and Julius Rosenberg in 1950.

The second chapter deals with the 1945 cases of *Amerasia* and Igor Gouzenko. The seventh chapter ends with the 1962 death of Robert Soblen, then in England and about to be returned to the United States after an unsuccessful flight to avoid a prison term for an espionage conviction related to his activities in the 1940s and 1950s. The spy cases of the 1940s and 1950s had their origin in the pre–Cold War era and reflected a time when American counterintelligence was so weak and the risk of public scandal so slight that the political activities of American Communists overlapped and were entangled with Soviet espionage. Those Americans who spied for the USSR in that era were by and large motivated by an ideological commitment to communism, admiration for the Soviet Union, and rejection of capitalism and the American social order. To a small segment of Americans, the Great Depression of the 1930s signaled the death spiral of capitalism, and the world could only choose between fascism and communism. Assisting Soviet espionage appeared to some of that generation to be but another way of ushering in the inevitable triumph of worldwide socialism.

These cases dating from 1945 to 1962 not only shaped public attitudes but put an end to that earlier era. The CPUSA's assistance to Soviet espionage, once a major asset for Soviet spying, turned into a liability. The Communist Party, while not a mass movement, nonetheless had a substantial membership, about sixty thousand in 1945. This membership, moreover, was constantly in flux. Each year thousands of members dropped out from disillusionment, boredom, or fatigue at the heavy demands the party placed on its adherents. At the same time, party organizers recruited thousands of new members to replace the dropouts and increase the CPUSA's size. Compared with the sprawling disorganization of other American political parties, the CPUSA was disciplined and semi-covert, and even maintained a party security network designed to identify government infiltrators. Nonetheless, an organization with sixty thousand members with thousands of new adherents coming in or dropping out each year was highly vulnerable to penetration by professional security officers conducting a sustained investigation. Once American counterespionage agencies, greatly strengthened by the World War II mobilization, turned their attention to Soviet espionage, the porousness of the American Communist Party to investigation led to the collapse of the multiple Soviet spy networks based on American Communists. Additionally, the spy trials irredeemably tainted the CPUSA with espionage and betrayal and contributed to the political isolation of the American Communist movement.

Soviet espionage did not end with Soblen's death in 1962, but Soviet spying of the 1960s and the later decades of the Cold War was of a different quality from that of the 1940s and 1950s. Due to the risk, Soviet espionage agencies stopped using the CPUSA as an auxiliary to their work. The ideological attraction of communism also receded when the American economy regained its dynamism after the Great Depression and the realities of Soviet totalitarianism in the Stalin era became common knowledge. In the 1960s and thereafter, while ideological attraction occasionally led some Americans to spy for the Soviet bloc (New Left radicals Theresa Squillacote and Kurt Stand, convicted in 1998, are examples), most Soviet spies were motivated by greed for money, personal discontent and resentments, adventurism, and sexual blackmail. The most notorious, Aldrich Ames (convicted 1994) and Robert Hansen (convicted 2001), had no discernible political agenda. Ames, a CIA officer, sold American intelligence secrets to the Soviet KGB for money. Hansen, an FBI agent, turned over American counterintelligence information to the KGB out of greed and a twisted personality that thrived on betraying his colleagues and his country. John A. Walker Jr., a U.S. Navy warrant officer, betrayed American naval secrets to the USSR for eighteen years and along the way recruited other navy personnel – his brother, an officer; his son, a petty officer; and a civilian communications specialist – into espionage as well. Walker (convicted in 1985) had no known sympathy for the left, even flirting with the Ku Klux Klan, and was motivated entirely by greed, as were the other members of his spy ring.

Other trials and legal proceedings in the early Cold War era involved internal political subversion, state and federal statutes on sedition, and the balancing of democratic free speech rights with agitation for revolution and the destruction of the Constitution. These are important matters but a subject separate from espionage for a foreign power. Similarly, the attitude of private bodies such as trade unions and political organizations to the legitimacy of association with Communists is consequential but irrelevant to espionage. The cases dealt with in the book focus on those involving Soviet espionage.

A Word about Trials and History

Occasionally, a prominent trial throws light and attention on some broader problem or issue. What began as a simple criminal prosecution becomes part of a larger debate about the kind of society America was or was becoming. Questions about the evidence become questions about the fairness of the American judicial system or the ability of juries to free themselves from prior prejudices. Commentators insist that the issues and facts of the case have a larger, more cosmic significance than the fates of the accused.

Criminal trials, however, are supposed to be about the particular facts of a case. Did the defendants actually do what they are accused of doing? Over the centuries, legislatures and higher courts have evolved a complex set of rules designed to ensure that juries hear only evidence pertinent to the charges. Prejudicial testimony likely to inflame emotions without throwing light on the facts of the case is not apt to be allowed. Hearsay evidence, or accounts of what someone was told by other parties, is usually forbidden. Irrelevant information is not permitted into testimony. Prosecutors themselves will often decide to bring charges only on a narrowly defined issue where the evidence is ample (and legally admissible), even though they are convinced of the guilt of a defendant on a much broader array of crimes. When that happens, the evidence dealing with these other activities will not be introduced into trial proceedings. The complex rules of the American justice system are themselves also a source of injustice on occasion. When police overlook a procedural rule or obtain evidence by irregular or illegal means, or a prosecutor forgets to file the right motion, a court may exclude relevant evidence from the trial or dismiss a conviction on technical grounds, allowing the obviously guilty to go free.

Trial proceedings, consequently, offer an intensely focused look at the facts of history. But students of history must place trial proceedings in a broader context to properly access their meaning by bringing into consideration the broader array of evidence that trial procedures exclude. And, of course, the passage of time brings new evidence to light and allows the luxury of hindsight denied to those participating in the event at the time.

Spy Trials and McCarthyism

When critics of the American regime have been charged with crimes, their defense not only has been to claim innocence but often also to counter-charge that the criminal justice system was being used to railroad dis-senters or instill fear in dissidents. Some criminal cases become symbols of the alleged unfairness of the judicial system and the American political order.

No period in American history has been so defined by charges of crim-inalizing dissent as the McCarthy era. Senator Joseph McCarthy of Wis-consin gave his name to a phenomenon that has come to define a dark age in American life. Variously labeled "a nightmare in Red," "the time of the toad," a "scoundrel time," "the Great Fear," and "the American inquisi-tion," the late 1940s and early 1950s have been portrayed as an era when, obsessed by fear of Communist subversion and Soviet spies, Americans sacrificed their civil liberties and engaged in a massive witch-hunt against alleged Communists.

Although McCarthy gave his name to this era, commentators have stressed that the assault against Communists began long before he first burst into prominence in 1950 and continued after the Senate effectively ended his political career by censuring him for misconduct in 1954. McCarthy himself never prosecuted anyone for any crime; his defining tactic was to accuse people of being Communists or serving the Commu-nist cause and to launch congressional investigations that carried no legal penalty other than contempt of Congress or perjury for refusing to answer questions or testifying falsely.

The most prominent alleged victims of McCarthyism broadly defined are Alger Hiss and Julius and Ethel Rosenberg. For decades scholars and activists have waged a campaign to demonstrate that their trials for working on behalf of the Soviet Union were tainted by anti-Communist hysteria and their convictions were miscarriages of justice. But Hiss and the Rosenbergs are only three of the many people during this era accused and tried for espionage or crimes related to their espionage, such as perjury or failing to register as the agent of a foreign power. (Hiss, for example, was found guilty of perjury for lying about his espionage activities.) These cases have raised serious and continuing questions about the American legal system, the competence of American counterintelligence agencies, the integrity of the FBI, and the nature of the Cold War.

Politics of the Early Cold War

The early Cold War spy cases garnered intense public attention at the time because of the rapidly shifting political context. As World War II drew to an end in 1945, only a few Americans worried about a Communist threat. After nearly four years of total war against fascism in alliance with the Soviet Union, there was widespread hope that the postwar world would see a continuation of the cooperation that had sealed victory against Germany and Japan. The CPUSA had never been able to become a mass political movement, even during the Great Depression, although it had managed to create a formidable array of affiliated and cooperating organizations and had built centers of strength in the trade-union movement, among some ethnic groups, in student and youth organizations, and in intellectual circles.

The Nazi-Soviet Pact of 1939 had only temporarily stalled the CPUSA's efforts to gain influence in American life but had convinced some disillusioned liberals that Communists could not be trusted to put the interests of the United States ahead of the Soviet Union. Other anti-Communists had launched investigations of American communism in the late 1930s under the aegis of the Dies committee (U.S. House Special Committee on Un-American Activities). During World War II, a series of investigations and revelations had convinced some counterintelligence officials that Communists and the USSR were only *temporary* allies of the United States. As the war wound down, moreover, the Soviet Union sent a remarkable signal via the CPUSA that a new era of conflict was about to begin.

In 1944, flush with enthusiasm about the prospects for postwar cooperation between the two superpowers, Communist Party leader Earl Browder had hailed the results of the December 1943 conference in Tehran of Stalin, Roosevelt, and Churchill as a new landmark in the relationship between capitalism and communism. By Browder's lights, the Tehran meeting where the three agreed on a common war policy against Nazi Germany had demonstrated that the United States and Great Britain had accepted the legitimacy of the USSR, which, in turn, had given up the dream of overthrowing world capitalism. The two systems would peacefully coexist in the postwar world. To Browder, the logical conclusion was that the CPUSA had to change its orientation from seeking to destroy capitalism to supporting the conciliatory policy of the Roosevelt administration against those whose visceral hostility to the Soviet Union represented the far greater danger. Declaring that a socialist America was not on the post-war agenda, Browder argued for the dissolution of the CPUSA as an independent political party and its reconstitution as an advocacy association that would function within the two-party system.

Browder's plan met with some resistance inside the Communist movement, but his assurance that he had the support of the Soviet Union dampened dissent. In fact, his proposal had caused disquiet in Moscow, not only because it called into question key elements of Marxist-Leninist theory, but also because Joseph Stalin had no intention of abandoning the class struggle or remaining an American ally. In the spring of 1945, Jacques Duclos, a French Communist only recently returned from Moscow, published an article in a Paris magazine denouncing Browder. When he refused to repudiate his views, the longtime leader of the CPUSA was expelled from the party he had dominated for more than a decade. Browder later expressed his belief that his expulsion marked the opening volley of the oncoming Cold War, a signal sent by the Soviet Union to Communist parties in the West that the end of World War II would mark a resumption of the class war in capitalist nations. After the dissolution of the USSR, newly opened Russian archives showed that Duclos had, as suspected, not written the article published in his name. It was simply a translation of a scathing critique of Browder's policy published in a secret political journal that circulated only among the elite of the Soviet Communist Party. The only text added comprised a few paragraphs inserted to provide not very convincing justification for Duclos, a French Communist leader, commenting on American Communist policy.

While a handful of observers sensed the meaning of the Duclos article, most Americans were oblivious to what was transpiring in the Communist milieu. It was Soviet actions over the next few years, particularly in Eastern Europe, that brought home the realization that the end of the most destructive conflict in human history had not ushered in an era of international amity. While tensions between the United States and the USSR ratcheted up over events in Poland, Berlin, and Czechoslovakia, former British prime minister Winston Churchill warned of an iron curtain descending through the middle of Europe, and the Truman administration launched the Marshall Plan to rebuild Western Europe's capitalist infrastructure.

With growing concern about Soviet intentions and increasing nervousness about its military capabilities, highlighted by news of its explosion of an atomic bomb in 1949, American policy makers struggled to define a new foreign policy and build public support for it. In the late 1940s and early 1950s charges of Soviet espionage at several highly publicized spy trials as well as a series of congressional hearings shaped public perceptions of the Cold War. To most of the American people the trials drove home the point that the United States faced not only a dangerous foreign enemy but also a serious issue of domestic security.

That Communists disliked the American system of government was no secret. Ever since its founding in 1919, the American Communist movement had maintained a steady drumbeat of criticism of American political, economic, and cultural institutions. The manifesto of the American Communist Party's 1919 founding convention declared, "Communism does not propose to 'capture' the bourgeoisie parliamentary state, but to conquer and destroy it. . . . It is necessary that the proletariat organize its own state *for the coercion and suppression of the bourgeoisie*" (emphasis in the original). For a brief period between 1936 and 1939 and again from mid-1941 to 1945, the CPUSA had adopted a patriotic pose, diligently searching for American roots and forebears and trumpeting its devotion to the American dream. The party happily proclaimed that "Communism Is Twentieth Century Americanism" – until a secret directive from Moscow expressing disapproval of so chauvinistic a slogan led to its quiet retirement. With the exception of those interregnums, the CPUSA made few bones about its distaste for both capitalism and democracy and its desire to replace them with a society modeled on Soviet Russia.

There had been periodic hearings during the 1920s and 1930s at which congressional inquisitors had elicited from Communist witnesses fervent paeans of praise for Soviet "democracy" and denunciations of alleged American repression, while also hearing from others often wildly exaggerated charges about the role that Communists were playing in American life. During the last half of the 1930s, a special House committee, named for the rabidly anti–New Deal Democratic representative from Texas, Martin Dies, heard from a mixture of sensible and alarmist anti-Communist witnesses about Communist efforts to infiltrate a variety of American institutions, particularly the labor movement and various New Deal agencies.

Congressional hearings, however, were performances of a sort rather than trials. While witnesses were under oath and could be questioned by congressmen or committee staff, there was no judge present to force a reluctant witness to speak on the spot, and evasive answers or even evading questioning altogether was frequent. Enforcing testimony through contempt-of-Congress prosecutions sometimes brought results, but such prosecutions were difficult to bring, often unsuccessful due to the vagueness of congressional questioning, and so long delayed by legal proceedings that both the public and Congress had lost interest by the time of any resolution. Congressmen and their staffs were often more interested in publicity and headlines than proving anything, and much of what they investigated was not a crime but a political or social situation to which they wished to bring public attention. Beginning in 1945, however, Americans were subjected to a series of sensational charges of espionage on behalf of the Soviet Union directed mainly, but not exclusively, at the U.S. government. From the very onset of these cases, critics charged that they were thinly veiled efforts to intimidate progressive-minded people or stir up support for the Cold War and animosity toward the Soviet Union. The government was, it was alleged, engaged in politically motivated use of the criminal justice system. As proof, there was the relative lack of success enjoyed by government prosecutors.

The U.S. government's success in prosecuting and convicting spies was in one sense not very impressive. Historical evidence that has become available since the end of the Cold War shows that several hundred Americans spied for the Soviet Union, but only a fraction of these, several dozen, were ever prosecuted. Several cases collapsed or were plea-bargained to relatively innocuous charges. Some sensational cases were characterized by bitterly disputed evidence that continued to be challenged as tainted for years after the trials. The credibility of important witnesses was, in many minds, deeply suspect. The government's own conduct was frequently questioned and sometimes condemned by appeals courts.

The earliest espionage case we discuss involves the journal *Amerasia*. The investigation into the *Amerasia* case began in mid-1945 with security agents of the Office of Strategic Services (OSS, American's World War II intelligence agency) and the Federal Bureau of Investigation conducting secret searches of the office of *Amerasia*, secretly photographing and removing evidence, wiretapping the office and residential phones of those on the *Amerasia* staff, and bugging their homes and meeting places, all done without benefit of a search warrant or court authorization. By the standards of peacetime American criminal and civil law, the wiretaps and warrantless secret searches and seizures of evidence were "illegal." But it was not peacetime, America was still at war, and *Amerasia* had obtained secret documents that if revealed to the Japanese would endanger the lives of anti-Japanese resistance leaders in Thailand. What was being investigated was not ordinary crime but possible espionage that threatened the war effort and national security.

The U.S. Congress had not passed a comprehensive wartime (or peacetime) espionage and internal security law. Instead, American security services operated under variegated espionage and antisubversion laws that overlapped in some areas and left other matters unaddressed along with a hodgepodge of presidential directives and executive orders (some peacetime, some wartime) often designed to fill the gaps in statutory law, along with guidelines from U.S. attorney generals (for the FBI) and various U.S. Army generals and Navy admirals (for the OSS and military security offices). Federal judges took no consistent stand on the matter. During World War II, federal courts, including the U.S. Supreme Court, sometimes treated as legally acceptable (citing wartime necessity and the president's constitutional authority as commander in chief) or more often turned a deliberately blind eye toward investigatory actions by American security agencies that would have been impermissible in ordinary criminal investigations.

As the sense of wartime emergency receded, attitudes regarding what was legal and illegal in security investigations were in flux. This ambiguity would increase with the end of World War II and the beginning of the Cold War. Would legal standards revert to earlier peacetime practices? The Cold War was not a formally declared military conflict but neither was it peace in the traditional sense. From the late 1940s until the collapse of the USSR in 1991 the United States existed in a state of semimobilization (including military conscription for half that period), maintained powerful military forces in the heart of Europe, and fought a series of regional wars across the globe connected to the central conflict with a nuclear-armed Soviet Union.

The Cold War also did not start with a sudden act such as the Japanese attack on Pearl Harbor that propelled the United States into World War II. Instead, it was a conflict that gradually developed in the late 1940s. And while there were partial precedents in American history, the Soviet Union's extensive use of espionage and the American Communist Party's role as the internal ally of America's chief foreign foe were unusual. This presented, in turn, unusual challenges to how the U.S. government and the legal system would deal with espionage and related internal security matters. The matter was never settled. Congress passed a number of new statutes but never created a comprehensive set of espionage and security laws. A series of Supreme Court decisions that upheld some of the new laws but struck down others in whole or in part as unconstitutional also kept the legal situation in a state of flux. By the end of the Cold War era, however, some of the anomalies and gaps in American security law were removed. For example, secretly listening in on telephone conversations, "wiretapping," was an indispensable tool for counterespionage, but federal law on wiretapping was a confused muddle from the 1930s to the late 1960s.

In 1934, when it passed the Federal Communications Act, Congress created the Federal Communications Commission (FCC) to oversee federal regulation of radio broadcasting. The law also transferred federal regulatory authority over telephone communications to the FCC. One section of the new act read: "No person not being authorized by the sender shall intercept any communication and divulge or publish the existence, contents, substance, purport, effect or meaning of such intercepted communication to any person." From the history of the legislation, it is not clear that Congress intended this section to apply to telephone communications, and under earlier legal decisions wiretapping evidence gathered by law enforcement authorities had been found admissible in court under common-law standards. But in the 1937 case of *Nardone v. United States*, the U.S. Supreme Court ruled that the language of the section did not differentiate between radio and telephone communications and also rejected the government's view that Congress in any case intended the prohibition to extend only to private parties and did not intend to prohibit law enforcement interception of telephone calls. The court then interpreted the new law as effectively banning evidence gained by law enforcement wiretaps from use in federal court proceedings.

Several times after the *Nardone* decision one or another house of Congress passed bills authorizing law enforcement wiretaps, but nothing passed both houses and became law. Frustrated by congressional inaction and concerned about espionage and Nazi fifth-column activity, President Roosevelt in 1940 specifically authorized wiretapping for national security purposes. U.S. Attorney General Robert Jackson, later appointed to the Supreme Court by President Roosevelt, interpreted the *Nardone* ruling as a prohibition only on disclosing wiretap evidence *in court* and a requirement that the recorded conversations had to be kept secret but *not* a general prohibition of wiretapping. Consequently, federal judges, citing the *Nardone* decision, continued to refuse to allow wiretap evidence to be introduced in court, but under the Roosevelt-Jackson policy (continued by later administrations), the FBI and other executive branch security agencies used wiretaps to gather information that could then be used to obtain nonwiretap evidence, which could be used as evidence in a court.

As several of the early Cold War spy cases discussed here illustrate, the mismatch between the executive branch's policies on national security wiretapping and the judicial branch's standards of admissible evidence produced deception, suspicion, and confusion until 1968 when the Congress passed the Omnibus Crime Control Act. This act authorized law enforcement wiretapping if the investigators obtained a judicial warrant and allowed warrantless national security wiretapping if authorized by the president. But in 1972 in the Keith case (*United States v. United States District Court*), the Supreme Court held that warrantless national security wiretaps of American citizens were unconstitutional but left the issue of wiretaps of foreign agents unclear. Congress responded in 1978 with the Foreign Intelligence Surveillance Act establishing a special "Foreign Intelligence Surveillance Court" to provide for timely and secret approval of national security wiretaps and other electronic surveillance of anyone, foreigner or citizen, in the United States.

It must also be kept in mind that espionage is an extraordinarily difficult crime to prove. Unlike so many other crimes, its most successful practitioners leave no trace of their activities. When someone robs a bank, money is missing, but the optimal situation for a spy is to steal a secret without anyone knowing anything has happened. Unless a person is caught in the act of illegally removing a document or item and handing it over to an unauthorized individual, it may be very hard to prove that he has done anything wrong. A careful spy would not keep souvenirs or evidence of his activities. Absent an actual physical surveillance of spying, an accomplice or participant in the crime is usually the government's major source of information. That too creates difficulties, since major witnesses are then tainted by association with the crime and can be plausibly accused of trying to curry favor with the prosecution and escape their own punishment.

There are other problems in prosecuting espionage cases, however. The U.S. government has to weigh the advantages and disadvantages of going public with espionage charges. As will be illustrated with several of the early Cold War spy cases, to prove that the information taken was valuable might require revealing in open court (and thus delivering to a foreign adversary) information that the government is not sure the spy actually transmitted or expose other secrets. Testimony by government agents under cross-examination also might expose resources, tactics, and methods used by counterintelligence agencies and enable other spies to escape detection more easily or to avoid actions that might make them vulnerable.

Sending guilty people to jail is only one of the motivations of spy chasers, and not a very important one. Their first priority is usually to stop the spying. Indeed, not only to stop it, but by surveillance and disruption, to prevent the spy from actually carrying out any espionage. That means that rather than wait to catch suspects in the act of stealing and transmitting information, counterespionage agents may prefer to remove them from positions where they have access to sensitive information. To do this, however, makes successful criminal prosecution very difficult because American criminal law is geared toward a crime having actually occurred and authorities arresting and trying the person responsible for a specific criminal act. Successful counterintelligence, however, often aims to prevent the spy from ever being able to carry out a specific act of espionage, but absent that specific act, conviction in an ordinary criminal trial is difficult. (Many of the same considerations apply to contemporary counterterror operations where the chief goal is to prevent acts of terror from happening, not successfully prosecuting terrorists after they have killed and wounded hundreds.)

Counterintelligence agents may well be willing to allow guilty people to go free rather than expose a valuable human or technical source providing information from inside the espionage ring. They may choose to quietly elicit a spy's cooperation and knowledge in return for immunity. In rare cases a counterespionage service may hope to "turn" the spy and use him as a double agent to feed disinformation to an adversary.

And, finally, espionage trials in the Cold War era were subject to the same legal rules as other criminal cases. Juries may not hear certain kinds of evidence because of the requirements of the legal system. If evidence has been gathered illegally, as a result of an unauthorized wiretap or a faulty search and seizure, it may not be used against a defendant, even if the material is authentic and directly relevant to guilt or innocence. Some perfectly sensible evidence developed by counterespionage officers cannot be used in court because of its unusual nature. One area of strength of American intelligence is its superb technical capacity for electronic interception and code breaking. When American cryptographers intercept and decode an electronic message between a hostile foreign intelligence agency and one of its spies inside the United States, there is little doubt about the spy's guilt. But such decryptions will not be introduced in court for obvious reasons. Once the hostile intelligence agency realizes its code has been broken, it will introduce a new code, one that may take years to decipher. From a counterespionage point of view, the advantages of continuing to read an opponent's espionage messages far out weigh what is gained by prosecuting one spy. Better simply to identify the spy and remove his ability to do any damage but allow him to go free.

Old criminal cases are often revisited years later because they are intrinsically interesting; the passage of time has cooled emotions, new evidence has emerged, or new witnesses come forward or are discovered. Not often, but occasionally, there are enough smoking guns that courts, historians, and sometimes even legislatures are persuaded that an injustice was done; then pardons are issued, convictions expunged from the record, and compensation provided.

A wholesale reevaluation of the espionage cases of the Cold War has been underway among historians in the past decade, prompted by an extraordinary opening of archives. In the 1980s under the impact of the Freedom of Information Act (FOIA), passed in the wake of Watergate, the files of the FBI became available for the first time. Although subject to limits, the FOIA enabled historians Allen Weinstein and Ronald Radosh to revisit the Hiss and Rosenberg cases. Their conclusions that Hiss and Julius Rosenberg were spies were not universally accepted. But after the collapse of the Soviet Union, a variety of Russian archives opened their doors to American scholars. That, in turn, led to the willingness of American intelligence agencies to release the Venona files, an invaluable set of about three thousand intercepted and decoded international cables sent between the headquarters of Soviet intelligence agencies in Moscow and their field officers in the United States and elsewhere. As a result of all this new information, historians now know much more about the truth of the charges of espionage that were so widely disputed for many years.

Most of those whom the government knew committed espionage were never charged with anything. Some of those who committed espionage were charged with other crimes – like perjury, conspiracy to commit espionage, unauthorized possession of government documents, or contempt of court.

Some of those convicted of espionage or espionage-related crimes never served a day in prison.

Looking at the spy trials of the Cold War can tell us something not only about that conflict but also about the limitations of the legal system in approaching the truth about espionage. We may admire the protections that system provides to people accused of crimes and recognize that there is no better way to proceed, but it is important to be realistic about the ways in which it can obscure or even confound the truth. Anyone relying on the results of the legal system to evaluate how extensive Soviet espionage was will be seriously misled. By the same token, anyone studying Soviet espionage will be puzzled by why so few perpetrators were ever successfully prosecuted. And the frustrations and limitations of the legal system help explain the sometimes disproportionate punishment of a few of those who were convicted.

Altogether, an understanding of how these spy cases were conducted at the time and how they look in the light of post–Cold War evidence allows us to better assess the history of the American politics and public opinion regarding communism and anticommunism in the early Cold War.

FURTHER READINGS

Soviet Espionage in the Early Cold War

Andrew, Christopher M., and Oleg Gordievsky. *KGB: The Inside Story of Its Foreign Operations from Lenin to Gorbachev*. New York: HarperCollins Publishers, 1990.

Comprehensive history of the KGB according to a former leading official of the KGB London station who defected to Great Britain in 1985. Based both on Gordievsky's personal knowledge and Andrew's espionage scholarship. Gives a history of Soviet intelligence activity in the United States in the 1930s and 1940s said to be based in part on Gordievsky's preparation of an internal KGB history prior to his defection. Maintains that the Rosenbergs were Soviet agents as were Alger Hiss and Harry Dexter White as well.

Andrew, Christopher M., and Vasili Mitrokhin. *The Sword and the Shield: The Mitrokhin Archive and the Secret History of the KGB*. New York: Basic Books, 1999.

Based on notes and documents of KGB officer and archivist who defected to the British Secret Intelligence Service in 1992. Mitrokhin's material covers sixty years of KGB operations, with most in the Cold War period but going back to the 1930s as well. Identifies hundreds of British, Italian, French, German, and other Europeans who assisted Soviet intelligence before and during the Cold War. Identifies numerous CPUSA members and officials who assisted Soviet intelligence. Says of Vasili Zarubin, chief of KGB operations in the United States from December 1941 until mid-1944, "Zarubin's recruitment strategy was simple and straightforward. He demanded that the leaders of the Communist Party of the United States (CPUSA) identify supporters and sympathizers in government establishments suitable for work as agents." Says Soviet espionage in the United States seriously weakened after World War II by "the post-war decline and persecution of the CPUSA."

Haynes, John Earl, and Harvey Klehr. *Venona: Decoding Soviet Espionage in America*. New Haven: Yale University Press, 1999.

Comprehensive and detailed analysis of what the Venona decryptions indicate about the extent of Soviet espionage. Integrates the Venona evidence with other documentation. Identifies several hundred Americans, chiefly Communists, who assisted Soviet espionage against the United States. Discusses at length the evidence regarding the espionage activities of Elizabeth Bentley, Harry Dexter White, Lauchlin Currie, Julius Rosenberg, Laurence Duggan, Maurice Halperin, Duncan Lee, Cedric Belfrage, Gregory Silvermaster, Alger Hiss, Victor Perlo, and others. Sees the CPUSA's role as key to Soviet espionage during World War II but as a source of ultimate weakness because the CPUSA could function as an auxiliary to Soviet espionage only as long as American security agencies were preoccupied with other targets and during a period when communism was perceived as nonthreatening. When those conditions changed, Soviet espionage suffered major reverses and the CPUSA became tainted with disloyalty.

Romerstein, Herbert, and Eric Breindel. *The Venona Secrets: Exposing Soviet Espionage and America's Traitors*. Washington, D.C.: Regnery, 2000.

Discusses the Venona decryptions and provides a history of Soviet espionage in the United States in the 1930s and 1940s that treats the CPUSA as an integral part of Soviet espionage operations.

Sibley, Katherine A. S. *Red Spies in America: Stolen Secrets and the Dawn of the Cold War*. Lawrence: University Press of Kansas, 2004.

Thorough scholarly survey and examination of key episodes of Soviet espionage. Makes use of all of the latest evidence with particular attention to extensive FBI investigative files.

Weinstein, Allen, and Alexander Vassiliev. *The Haunted Wood: Soviet Espionage in America – The Stalin Era*. New York: Random House, 1999.

Based on hitherto secret documents provided by the Russian Foreign Intelligence Service from the KGB's archives. Discusses the espionage activities of Alger Hiss, Whittaker Chambers, Laurence Duggan, Martha Dodd, Elizabeth Bentley, Ted Hall, Julius Rosenberg, David Greenglass, Boris Morros, the members of the Silvermaster group, the members of the Perlo group, and many others. Discusses documents showing that one member of Congress, Representative Samuel Dickstein, was bribed by Soviet intelligence to provide various services. Discusses the assistance provided Soviet intelligence by Earl Browder and the CPUSA.

The American Communist Movement

Draper, Theodore. *The Roots of American Communism*. New York: Viking Press, 1957.

Well-written and indispensable scholarly study of the origins of the American Communist Party. Emphasizes the power of Soviet Bolshevism in inspiring and shaping American communism and the rapid subordination of American communism to Soviet leadership. Draper, a young Communist in the late 1930s who later left the party, amassed a rich collection of primary source material in preparing this and his subsequent volume on Communist history.

Draper, Theodore. *American Communism and Soviet Russia*. New York: Viking Press, 1960.

Well-written and thorough scholarly study of the Communist Party in the 1920s. This key history of American communism finds that Soviet policies expressed through the Communist International decisively shaped the American Communist Party in its formative first decade of existence.

Howe, Irving, and Lewis A. Coser. *The American Communist Party: A Critical History, 1919–1957*. Assisted by Julius Jacobson. Boston: Beacon Press, 1957.

Comprehensive one-volume political history of the Communist Party up to 1957. Emphasizes its obedience to Moscow and its hostility to democracy. Howe and Coser were leading left anti-Communist intellectuals of the 1950s, and sections of the book have a polemical tone.

Isserman, Maurice. *Which Side Were You On? The American Communist Party during the Second World War*. Middletown, Conn.: Wesleyan University Press, 1982.

Well-researched and scholarly political history of the Communist Party from the late 1940s to the end of World War II. Concentrates on the Communist Party's internal political life. Maintains that the generation of Communists who joined the party in the 1930s was oriented toward a democratized and Americanized Communist movement but was frustrated by the structure of the Communist Party.

Klehr, Harvey. *The Heyday of American Communism: The Depression Decade.* New York: Basic Books, 1984.

Most thorough and comprehensive history of the CPUSA in the 1930s, the era of its greatest growth and influence. Discusses both the CPUSA as an institution and the involvement of Communists in the labor movement, liberal and New Deal politics, cultural and intellectual circles, and other arenas.

Klehr, Harvey, and John Earl Haynes. *The American Communist Movement: Storming Heaven Itself.* New York: Twayne, 1992.

Comprehensive history of the American Communist Party from origins to 1991. "Every different era in the history of the American Communist movement has been inaugurated by developments in the Communist world abroad. The Russian Revolution led to the formation of the first American Communist party. Soviet pressure led to the abandonment of an underground Communist party. Comintern directives led American Communists to adopt an ultra-revolutionary posture during the late 1920s. Soviet foreign policy needs midwifed the birth of the Popular Front in the mid-1930s. The Nazi-Soviet Pact destroyed the Popular Front in 1939 and the German attack on the USSR reconstituted it in 1941. The onset of the Cold War cast American Communists into political purgatory after World War II and Khrushchev's devastating expose of Stalin's crimes in 1957 tore the American Communist party apart."

Starobin, Joseph R. *American Communism in Crisis, 1943–1957.* Cambridge, Mass.: Harvard University Press, 1972.

Well-researched, poignant scholarly study by the former foreign editor of the Daily Worker. Argues that Browder was leading the Communist Party in the direction of a positive participation in American politics when he was expelled. Maintains that the American Communists were caught up in a "mental Comintern" that caused them to slavishly follow what they thought, occasionally erroneously, were Moscow's wishes. Suggests that Moscow made little effort to understand the condition of the American Communist Party and regarded it with minimal interest.

The Politics of Post–World War II Anticommunism

Caute, David. *The Great Fear: The Anti-Communist Purge under Truman and Eisenhower.* New York: Simon and Schuster, 1977.

Highly influential revisionist work. Maintains that mass hysteria, repression, and political purges swept America in the late 1940s and 1950s. Asserts that the nation was "sweat drenched in fear" and treats opposition to communism as intellectually and morally indefensible.

Chase, Harold William. *Security and Liberty: The Problem of Native Communists, 1947–1955.* Garden City, N.Y.: Doubleday, 1955.

Discusses the trade-off and difficulties of balancing effective countersubversion polices with civil liberties.

Haynes, John Earl. *Red Scare or Red Menace? American Communism and Anticommunism in the Cold War Era.* Chicago: Ivan R. Dee, 1996.

Scholarly survey providing a summary history of the CPUSA and emphasizing the variety of anti-Communist constituencies mobilized after World War II and the extent to which pre–World War II antifascism provided models and precedents for post–World War II anticommunism, and holding that, for all of its excesses, domestic anticommunism was a rational response to a real threat to American democracy.

Hook, Sidney. *Political Power and Personal Freedom: Critical Studies in Democracy, Communism, and Civil Rights.* New York: Criterion Books, 1959.

Discussion by a leading anti-Communist liberal philosopher of how a democratic society should deal with an antidemocratic totalitarian movement.

Kutler, Stanley I. *The American Inquisition: Justice and Injustice in the Cold War.* New York: Hill and Wang, 1982.

Highly critical of anticommunism. Sees the threat of espionage and communism as minor and insufficient to justify government security policies.

Lamphere, Robert J., and Tom Shachtman. *The FBI-KGB War: A Special Agent's Story.* New York: Random House, 1986.

Memoir by a veteran senior FBI agent deeply involved in counterintelligence. Discusses links between the Communist Party and Soviet espionage.

Moynihan, Daniel P. *Secrecy: The American Experience.* New Haven: Yale University Press, 1998.

A survey of the role of secrecy and security in the modern American state by an innovative intellectual and a U.S. senator.

O'Neill, William L. *American High: The Years of Confidence, 1945–1960.* New York: Free Press, 1986.

Depicts the era as basically healthy and progressive and rejects the revisionist view of the time as a fear-ridden nightmare.

Schrecker, Ellen. *Many Are the Crimes: McCarthyism in America*. Princeton, N.J.: Princeton University Press, 1999.

Influential revisionist book of the late 1990s. A thoroughly researched and broad academic denunciation of any form of opposition to communism. Conflates all varieties of opposition to communism with McCarthyism. Sees opposition to communism as responsible for slowing the development of feminism, driving talented musicians from major orchestras, producing bad movies and dull television programming, severing the connection between art and social responsibility, retarding the natural sciences, crippling American higher education, and leading to Richard Nixon.

Sirgiovanni, George. *An Undercurrent of Suspicion: Anti-Communism in America during World War II*. New Brunswick, N.J.: Transaction Publishers, 1990.

Surveys the spectrum of anti-Communist and anti-Soviet agitation in World War II, including conservative Catholics and Protestants, southern Democrats, partisan Republicans, the right-wing press, anti-Communist AFL and CIO leaders, and anti-Communist Socialists.

Whitfield, Stephen J. *The Culture of the Cold War*. Baltimore: Johns Hopkins University Press, 1991.

Thorough, highly readable, and detailed survey with much original scholarly research examining how the Cold War with the Soviet Union and concerns about domestic communism influenced American popular and elite culture.

2

The Precursors

WHILE MOST AMERICANS CELEBRATED THE ACCOMPLISH-
ments and heroism of our Soviet allies during World War II, reveling
in the Red Army's pulverizing of Nazi forces and hoping that the United
States, Britain, and the Soviet Union would continue their cooperation
into the postwar world, counterintelligence agencies were less sanguine.
Although the FBI had focused much of its wartime activities on Nazi and
Japanese activities, by 1943 it was unable to ignore growing signs that
America's Soviet ally covertly was behaving in an unfriendly manner.

Neither the Soviet Union's joining the fight against Hitler nor Stalin's
dissolution of the Communist International (Comintern) during the war
could erase the long-standing hostility to communism that animated many
Americans or the suspicion of some that Communist subversion was a continuing problem. While the Communist Party, USA (CPUSA) had abandoned its rhetorical denunciations of capitalism, proclaimed its absolute
commitment to winning the war, and, by 1944, forsworn even a postwar
effort to transform America into a socialist society, a series of events
and investigations convinced FBI chief J. Edgar Hoover and other high
government officials that communism remained a danger to American
security.

Only a small fraction of the evidence that Communists and communism
remained a threat became public before 1947. What did become known,
moreover, was often fragmentary and confusing, occasioning angry claims
from admirers of the USSR that mendacious forces in the government
were intent on undermining American-Soviet cooperation. Nevertheless,
it helped to galvanize the considerable reservoir of anticommunism that
had been put into abeyance by World War II, to shape elite opinion, and
to convince policy makers that the defeat of Nazism would not inaugurate
a new era free of internal as well as external dangers.

To the FBI, the most disturbing sign was the discovery during World War II of a massive Soviet-directed espionage operation aimed at virtually every major American military and defense secret. Soviet spies were busily engaged in ferreting out information about avionics, radar, sonar, and proximity fuses, among other classified matters. They were reporting on sensitive diplomatic, military, and political developments within the American government. And the FBI itself learned about the U.S. Army's Manhattan Project, America's crash effort to build an atomic bomb, only when it stumbled across one of the Soviet's efforts to steal its secrets.

The general public, meanwhile, remained largely oblivious to Soviet espionage. During the 1920s and 1930s there were periodic newspaper reports about Soviet industrial espionage, largely revolving around Amtorg, the USSR's American-based agency to stimulate trade and obtain industrial goods. Several congressional investigations had featured charges that Amtorg employees were actually spies whose main job was to steal industrial secrets. But there was little follow-through, and the stories quickly faded away. The FBI and military security agencies had investigated a handful of Soviet-inspired espionage cases in the 1930s with minimal results.

That began to change in the late 1930s but only slowly. Walter Krivitsky, then a senior KGB officer in Western Europe, defected in France in 1937. After his arrival in the United States in 1938, he teamed up with journalist Isaac Don Levine to write a series of sensational articles for the *Saturday Evening Post*, one of the most widely read magazines of the day, detailing Stalin's bloody purges, betrayal of the Spanish republic, and plans to cooperate with Hitler. His 1939 autobiography, *In Stalin's Secret Service*, expanded on those themes and sold well. While Krivitsky's political exposés generated the most vitriolic public responses from pro-Soviet partisans, his claims of espionage were not ignored. The FBI questioned him, the Passport Office solicited his help in identifying fake American passports used by Soviet agents, and he testified before the Dies committee (U.S. House Special Committee on Un-American Activities) on past Soviet espionage directed at the United States, also identifying American Communist leader Earl Browder's sister, Margaret, as a Soviet agent in Europe.

Whittaker Chambers, another Soviet spy who had quietly defected in 1938, met Krivitsky through Levine and the two spent hours discussing their espionage careers. Eventually convinced that informing was a moral necessity, Chambers met with presidential adviser Adolf Berle in September 1939, shortly after the Nazi-Soviet Pact had been signed, to expose the spy ring within the American government that he had supervised. Levine, who was present at the meeting, jotted down the names mentioned by Chambers, while Berle made a more elaborate set of notes that he entitled "Underground Espionage Agent." Although there were minor discrepancies, both lists contained the names of such government employees as Alger Hiss, his brother Donald, and Laurence Duggan of the State Department as well as Lauchlin Currie in the White House. Despite Berle's assurance that the problem would be dealt with, there was little follow-up. Not until several years later, in 1943, and then at the FBI's initiative, did he turn over his notes on the 1939 meeting to the FBI. And by the time the FBI first interviewed Chambers, in 1942, he was once again reluctant to talk. His reticence probably was related to Krivitsky's fate.

Krivitsky had made a brief visit to Great Britain to help unearth spies, but in August 1940 he was shaken by Trotsky's assassination. Soviet agents had been keeping Krivitsky under surveillance in the months before February 1941, when his body was discovered in a Washington hotel with a bullet through his head. Officially labeled a suicide, his death has remained a mystery, with enough discrepancies to convince some observers that he was the victim of a carefully plotted murder. Combined with the lack of action on his exposé to Berle and the American-Soviet alliance during the war, Krivitsky's death likely convinced Chambers that going public or even talking to security officers was futile and possibly dangerous. His story and evidence about Alger Hiss's espionage would remain a secret until 1948.

Amerasia: The First Cold War Spy Case

The first significant public exposure to Soviet espionage came just after the end of combat in Europe but while war continued in the Pacific. On June 6, 1945, the FBI arrested six people associated with the pro-Communist magazine *Amerasia* and accused them of espionage. John Stewart Service was a prominent State Department "China Hand," as the small group of diplomats who specialized in China matters was known. Emmanuel Larsen was a State Department staff specialist (rather than a diplomat), and Andrew Roth was a wartime naval officer assigned to the Office of Naval Intelligence. Kate Mitchell and Philip Jaffe edited *Amerasia*. Mark Gayn was a well-known journalist. Right-wing columnists and writers hailed the arrests as confirmation of their complaints about lax security and the unreliability of Communists and their sympathizers. Left-wingers worried about "red-baiting" and overeager government gumshoes intruding into freedom of the press.

Although only Jaffe and Larsen were ever convicted of any offense – and in their case it was merely unauthorized possession of government documents – the *Amerasia* case remained a staple in American political life for the next half a decade. Liberals and New Dealers saw the arrests as part of a campaign to stifle freedom of the press and continue support for the corrupt and undemocratic Chiang Kai-shek government in China. Conservatives concluded that the collapse of the case proved that there had been a cover-up designed by a pro-Communist bloc in the State Department. The triumph of the Chinese Communists in 1949 and Senator Joseph McCarthy's subsequent charge that the State Department was saturated with Communists resurrected the case. It played a prominent role in the U.S. Senate's Tydings committee hearings held to examine McCarthy's charges. The *Amerasia* affair contributed to the firings of several senior diplomats who specialized in Chinese matters from the State Department.

Despite its prominence at the time, historians have largely ignored the *Amerasia* case. There was no dramatic trial as in the Hiss and Rosenberg cases, the other two prominent spy cases of the postwar era. Indeed, many people doubted that the case involved espionage at all.

The *Amerasia* arrests were the product of an investigation lasting three and a half months that was sparked by *Amerasia* itself. Its January 26, 1945 issue included an article on British policy in Asia; when an intelligence analyst in the Office of Strategic Services (OSS) read the section on Thailand, he was startled and disconcerted to discover that a large portion of it was a nearly verbatim copy of a top secret report he himself had written earlier. While the stolen paragraphs in *Amerasia* did not include this information, what made the report particularly sensitive was its detailed discussion of the leaders of the resistance movement in Thailand then waging a guerrilla campaign against Japanese occupying forces. If this OSS report got into the hands of the Japanese they would be able to decapitate the Thai resistance. OSS investigators were determined to uncover how the OSS report had made its way to the journal.

OSS security officers quickly learned that the magazine's editor, Philip Jaffe, had a long record as a Communist sympathizer and Soviet admirer.

This was not reassuring. While the Soviet Union was an American ally in the war against Nazi Germany, the USSR was not an American ally in the war against Japan. (The USSR did not declare war on Japan until August 8, 1945, a few days after the atomic bomb was dropped on Hiroshima and just prior to Japan's surrender.) After a few weeks of surveillance, on March 11, 1945, OSS security men broke into the magazine's offices at night and found a trove of government documents. Hundreds of memos, reports, and papers from the U.S. State Department, Navy, War Department, and Office of War Information were scattered about, as well as other OSS material. Convinced that a handful of documents would not be missed from the mess, the investigators took several and left, leaving behind no sign of their surreptitious entry.

OSS officials concluded that they had stumbled onto a nest of spies. Within a day of getting a report about the material, General William Donovan, chief of the OSS, met with the secretary of state, whose department was the source of many of the purloined documents. After consultations with the secretary of the navy, everyone agreed to turn the investigation of the case over to the FBI. By March 15 the FBI had launched a major probe, ordering twenty-four-hour surveillance of Jaffe and placing wiretaps on *Amerasia*'s office phones and the home telephones of its editors, actions necessitating clandestine entries into their homes.

For the next few months the bureau closely shadowed Jaffe and several other people with whom he came into contact. Agents entered hotel rooms, private residences, and offices without warrants to search and listened to conversations on bugged phones and in hotel rooms with hidden microphones, gathering a great deal of evidence that Jaffe and several of his contacts were engaged in a plot to gather secret information from American government sources and transmit it to the Soviet Union. Virtually none of this evidence, however, was ever made public.

As the FBI learned more about Jaffe, it became convinced that he was the major figure in the conspiracy. Born into a poor family in the Ukraine in 1895, he came to America a decade later. His father eked out a meager living in New York; Philip was a hustler who attended several colleges before landing a job with a messenger service and marrying the boss's daughter. He finished college at Columbia in 1920, took care of his sick wife, and saved the family business from collapse before starting his own company in 1923. After several rocky years, the Wallace Brown Corporation, which sold greeting cards by direct mail and used a network of housewives to peddle them door to door, was prospering, and Jaffe became more engaged in radical political activities, flirting with a tiny Communist sect whose founders included some of his old classmates and friends. But he soon fell under the influence of a relative, a young Chinese student, Chi Ch'ao-ting, who had married Jaffe's cousin. Chi had come to the United States to study – he eventually earned a Ph.D. at Columbia University – but he had also joined the CPUSA in the 1920s; when Jaffe first met him, he had just returned from Moscow where he had served as an interpreter at a congress of the Communist International. Under Chi's influence, Jaffe became active in Communist fronts, most notably as a founding member and executive secretary of the American Friends of the Chinese People and editor of its paper, *China Today*, first published in 1933, and dedicated to advancing the cause of the Chinese Communists. During World War II, Chi became the aide to the minister of finance in the Kuomintang government, concealing his secret membership in the Communist Party. (Chi received his posting to the Kuomintang government with the assistance of secret Communist sympathizers in the U.S. Treasury; see Chapter 3.) After the Communists seized power in China, he became a high-ranking diplomat; years later the Chinese Communist Party revealed that he had served it as an undercover operative during the war.

In the mid-1930s, however, Communists adopted their "Popular Front" policy, downplayed their revolutionary Marxism-Leninism, and sought to present themselves as part of a broad antifascist front. In this more moderate posture, *China Today*, deemed too overtly Communist, was jettisoned and replaced by a new magazine, *Amerasia*, which attracted a distinguished editorial board of largely non-Communist scholars and policy makers. Despite its new aura of respectability, the magazine was under the control of Jaffe, Frederick Vanderbilt Field, a wealthy secret Communist, and Thomas A. Bisson, an ostensibly independent writer, whose covert ties to Soviet intelligence did not become public knowledge until long after his death and the release of the Venona decryptions.

Shortly after launching the magazine, in April 1937, Jaffe took a four-month trip to the Far East with his wife. In China they met Bisson, the scholar Owen Lattimore, and Edgar Snow, whose flattering portrait of the Chinese Communists, *Red Star over China*, had just been published. In June they all traveled together to Yenan, Communist headquarters, where they met with Mao Tse-tung, Chou En-lai, and other Chinese Communist Party leaders, cementing Jaffe's loyalty to their cause.

After returning to the United States, Jaffe basked in the success of his new magazine, which published contributions by Roosevelt administration officials, distinguished scholars, and covert and overt Communists. Subscriptions soared past 1,700, an impressive total for a highly specialized journal, with one-third going to government agencies, and *Amerasia* becoming a familiar presence in debates about American policy in the Far East. For Jaffe, whose yearnings for an academic career had foundered because of his need to go into business to support a family, the opportunity to interact with scholars and policy makers was a heady experience. He became a frequent contributor to symposia and panel discussions and reveled in his newfound status as an expert on China policy.

That status, however, rested on Jaffe's own financial subsidy that kept the journal alive. By 1941 Field had left to pursue other Communist causes, and Jaffe was the sole support of the operation. During World War II, *Amerasia* became even more of a one-man operation. Jaffe's main aide was assistant editor Kate Mitchell, from a wealthy Buffalo, New York, family, who did much of the writing as onetime contributors reduced their submissions due to wartime pressures. Jaffe also began to work closely with a former *Amerasia* employee, Andrew Roth, a young lieutenant in the Office of Naval Intelligence, specializing in Japan, whose interests in the Far East had been stoked by a college class he had taken with Chi Ch'ao-ting. Sympathetic to communism and critical of American policy on how to democratize Japan after the war, Roth provided Jaffe with an entree to potential authors and sources of inside information for *Amerasia*, kept him informed of Washington gossip on Asian policy, and helped him obtain reports produced by government agencies.

During one of Jaffe's trips to Washington in the spring of 1944, Roth, introduced him to Emmanuel (Jimmy) Larsen, a civilian State Department employee then on loan to the Office of Naval Intelligence. As a young boy, Larsen had lived in China; he had graduated from a Danish university and then returned to China to work for two decades in a variety of jobs. In the mid-1930s he returned to the United States and took a government job, where he continued to pursue a private obsession with accumulating biographical information on prominent figures in Chinese history. Larsen had no discernible political interests, but he and Jaffe got along well, united by a shared obsession with biographical data; Larsen even sold Jaffe a copy of his files, an action that undoubtedly stimulated thoughts of future cooperation in both men.

The FBI quickly became aware of Jaffe's various contacts in Washington. When he prepared for a trip to the capital in late March, agents inventoried the documents on desks in the Office of Far Eastern Affairs at the State Department in hopes of tracing anything that later turned up in Jaffe's possession, and another group of agents in New York broke into *Amerasia*'s offices and photographed a number of classified documents strewn about, including some with Emmanuel Larsen's name on them. That same day a wiretap picked up a mysterious conversation about "bananas" that appeared to be in code between Jaffe and someone at a phone registered to Emmanuel Larsen. The following day agents watched Larsen meet Jaffe at his hotel, saw Roth join them, and, after Larsen left, Roth and Jaffe pore over documents that Roth had brought with him in a thick manila envelope. Over the next two months, electronically bugged hotel rooms provided agents with recordings of conversations in which Roth and Jaffe discussed getting confidential material from Assistant Secretary of the Treasury Harry Dexter White (see Chapter 3). They watched Roth's wife meet in Washington with her husband and Larsen, leave the luncheon with bulging envelopes, take them with her to New York, and pass them on to Jaffe. They observed Roth meeting with Chi Ch'ao-ting and with State Department officials. They saw both Roth and Larsen pass documents to Jaffe.

The next person to become a suspect was Mark Gayn, a journalist for *Collier's* and *Time* magazines and a correspondent for the *Chicago Sun* newspaper. Born in Manchuria as Mark Ginsbourg, the son of a Russian exile, he lived in the Soviet Union as a teenager before the family moved to China. After attending college in the United States, Mark became a correspondent in China in the mid-1930s. His regular columns for mainstream American publications often boasted about his "confidential sources." When he met with Jaffe, he too became an object of FBI surveillance.

Until mid-April, however, the FBI had not determined that any espionage was taking place because it could not clearly establish that any information had been given to agents of a foreign power, a necessary legal component for a formal charge of espionage. Roth was writing a book on Japan, Jaffe was editing a magazine, and Gayn was a journalist. This leaking of confidential information might be dangerous and illegal but was not necessarily espionage. While Jaffe had visited CPUSA headquarters, there was as yet no positive evidence that he had given anyone there confidential government papers. Everything changed when John Stewart

Service, a foreign service officer, returned from China in the middle of April.

Service had been born in 1909 in China, where his parents worked with American missionary programs. Shortly after graduating from Oberlin College, he joined the State Department, became a foreign service officer (i.e., a career diplomat), and was posted to China. During World War II he grew increasingly disillusioned about corruption and incompetence within the Kuomintang government. His reports buttressed the negative opinions of Chiang Kai-shek held by General Joseph Stilwell, commander of the Far East theater. In July 1944 Service was part of the first official American delegation to visit the Chinese Communists at their Yenan base and was impressed by their discipline, spirit, and potential. The Chinese Communists put on an elaborate "Potemkin village" display that presented life in Communist Yenan as a communal utopia, and Service accepted it at face value and was naively oblivious about their long-term goals to build a totalitarian state modeled on Stalin's USSR. Convinced that a civil war would follow the defeat of the Japanese, and that the Communists would win, he believed that the United States should build ties to them.

Service found himself in a precarious position by early 1945. Stilwell was removed from his position, recalled to the United States, and placed under a gag order to prevent him from expressing his scathing criticisms of Chiang. Service's attacks on Chiang and defense of Stilwell angered the new American ambassador to China, Patrick Hurley, who suspected, accurately, that Service was going behind his back and helping to spread Stilwell's views within the press and undercut Hurley's own diplomatic efforts. Service was sent back to Washington in April and given a desk and few responsibilities. Encouraged by another "China Hand," John Carter Vincent, and Lauchlin Currie, a Roosevelt aide (and covert source for Soviet intelligence – see Chapter 3), Service decided to leak information to discredit Hurley, Chiang Kai-shek, and the Kuomintang government.

The first journalist with whom he met was Mark Gayn. A day later, Andrew Roth suggested Service meet with Philip Jaffe. From the first moment an FBI wiretap picked up Jaffe's conversations with Service, it became apparent that the stakes had been raised. Service admitted leaking diplomatic material, offered to provide Jaffe with sensitive internal government reports, and seemed to be aware of *Amerasia*'s left-wing reputation. Within a day, he was bringing material for Jaffe to read. And several days later FBI agents observed a meeting at Jaffe's New York home attended by a Chinese Communist Party representative to the United Nations Conference, an encounter that could have provided an opportunity to pass along confidential diplomatic and military information.

Early in May, Jaffe met with Joseph Bernstein, a former *Amerasia* employee. While the FBI could not overhear their conversation, Jaffe soon met with Earl Browder. The significance of these meetings became clear on May 7, when Jaffe returned to Washington, and the FBI listened in to a conversation with Roth in his hotel room in which Jaffe explained to Roth why he was so anxious to cultivate Service.

The listening FBI heard Jaffe tell Lieutenant Roth that Joseph Bernstein claimed to be a Soviet spy and needed Jaffe's help in obtaining material from the Far Eastern Division of the State Department. Jaffe also explained that he was unsure that Bernstein was what he claimed to be, and that was why he also had met with Earl Browder. Browder, Jaffe said, had advised him to insist on meeting Bernstein's Soviet controller rather than trusting Bernstein's self-identification. Although he had not yet followed through, Jaffe explained to Roth that this contact was the culmination of his dream to work on behalf of the Soviet Union and the real reason he had first begun to cultivate Emmanuel Larsen. Roth was alarmed and pointed out to Jaffe that he could serve Soviet interests by continuing to leak secrets through his magazine's published articles without the risk of giving material directly to covert Soviet agents, but Jaffe was adamant that this was not sufficient, and Roth eventually acquiesced. Over the next few weeks FBI agents monitoring wiretaps heard Service telling Jaffe that certain information he had given him was confidential, heard Bernstein and Jaffe using a primitive code substituting "cigarettes" for documents, and heard Jaffe passionately explain to Roth that "the first test of a real radical is, do you trust the Soviet Union through thick and thin, regardless of what anybody says," because it is "the one shining star in the whole damned world, and you got to defend that with your last drop of blood."

Although the FBI never observed the actual transfer of documents to Bernstein, it suspected that he was, in fact, a Soviet agent. A graduate of Yale, where he was a member of a Communist student group, Bernstein had worked in Europe as a journalist and translator. Back in the United States in 1938, he associated with several literary figures close to Willi Münzenberg, the master propagandist of the Communist International. When he had applied for a government job in 1940, discrepancies in his record had prompted an investigation that resulted in rejection. He had told Jaffe that he had long been a Communist Party member but had been instructed to drop his membership when he went to work for Soviet intelligence. Years later, a decrypted Venona cable identified Bernstein as a GRU (Soviet military intelligence) agent operating under the cover name of Marquis, who had been working for the Soviets since at least 1943.

By late May 1945 the FBI was under pressure to make arrests by the OSS and other agencies whose documents had been stolen. Several intercepted comments suggested that some of the defendants might be getting suspicious about the wiretaps and surveillance. Roth's transfer to a new posting had been held up to keep him in Washington, but further delays might prompt him to begin to wonder if something was wrong. More than two months had gone by since the opening of the investigation. If spying was going on, every day without an arrest increased the risk that crucial information might be transmitted to unauthorized parties. Although the FBI had no direct evidence that Jaffe had passed classified documents to either the Chinese Communists or Bernstein, further surveillance might not turn up anything since Jaffe and Roth had discussed simply providing Bernstein with oral reports. Finally, the Bernstein connection was due to electronic eavesdropping, so even if Jaffe changed his mind and was caught in the act of giving him government documents, any evidence might still be inadmissible in court.

The major problem for government prosecutors, in fact, would be the admissibility of much of their evidence. The initial investigation by the OSS had quickly led to a surreptitious entry into *Amerasia*'s offices. No warrant had been obtained. The wiretaps on all the suspects had, likewise, been placed without warrants or court orders. Although the law, court decisions, and presidential directives were not clear about whether the OSS and FBI actions were permissible on intelligence and national security grounds during wartime (and World War II was still raging), using the evidence in a legal proceeding was fraught with difficulties. The FBI, for its part, argued that in wartime the government had the right to take extraordinary measures to recover its own property. Justice Department officials, moreover, were confident that if some of the defendants were arrested with government documents in their possession or some could be induced to confess and cooperate, the issue of tainted evidence would never arise.

Because the arrests might affect the upcoming United Nations conference and relations with the Soviet Union due to *Amerasia*'s Communist links, President Truman was informed; he ordered Justice Department prosecutors to go ahead immediately. On June 6, Jaffe, Service, Roth, Larsen, Gayn, and Kate Mitchell were arrested and charged with conspiracy to commit espionage. A horde of classified government documents was found in Jaffe's and Mitchell's offices, Gayn's home, and Larsen's apartment. Additionally, the FBI had found a copy of a classified document in Lieutenant Roth's handwriting in Jaffe's office, as well as documents given to Jaffe by Service. None of those arrested confessed to anything, but both Larsen and Service dropped hints that they would be open to helping the government.

The government press release announcing the arrests said nothing about the exact content of the evidence or documents seized by the FBI. The media, spurred on by some impolitic comments by State Department officials suggesting the arrests were part of a crackdown on unauthorized leaking to journalists, began to question if there was less to the case then met the eye. The government was accused of "red-baiting," engaging in vendettas against whistleblowers, and trying to muzzle reporters, three of whom were under arrest. There was no public evidence that any of the documents had been passed to an agent of a foreign government, and no Soviet citizen or other foreign national had been arrested. While many of the seized documents were innocuous, there was resistance to using the more sensitive ones in court, because that would expose the information in them and thus deliver them to the USSR and the Chinese Communists, the very entities from which the government wanted the information kept. Still, classified documents had been found in the possession of people who had no right to them; FBI wiretaps and bugs offered conclusive proof that at least two of the defendants were conspiring to turn sensitive material over to a Soviet agent, and other defendants had knowingly furnished material to unauthorized persons. Finally, several of those arrested had hinted that they would be willing to cooperate with prosecutors; obtaining their evidence could very well force guilty pleas from some of the others.

Between the arrests in June and the final disposition of the court case in October, however, nothing went right for the prosecutors. Some of their problems were linked to the evidence – both its nature and the way it was obtained. More seriously, political pressure brought to bear on the prosecutors eviscerated their case and their enthusiasm for pursuing it. John Service and Kate Mitchell hired well-connected, powerful lawyers who skillfully manipulated the system to protect their clients. Rather than pushing hard to obtain their testimony against their codefendants, the chief prosecutor caved in and watched his entire case collapse. The debacle became fuel for long and bitter complaints by conservatives that Communist sympathizers had managed to cover up espionage and prevent a full airing of the facts of the case. The truth was far more complicated but almost as seedy.

The government began presenting the case to a grand jury on June 21, just two weeks after the arrests. Robert Hitchcock, the lead prosecutor, planned to indict all six on charges of embezzling government property and use that charge to induce one or more to cooperate, enabling him to then file charges of conspiracy to commit espionage against the holdouts. It appears the grand jury followed his bidding (although these embezzlement indictments were never filed). But Hitchcock soon faced intense political pressure to cut a deal for several of the defendants.

Almost immediately after his arrest John Service heard from his old boss, General Stilwell, who assured him of his support and offered to testify on his behalf, a step that would enable Stilwell to make public his stinging criticisms of the Kuomintang regime. Although Service was initially attracted to the idea that a trial would make public the disagreements within the American government about China policy, he soon saw the downside of a trial with all its attendant publicity. Some of his State Department superiors and friends worried that they would be dragged into an ugly debate and counseled against girding for a fight. Service himself worried that a trial would destroy his State Department career, since even an acquittal might reveal his role in leaking damaging government information to the press. While his lawyer mused about relying on technicalities to challenge the admissibility of incriminating documents taken from his desk by the FBI, White House aide Lauchlin Currie was maneuvering to hire Thomas Corcoran, a legendary Washington fixer, to get Service off the hook. Currie had used Service to leak material, so he undoubtedly felt a personal obligation to help him. But unbeknownst to Service, Currie was also cooperating with Soviet intelligence and no doubt feared what a full investigation might uncover.

Once a top Roosevelt aide, "Tommy the Cork," as he was known, had gone into private practice in 1940 and quickly became one of the most effective lobbyists in the capital. Suspicious of his tactics and worried about his political loyalty, Harry Truman ordered the FBI to wiretap Corcoran's phones shortly after becoming president. The surveillance was in place just in time for the FBI to follow his extraordinary manipulation of the Justice Department on behalf of Service. Corcoran had no ideological ax to grind in the case, but he did have a very practical reason to aid Service. One of his private clients, China Defense Supplies, channeled aid to Chiang Kai-shek; Corcoran was even an officer of the company. His motive in helping a vocal critic of the Chinese government was quite practical. A trial would put Stilwell on the stand to denounce the Kuomintang regime's corruption, damage China's image in the United States, and, given the nature of some of the classified documents, embarrass both Chiang and his wife with details of their less-than-exemplary personal lives.

Corcoran quickly began working his connections. He assured the newly appointed attorney general Tom Clark that he had defused potential opposition to his confirmation and badgered Assistant Attorney General James McGranery with stories of Service's integrity, political connections, and distance from the other defendants. When the Justice Department sought to have Service testify against the others, Corcoran warned that putting Service in that position would ruin his career. Corcoran's campaign succeeded. While Hitchcock insisted on having Service appear before the grand jury, he assured Corcoran that he had nothing to fear. In early August Corcoran informed Service that his appearance was "double riveted from top to bottom," he would not be in any jeopardy or have to answer any tough questions, and he would not have to testify against Jaffe or Roth. With the lead prosecutor signaling his sympathy, the grand jury voted not to indict Service on any charge.

At the same time that Corcoran was ensuring that Service would not have to testify against his codefendants to escape prosecution, Kate Mitchell's lawyers were delighted to discover that the prosecutor did not seem zealous to negotiate a plea or force her to testify against anyone else. The Justice Department's Hitchcock even offered to show Mitchell the questions he intended to ask her, and he brushed aside Gayn's offer to plead to a lesser charge as unnecessary. When they went before the grand jury, he questioned them in a perfunctory manner, and neither was indicted. After he left government employ in December 1945, prosecutor Hitchcock became a partner in the Buffalo law firm whose senior partner, Kate Mitchell's uncle, had negotiated the dismissal of the charges against her.

The grand jury voted to indict Jaffe, Larsen, and Roth on August 10, 1945. Noting that even their indictments were not unanimous, Hitchcock advised his superiors and the FBI that a plea deal resulting in no jail time was the government's best hope of securing convictions. While the FBI continued to demand that the defendants pay some price for stealing classified documents, Larsen persuaded his building superintendent to sign an affidavit that the FBI had searched his apartment without a warrant, and his lawyer was about to inform the press that he was moving to suppress all the government documents seized after his arrest. Afraid that once Larsen's motion became public, Jaffe would conclude that the same tactic had been used against him, the Justice Department quickly worked out an agreement that Jaffe would plead guilty to unauthorized possession of government documents and pay a $5,000 fine but get no jail time. Hitchcock told the judge on October 10 that he agreed with Jaffe's attorney that the whole case was a result of an excess of journalistic zeal on *Amerasia*'s part and had nothing to do with espionage. The judge reduced Jaffe's fine to $2,500. A few months later, Larsen pleaded *nolo contendere*, and Jaffe, no doubt delighted that his own forays into espionage would escape scrutiny, paid his $500 fine for him. In subsequent interviews with the FBI, Jaffe minimized Lieutenant Roth's role in the whole affair, and, despite contradictions between his story and the evidence gained from wiretaps and bugs, Justice Department attorneys concluded that they would not be able to convict Roth; the charges against him were dismissed in February 1946.

Apart from Jaffe and Larsen, none of the others involved in the *Amerasia* case were ever brought to court. Kate Mitchell faded into obscurity, became a heavy drinker, and died in the early 1960s. Mark Gayn remained a newspaper reporter, getting into trouble after filing a story from Korea based on classified information. He privately broke with communism but was unable to obtain an American passport and visa for his second wife, a Hungarian, and settled in Canada where he worked for the *Toronto Sun* for many years. Andrew Roth became a foreign correspondent for the *Nation* magazine; when he was threatened with the nonrenewal of his passport, he decided to remain in Great Britain where he established himself as a successful left-wing journalist and publisher. John Service was reinstated by the State Department after the grand jury refused to indict him and posted to Japan as an aide to General Douglas MacArthur. As will be seen, however, *Amerasia* came back to haunt him.

In the years after the *Amerasia* case, the American National Security Agency in the Venona project decoded nearly three thousand cables sent between Soviet intelligence officers in the United States and their headquarters in Moscow. The decryptions identified *Amerasia* employees Joseph Bernstein and Thomas Bisson as Soviet spies. Joseph Bernstein was, in fact, working for the GRU, just as Jaffe had told Andrew Roth. Although the FBI continued to investigate Bernstein for years, it was never able to gather any legally usable evidence that he had spied. In 1949 the FBI arrested Judith Coplon, a Justice Department counterespionage analyst (see Chapter 6) as a Soviet spy. One of the documents in her possession was an FBI report she had stolen that indicated that an agent had observed Bernstein receiving something from another suspected Soviet spy and passing it to a Communist Party official. After the document was made public as evidence in the Coplon case, the FBI assumed that Bernstein, alerted that he was under surveillance, ceased any further espionage. Although questioned by the FBI and a grand jury, Bernstein refused to admit anything. He died in 1975.

Thomas Bisson, an economist specializing in Asia matters, had worked for the Board of Economic Warfare in World War II. Bisson, whose pro-Communist sympathies were not well concealed, had been called to testify before a congressional committee in 1943, but he emphatically denied any Communist sympathies in sworn testimony. He then worked for the Institute for Pacific Relations and for *Amerasia*. At the end of World War II he got a job as a senior economic adviser to the Supreme Commander Allied Powers (SCAP), the American occupation authority in Japan. He advised SCAP to support the plans of the Japanese Socialist Party, then leading the Japanese government, to rebuild the Japanese economy along Marxist lines. When center-right parties won the Japanese election of 1949 and took control of the government, Bisson returned to the United States. Years later deciphered Venona messages showed that Bisson had been a Soviet source during World War II, turning over confidential Board of Economic Warfare materials to the Soviet GRU in 1943. He, too, was never prosecuted.

The first major spy prosecution of the nascent Cold War era had collapsed in ruins, but the *Amerasia* spy case as a political issue was just beginning. An enraged J. Edgar Hoover, convinced that the Justice Department had deliberately mishandled the prosecutions, began to leak material. Almost immediately after Jaffe's plea bargain, a conservative congressman demanded a congressional investigation. Assistant Attorney General James McGranery and Tom Corcoran worked unsuccessfully to prevent an inquiry. The House of Representatives voted to undertake a probe under the direction of Congressman Sam Hobbs (Democrat, Alabama). Working in secret, the Hobbs committee heard from an embittered Emmanuel Larsen, who had lost his government job and who irrationally thought himself an innocent victim and blamed the whole mess on a pro-Soviet cabal headed by Under Secretary of State Dean Acheson. A slew of government witnesses from the OSS, Justice Department, and FBI pointed the finger at each other for mishandling the investigation. Despite hints that someone had engaged in a cover-up of espionage, Hobbs, a conservative southern Democrat, had no desire to embarrass the Truman administration or step on the FBI's toes. The final report, issued in October 1946, denounced the State Department and Office of Naval Intelligence for lax security and personnel policies, but the actual hearings were closed to the public and the report received little attention.

The next flurry of attention came from Emmanuel Larsen. Unemployed and bitter, Larsen convinced himself that he had been made a scapegoat. He was particularly galled that Service had not been indicted, had retained his government job, and received generous support from colleagues in the State Department. Larsen wrote an article for the inaugural issue of Isaac Don Levine's anti-Communist magazine, *Plain Talk*, in October 1946, claiming that a secret Communist clique at the State Department determined to eliminate pro-Chiang officials was responsible for leaking material to Jaffe. Service, Larsen claimed, had framed him to protect this clique. Although the article made a splash, Larsen soon sank back into obscurity, now nurturing a grudge against the conservative anti-Communists he felt had lost interest in the *Amerasia* case and abandoned him.

By 1948 *Amerasia* had been overshadowed by the startling testimony of Whittaker Chambers and Elizabeth Bentley, both former couriers for Soviet intelligence, before the House Committee on Un-American Activities. Their charges that dozens of former and current government employees had worked for the Soviet Union mesmerized the country. None of those they named had been arrested in the *Amerasia* case. But both Bentley and Chambers had identified Lauchlin Currie as a source, although neither one had met directly with him. Currie, by now a private citizen, appeared before the committee, answered all the questions he was asked, indignantly denied the charges, but in 1950 left the United States, taking a consulting job in Colombia and later became a Colombian citizen. Only after his death did the decoded Venona cables demonstrate that, in fact, Currie had worked for Soviet intelligence.

Sequel to *Amerasia*: Joseph McCarthy

The charges against Alger Hiss also refocused attention on the State Department as a place infiltrated by Soviet agents. Disenchanted by the department's slow response to President Truman's loyalty-security program and sensing a potentially useful issue for his reelection campaign, one obscure conservative senator caused an uproar in February 1950, shortly after Hiss's conviction for perjury. Joseph McCarthy of Wisconsin was a first-term Republican senator whose undistinguished career had left him politically vulnerable. On the advice of several consultants, he decided to use the Communist issue. Speaking to a Republican group in Wheeling, West Virginia, he denounced the State Department as a nest of spies and included John Stewart Service prominently on the list. Back in Washington, a special subcommittee of the Foreign Relations Committee was set up to investigate McCarthy's charges that "card carrying Communists" were rife in the department. Chaired by Millard Tydings of Maryland, a McCarthy critic, the subcommittee began hearings that Democrats hoped would expose the thin evidence upon which McCarthy had based his claims. McCarthy's charges were, in fact, based on thin evidence. The list he had access to was not a roster of suspected spies but an obsolete list of State Department personnel about whom there were unresolved security risk questions, a much less dramatic matter. McCarthy met with Larsen in a desperate hope to buttress his charges with something substantive. Larsen, however, shied away from implicating himself in espionage and indicated he wanted nothing to do with the hearings.

McCarthy then took a different tack and implicated Jaffe and Service as tools of Owen Lattimore. Lattimore, McCarthy told the Tydings committee and the U.S. Senate, was "the top Russian spy," "one of the top espionage agents," and the "chief Soviet espionage agent in the United States," and he predicted that when the Lattimore case was exposed "it will be the biggest espionage case in the history of the country."

Lattimore was a pioneering scholar of the little-known cultures of the Chinese borderlands of Mongolia, Manchuria, and the Turkic-speaking regions of inner Asia. In 1941 Generalissimo Chiang Kai-shek, leader of the Nationalist Chinese government, requested that the United States recommend a political adviser to assist his relations with the United States during the war against Japan. The White House, on the advice of Lauchlin Currie, chose Owen Lattimore, and he served in Chiang's headquarters at Chungking during 1941 and 1942. Lattimore later served as deputy director of Pacific operations for the U.S. Office of War Information. In 1950 he was director of the School of International Relations at Johns Hopkins University that educated many aspiring American diplomats.

McCarthy's charges were explosive. Right away, however, there were problems with the case against Lattimore. He had never had been a State Department official, the ostensible place at which the espionage had taken place, although he had worked with the State Department and at various times was associated with American diplomats. McCarthy flung a lot of rhetoric at Lattimore, with vague charges that he had "access to all the files" at the State Department and "comes in whenever he cares to," but he had no evidence of specific acts of espionage. McCarthy, indeed, had no case that Owen Lattimore had engaged in espionage and only weak evidence that he was a concealed Communist.

McCarthy persuaded Louis Budenz, a former Communist *Daily Worker* editor, to testify to the Tydings committee that a high party official had told him to regard Lattimore's pronouncements about Asia as those of a Communist. Budenz, however, had no firsthand knowledge of Lattimore's Communist allegiance, and even this indirect evidence was weakened by the circumstances of its production. Budenz had defected from the CPUSA in 1945, had been interviewed extensively by the FBI, and had written a great deal about his activities in the party and of what he knew or had heard of the party's underground work. He had never publicly identified Lattimore as a Communist until 1950, nor had he done so privately to the FBI. This delayed recollection seriously undercut the credibility of what was interesting but nonetheless secondhand evidence. The timing of Budenz's naming Lattimore just when McCarthy needed some support appeared suspicious. Actually Budenz had identified Lattimore as a secret ally of the CPUSA in private discussion in 1948 with Alfred Kohlberg, prior to McCarthy coming on the scene. But Kohlberg, a fierce enemy of the "China Hands," had persuaded Budenz to keep this information away from the FBI until Kohlberg found a sympathetic congressman to whom to leak it. McCarthy was the recipient of the leak.

As the weakness of his spy case against Lattimore became clear, McCarthy changed the charge. In a rare half-retreat, he told the Senate "I may have perhaps placed too much stress on the question of whether or not he had been an espionage agent" and went on to attack Lattimore as having promoted and inspired among his contacts at the State Department an Asia policy that allowed the Communists to take control of China.

This, of course, was not espionage but the subtler matter of influencing U.S. policy for improper reasons, a charge that was even more difficult to prove.

McCarthy's charges about Lattimore, in any event, were soon competing with newspaper accounts of how the prosecution had either bungled or deliberately mishandled the original *Amerasia* prosecutions. Details from the Hobbs committee's secret hearings were leaked to the press, revealing for the first time just how extensive a collection of classified government documents Jaffe had accumulated. The appearance of impropriety of the chief prosecutor going to work in the law firm representing one of the defendants got noticed. The curious lack of prosecutorial diligence of the Justice Department occasioned comment. When the Tydings committee turned its attention directly to the *Amerasia* case in closed hearings, Justice Department officials minimized the seriousness of the whole affair and placed the blame for the fiasco on the bungling of the FBI investigation that had tainted the evidence.

Angry at the accusations leveled at the FBI and still convinced that it was Justice Department decisions that had destroyed the case and allowed guilty defendants to escape unscathed, J. Edgar Hoover threatened to have his aides testify that the Justice Department prosecutors knew quite well that the FBI had entered homes and offices without a warrant before approving the arrests. Hoover eventually worked out a deal with his nominal boss, Attorney General Peyton Ford, to avoid airing dirty linen before Congress. In particular, they agreed that there should not be a hint of the Corcoran tapes that revealed a successful effort to let Service escape not only prosecution but also even the need to testify against anyone else.

When Service, Larsen, and Jaffe appeared before the Tydings committee, the cover-up of a cover-up continued. Larsen repudiated his testimony before the Hobbs committee, suggesting that the transcript had been altered. He claimed that Isaac Don Levine had also changed his original article for *Plain Talk* to create a nonexistent pro-Communist clique in the State Department. He contradicted sworn statements he had previously made before the State Department Loyalty-Security Board about Service. None of this bothered the Democratic members of the committee, who were delighted that Larsen had punctured McCarthy's charges.

By the time Jaffe testified, he had broken with communism. Not only had his old friend Earl Browder been deposed as CPUSA leader, but also Jaffe's refusal to support Henry Wallace, the Communist-backed candidate for president in 1948, had sparked attacks on him in Communist publications. Although he toyed with the idea of exposing Joseph Bernstein's role for Soviet intelligence, his inability to obtain a guarantee of his own immunity from prosecution led Jaffe to invoke the Fifth Amendment more than one hundred times. The FBI continued to monitor Bernstein's activities for many years, but, without Jaffe's cooperation, it never developed enough evidence to prosecute him, despite the wiretap evidence that he had solicited Jaffe to cooperate in espionage and Venona decryptions confirming his work for the Soviets.

John Stewart Service was a far more cooperative witness but just as inaccurate and deceptive as Larsen. He presented himself as far more naive about Jaffe and *Amerasia* than he actually was. More seriously, Service lied about his relationship with Tom Corcoran and denied that Corcoran had done anything more for him than recommend another lawyer. While the minority Republican counsel bombarded him with questions clearly based on an FBI leak about the Corcoran wiretaps, Service refused to admit that he had been told the case had been fixed. The controversy also prompted the State Department's Loyalty-Security Board to reinvestigate Service. He brazenly lied to the board, denying that he had ever given Jaffe copies of a number of his government reports; his argument was accepted and Service was cleared for continued State Department employment. However, the next level Civil Service Loyalty-Security Review Board found his behavior during the episode ethically troubling, and the State Department fired him in 1951. He filed a lawsuit, claiming that the review panel had no authority to reconsider his case, given the State Department's Loyalty-Security Board's exoneration, and a unanimous Supreme Court agreed in 1957. Service was reinstated, but the State Department denied him a security clearance and assigned him to low-level positions for several years. Realizing his career as a diplomat was over, he resigned and entered graduate school at the University of California, Berkeley. Later in life he would continue to express admiration for Communist China and even for Mao's catastrophic Cultural Revolution.

The Tydings committee conducted only a superficial examination of the *Amerasia* case. The Democratic majority was not anxious to probe too deeply into allegations of malfeasance in either the State Department or the Justice Department. The majority rebuffed Republican requests to call Corcoran and Lauchlin Currie to testify. The panel split along partisan lines in its report, with the Democrats finding "not one shred of evidence" that the case had been fixed and the Republicans decrying a "whitewash." Its conclusions did nothing to end the controversy about Soviet spies or change anyone's mind about the validity of McCarthy's charges.

Because two of the Justice Department's principal figures in the original cover-up, Tom Clark and James McGranery, had become judges (Clark on the U.S. Supreme Court, McGranery a federal district judge), the Truman administration continued to fend off efforts to reopen the issue for fear of a major scandal. McGranery became attorney general of the United States in 1952 and lied during his confirmation hearings about his role in the *Amerasia* case. J. Edgar Hoover used the opportunity to remind his new boss that he had in his possession a wiretap of the conversation in which McGranery and Corcoran had discussed getting Service out of trouble and provided him with a copy. The first major espionage case of the postwar era may have fizzled out because of evidentiary problems and political interference, but the bitterness and sordidness it occasioned left a major residue. The lying and political manipulations spawned by *Amerasia* enmeshed two attorney generals – one of whom committed perjury – while several spies and would-be spies avoided prison.

Sequel to *Amerasia*: McCarran and Lattimore

The Tydings committee had exonerated Lattimore, but his troubles were far from over. Senator Pat McCarran, a conservative Democrat from Nevada, shared McCarthy's view that Lattimore was a Soviet agent. McCarran headed the Senate Judiciary Committee's Internal Security Subcommittee (SISS), the Senate equivalent of the U.S. House Committee on Un-American Activities. McCarran ordered a full-scale investigation of Lattimore and set out to prove that a cabal of concealed Communists in the government had manipulated America's China policy.

While the Tydings committee had been deferential to Lattimore, McCarran's committee was hostile. Senator McCarran subjected Lattimore to twelve days of examination in 1952, constantly interrupted him, made hostile and rude comments about his testimony, and asked him questions of such complexity and vagueness as to make an adequate reply impossible. Lattimore responded with equal animosity and impudence. His answers were often evasive, his tone sneering, and he had convenient lapses of memory on key points of his record. Neither McCarran nor Lattimore emerged from the affair looking very good. But McCarran, despite his single-minded effort, could not turn up any evidence that Lattimore had committed espionage or that he was a concealed Communist. He did, however, present plenty of evidence that Lattimore's views about communism and the Soviet Union were such that most Americans would not want him anywhere near those involved in setting American foreign policy.

In the late 1930s Lattimore had edited *Pacific Affairs*, a journal of the Institute for Pacific Relations, a think-tank funded largely by business firms and philanthropists interested in promoting American-Asian trade and cultural exchanges. Its membership included international business executives, diplomats, journalists, and scholars. The McCarran committee hearings as well as several later congressional investigations brought out that concealed Communists had infiltrated the Institute for Pacific Relations in the late 1930s. The secretary (director) of the American section of the Institute for Pacific Relations from 1938 to 1940 was Frederick Vanderbilt Field, a secret Communist totally loyal to the party, and one of the founders and funders of *Amerasia*. Field left the Institute for Pacific Relations in 1940 to become the chief founder and executive director of the American Peace Mobilization, the CPUSA's peace front while the Nazi-Soviet Pact was in effect.

As for Lattimore himself, the record showed that he vigorously defended Stalin's grotesque Moscow Trials and called the Soviet Union a democracy during the worst years of Stalin's dictatorship. He also took the view that there was little to chose from between Great Britain and Nazi Germany during the Nazi-Soviet Pact period, was a close associate of several of those who stole government documents in the *Amerasia* case, and had himself been on *Amerasia*'s editorial board for several years. Investigators also uncovered in the Institute for Pacific Relations files a 1938 letter in which Lattimore told a colleague that the institute needed to lag behind the public position of the Chinese Communists "far enough not to be covered by the same label – but enough ahead of the active Chinese liberals to be noticeable" and that it should back the Soviet Union's "international policy in general but without using their slogans and above all without giving them or anybody else an impression of subservience." Nor did he later change his views; in 1949, just prior to the Communist invasion of South Korea, he said he wanted "to let South Korea fall – but not to let it look as though we pushed it."

In 1944 Lattimore accompanied Vice-President Henry Wallace on a visit to the Soviet Far East. Lattimore, an acknowledged authority on that part of the world, served as Wallace's adviser. One of the places Wallace visited was Magadan, headquarters of Dalstroy, a Soviet agency that ran a network of Gulag labor camps in the Soviet Far East, extracting gold from the Kolyma prison mines and timber from a network of forest prison camps. The Kolyma gold mine prison camps were among the most lethal in the Gulag system and thousands of political prisoners died there from overwork and exposure.

For Wallace's visit to Magadan, the Soviets temporarily took down prison camp guard towers, locked the prisoners in their huts and took Wallace on a tour of a fake farm camp that was manned by Soviet security police pretending to be workers. Wallace was totally taken in and returned to the United States full of praise for what he had seen. This would later deeply embarrass him when the monstrous nature of the Gulag system and the Kolyma camps became well known in the West. Lattimore, as Wallace's expert adviser, should have warned the vice-president that he was seeing a Potemkin village. Instead, he went along with the Soviet facade and in his own right praised Dalstroy. Given Lattimore's reputation as an expert on that area of Asia, his later explanations that he, too, had been taken in had limited credibility.

None of this proved that Lattimore was a spy or even that he was a concealed Communist. The FBI, which did its own investigation, concluded that, although Lattimore was ardently pro-Communist in his sympathies, there was no reliable evidence that he was a Soviet agent or even a secret member of the CPUSA. Senator McCarran was not, however, satisfied with showing that Lattimore held pro-Soviet views. He was sure that Lattimore was a major Soviet spy and insisted that the Justice Department find something in the twelve days of testimony before SISS that could be the basis for a perjury charge. Because McCarran was a powerful Democratic senator, Truman's attorney general responded. After the Justice Department's regular prosecutors balked at seeking an indictment, Attorney General McGranery brought in Roy Cohn, a hard-driving, win-at-any-price attorney, to prosecute the case.

In December 1953 Cohn persuaded a U.S. grand jury to issue a seven-count indictment for perjury based on Lattimore's testimony before the Senate Internal Security Subcommittee. Some of the counts were on points where documents showed that Lattimore's testimony had been false or incorrect but the substance was minor, the incidents old, and nothing more than poor memory may have been involved. For example, one count charged perjury for Lattimore's testimony that he had not met with Soviet diplomat Constantine Oumansky between September 1939 and June 1941, the period of the Nazi-Soviet Pact, or his denial that when he had edited *Pacific Affairs* in the 1930s he had known that an author who used the nom de plume "Asiaticus" was a Communist. Other points were not overt acts but rather states of mind or matters of opinion inherently difficult to prove or disprove in a court, such as a count charging that Lattimore lied when he denied being sympathetic to communism.

Lattimore, however, was never tried. His attorneys quickly moved to have the indictment dismissed as insubstantial or not judicable. On May 2, 1954, U.S. Judge Luther W. Youngdahl threw out four of the seven counts, including that of perjury in denying sympathy with communism as not judicable or too vague to be fairly answered in a court of criminal law. The three counts Youngdahl left standing concerned minor matters of little apparent importance. Under continued pressure from Senator McCarran, prosecutors appealed Judge Youngdahl's ruling. In July a U.S. Court of Appeals restored two of the counts Youngdahl had dismissed, but supported his dismissal of two, including the key one of perjury for denying sympathy for communism.

This left prosecutors with five counts of perjury, but none of these counts involved matters of any substantive importance, and the Justice Department realized that a jury would be unlikely to send someone to prison for unimportant statements, no matter how false. Consequently, on October 7, 1954, prosecutors convinced a U.S. grand jury to issue a second indictment against Owen Lattimore for perjury: charging him with lying when he denied that he had followed or promoted the Communist line. Again, however, the charges were not matters of fact that a trial could adjudicate but involved lying about matters of political or ideological judgment that were ill-suited for resolution through a criminal trial proceeding. Lattimore's lawyers again appealed, the appeal was again heard by Judge Youngdahl, and in January 1955 he dismissed the new indictment, commenting, "to require a defendant to go to trial for perjury under changes so formless and obscure as those before the court would be unprecedented and would make a sham of the Sixth Amendment [to the Constitution] and the federal rule requiring specificity of charges."

Prosecutors appealed the ruling, and in June 1955 the U.S. Court of Appeals issued an evenly divided opinion. Under federal court rules, that upheld Youngdahl's dismissal of the second indictment. McCarran had died in September 1954, and in his absence the pressure to prosecute

Lattimore faded rapidly. After the reversal at the appeals court, the Justice Department dropped the matter.

Although Lattimore was victorious in avoiding the perjury charges with their implication of espionage, the revelations of his past sympathy for Soviet policies did not recommend him for faculty status in programs training Americans for U.S. government foreign service. He left Johns Hopkins University, and most of the rest of his academic career was spent at the University of Leeds in the United Kingdom.

Gouzenko: A Canadian Spy Case with American Repercussions

On its face the Gouzenko case only tangentially involved the United States. Most of those accused of spying on the basis of the evidence provided by Igor Gouzenko, a code clerk for Soviet military intelligence (GRU) in Ottawa, were Canadians. But the reverberations of the case caused significant tremors in America, providing early indications of the significant scope of Soviet spying, its use of local Communist parties as recruiting centers, and its interest in atomic espionage. The case also graphically illustrates the halting and tentative responses of Western intelligence agencies to the reality of Soviet espionage and the difficulty of developing adequate legal evidence to sustain convictions.

At the same time as Canadian authorities were secretly debriefing Gouzenko and carrying on covert surveillance of the people he implicated, the FBI was trying to assimilate and make sense of Elizabeth Bentley's secret charges about dozens of American government employees. Mindful of the implosion of the *Amerasia* case, which had foundered because of legally inadmissible evidence, prosecutorial blunders and political manipulation, and the failure to obtain the full cooperation of any of the conspirators, counterintelligence officials struggled with questions of how to respond to Soviet espionage.

Igor Gouzenko was a twenty-five-year-old cipher clerk working for the Soviet military attaché, Colonel Nikolai Zabotin, at the USSR's Canadian embassy (to be precise, the USSR's legation). Trained as an engineer, he had apprenticed at a military intelligence academy in Moscow and been sent to Canada in the summer of 1943 along with his wife. Under a strict security regimen, Gouzenko encrypted and encoded messages from Zabotin to GRU headquarters in Moscow and the responses. Many of the messages dealt with the significant spy operation focused on Canada that Zabotin oversaw. The local KGB resident, Vitaly Pavlov, was in charge of a larger espionage network and also had responsibilities for embassy security.

Gouzenko first began to consider defecting in September 1944 when he received orders transferring him back to Moscow. Because of a staff shortage, he was allowed to remain, but he and his wife had become enamored of life in the West. With one young son, born in Canada, and another on the way, the Gouzenkos decided they would not return if ordered. In August 1945 Gouzenko was recalled; he would depart as soon as his replacement arrived and was trained. Determined to remain in Canada, the clerk decided to defect and steal as many secret documents detailing Zabotin's spy ring as he could. On the evening of September 5, he went to the embassy, entered the secret cipher area, stuffed more than a hundred documents in his pockets and under his clothes, and left the building.

Gouzenko's saga over the next few days was graphic evidence of how uncomfortable Canadian officials were about confronting the issue of Soviet espionage. His first stop was a newspaper office, but the editors were gone for the day. Gouzenko nervously explained what he had done to a reporter, but the latter was dismissive and suggested he go to the police. At the Justice Ministry, a sentry informed him that the offices were closed. When he returned the next morning, he was taken to Parliament after insisting that he had to speak to the justice minister. Gouzenko impressed upon everyone to whom he spoke that his life was in danger and that he had information about Soviet espionage in Canada and the United States – including a spy close to American secretary of state Edward Stettinius – and efforts to obtain atomic information. When he was told that the minister would not see him, Gouzenko threatened to commit suicide. While some government officials thought these issues compelling, the prime minister, Mackenzie King, worried about doing anything that the USSR might perceive as an unfriendly act and mused that Gouzenko might be unbalanced.

Rebuffed at the Justice Department, the Gouzenkos returned to the offices of the *Ottawa Journal*, where no one thought tales of Soviet espionage might make for an interesting story. Efforts to apply for asylum in Canada brought news that the process might take months. Distraught, they went back to their apartment. Meanwhile government officials were arguing about how to respond; the consensus was that Gouzenko should be told to go back to the Soviet embassy and return the papers. No one in the government or press wanted to offend the USSR or be seen as provoking an international crisis.

The prime minister did agree to police surveillance of Gouzenko and agreed to try to obtain his documents if he did commit suicide. Back in their apartment, the Gouzenkos noticed strange men watching. When an official from the Soviet embassy knocked on the door, the frightened family slipped out onto a balcony shared by a neighbor, appealed for help, and took shelter with these neighbors. Later that night, four officials from the Soviet embassy broke into the Gouzenkos' apartment. When the police confronted them, they claimed diplomatic immunity and left.

The brazen Russian action convinced Canadian authorities to act. The next day, Gouzenko was given an appointment with the Royal Canadian Mounted Police, granted asylum, and moved to a safe and secure location. For the next few months the government imposed a strict gag order on everyone who knew what had happened while its investigators pored over the documents he had taken. Not a word of his defection reached the public. When the Soviets demanded to know where Gouzenko was and solicited Canadian assistance in locating him, asserting that he had stolen money from the embassy, the Canadian and American governments obligingly pretended to institute a nationwide search for the missing man.

As RCMP officers examined Gouzenko's documents and the extent of the Soviet espionage in Canada became apparent, authorities worried about the proper response and the potential consequences. By not arresting any of the people implicated by Gouzenko's documents, they hoped to keep the Russians confused about whether they were, in fact, holding him or if he was on the run. Prime Minister Mackenzie King began a lengthy process of consultations with the British and American governments to decide how to react. Any public announcement or arrests could spark a confrontation with the Soviet government at a crucial diplomatic moment. On September 20, 1945, Mackenzie King flew to Washington to meet President Truman. His diary entry indicates that he informed the president that the "Corby Case," as it was code-named, involved atomic bomb information and "also the statement [by Gouzenko] that an assistant secretary of the Secretary of State's Department was supposed to be implicated," a reference that was later taken to be Alger Hiss, who had been an assistant to Secretary of State Edward Stettinius.

Soon after leaving the White House, King sailed to London where he discussed the issue of arresting Alan Nunn May, a scientist whose espionage on behalf of the Soviets had been revealed by the documents. May had joined the British atomic bomb project in 1942 and in the summer of 1943 came to the Canadian Department of Scientific and Industrial Research to work on the natural uranium reactor at Chalk River, then part of the wartime joint British-American atomic project. The GRU approached him and recruited him as a spy while he was working at Chalk River, and he had the cover name "Alek" in Gouzenko's documents. May made three trips to the Manhattan Project's atomic reactor in Chicago and obtained uranium isotope samples for his own work at the Chalk River reactor. He then passed these along to the GRU before being scheduled to return to England to continue work on Britain's independent postwar atomic bomb project. Because one of the Gouzenko messages contained plans to have May meet a Soviet agent in London, intelligence agents had decided to allow him to depart in mid-September. He never kept the scheduled rendezvous, but it was decided to keep him under surveillance and not make any immediate arrest.

The British and American governments were concerned that the timing of any arrests not disrupt ongoing delicate negotiations about the international control of atomic weapons. The Canadians, used to playing a supporting role in international affairs, were very leery of doing anything that might complicate diplomatic activities or upset more powerful political forces. An additional concern was that hard evidence of espionage was lacking. Gouzenko's documents listed only code names, and he had never had any direct contact with any of the spies. While he would later testify that he had heard or learned the real names of some of the spies and this evidence was factually compelling, legally it was hearsay and inadmissible in court. Unless spies were caught in the act of passing information, convictions in a court of law were difficult since espionage by its nature was an activity carried out in secret that left few traces. By the end of 1946 several of the Russian intelligence officers involved, including Colonel Zabotin, had been recalled to Moscow, a sign that the Russians were afraid Gouzenko was in Canadian custody and talking; they would have obviously suspended any connections with Canadian spies for the duration.

The legal context in Canada differed drastically from that of the United States in regard to espionage-related matters and gave Canadian authorities wide investigatory powers. The Canadian War Measures Act, still in force in 1946, allowed suspects to be questioned in secret without benefit of legal counsel, but there was concern that any confessions obtained under such duress might not stand up in a trial. A few suspects were vulnerable because Gouzenko had obtained handwritten memos they had supplied, but the only way to ensure convictions was if suspects could be induced to confess. The Royal Canadian Mounted Police and prosecutors considered a plan to arrest those implicated, holding them incommunicado without access to family, friends, and lawyers and interrogating them. The prime minister would create a royal commission to question Gouzenko, assess the evidence (including secret material not deemed suitable for open proceedings), and issue a report that would influence public opinion without being entangled in legal issues. But there was no pressure or incentive to move quickly.

Whatever plans the Canadians had to keep the case quiet ended on February 3, 1946. Acting on the basis of a leak from within the American government, Drew Pearson included a report on his Sunday evening broadcast that a Russian spy had provided information about a large Soviet espionage operation directed against the United States and Canada and that the information was of such gravity that King had come to Washington to brief President Truman. The Canadian government quickly responded, creating a royal commission headed by two Supreme Court justices, and authorized suspects to be arrested, held indefinitely, threatened with contempt if they refused to answer questions, and presumed guilty. On February 15 thirteen civil servants were arrested, and Alan Nunn May was picked up and questioned in Great Britain; although their names were not released to the public, after five months Gouzenko's chickens had finally come home to roost.

May's situation was different from anyone else because he was questioned in England. After first denying any contact with the Russians, he broke down when confronted with incriminating evidence and confessed that he had been contacted in Canada by someone he refused to identify who wanted information about atomic research. He had turned over uranium samples and what other information he had. Although he had made arrangements to meet a Russian agent after he returned to England, he had decided to end the relationship. He justified giving atomic secrets to Stalin's USSR on the grounds that "this was a contribution I could make to the safety of mankind." Arrested in early March, May was charged with violating the Official Secrets Act, pled guilty, and was sentenced to ten years in a British prison.

The Canadian Royal Commission, meanwhile, moved slowly. As the press speculated about the identity of those arrested, it remained silent. After two weeks, mounting criticism of the secrecy and the inability of those arrested to see families or lawyers prompted the prime minister to urge more speed. The commission quickly issued its first interim report naming several Russian embassy officials as spies and recommending charging four civil servants with security violations. Meanwhile, on February 20, the Soviet Foreign Ministry issued a statement that its military attaché had received "from Canadian nationals with whom they were acquainted, certain information of a secret character." It denied the information was of any great import or significance due to the advanced nature of Soviet science and noted that the attaché had been recalled as soon as the government became aware of these activities.

The first Canadian commission report noted that two women, Emma Woikin, a cipher clerk employed by the Canadian Department of External Affairs, and Kathleen Willsher, a secretary at the British High Commission, had confessed to giving Soviet officials material from diplomatic cables. Woikin was a naive and lonely Doukhobor (a Russian Orthodox sect that had immigrated to western Canada), who hoped to move back to the Soviet Union. Willsher was a member of the Communist Party of Canada (CPC). They were swiftly convicted and sentenced to several years in prison. Two others were also implicated in the initial report. Gordon Lunan, an employee of the Canadian Wartime Information Board, admitted that he had met with a Soviet agent, supplied information, and also asked friends to provide material. He received a five-year sentence. Among Gouzenko's documents were several filled with incriminating comments that indicated Lunan supervised the activities of three other men, Edward Mazerall, Israel Halperin, and Durnford Smith. Edward Mazerall, a National Research Council of Canada employee, admitted that Lunan had asked him for information on radar, then a new and very secret technology, to pass along to the Soviet Union and that he had given him two reports he had written. Mazerall went to prison for four years.

The Canadian commission's second interim report, released in mid-March 1946, led to the prosecutions of Dr. Raymond Boyer, Harold Gerson, Matt Nightingale, and Dr. David Shugar. It also incriminated Sam Carr, head of the Canadian Communist Party, and Fred Rose, a Communist member of the Canadian Parliament from Montreal. Boyer, a chemist at McGill University cover-named "The Professor," worked on RDX, an advanced explosive. He acknowledged passing on secret information to Rose, knowing that it would be transmitted to the USSR, but justified his actions on the grounds that the data were not sensitive and that the Russians were allies. He was sentenced to two years in prison. Gerson, a geological engineer working in the Canadian Department of Munitions and Supply, was convicted of conspiring to violate the Official Secrets Act and jailed for four years. Nightingale, a Royal Canadian Air Force officer, and Shugar, a physicist working on anti–submarine detection, were acquitted even though documents indicated that Carr had tapped both men for assignments. They denied giving any information.

Fred Rose, born in Poland and active in the Communist Party of Canada since the mid-1920s, had been imprisoned in 1930–1931 for sedition. As a result of the Nazi-Soviet Pact, the CPC opposed Canada's participation in the war against Nazi Germany. After it was banned in 1940 as a disloyal organization, more than a hundred of its leaders were interned. Rose, along with party leader Sam Carr, secretly fled to the United States to avoid capture. After the Nazi attack on the Soviet Union in 1941, the CPC reversed course and supported the war effort. Rose surfaced and was briefly interned in 1942 for authoring antiwar pamphlets during the Nazi-Soviet Pact period. He was released in October 1942 after signing an "Understanding" that he would "do no act which might be of injury to the Dominion of Canada, of the United Kingdom, or any of His Majesty's Dominions, or any Allied or Associated Powers." Gouzenko's materials showed that Rose had at that point already volunteered his services to the GRU. Elected to Parliament in 1943 as a candidate of the Labour-Progressive Party, as the Canadian Communist Party then called itself, he was reelected in 1945. Gouzenko's material unambiguously identified him, and Boyer's admission that he had given Rose confidential material sealed his fate. He was sentenced to six years in jail, stripped of his parliamentary seat, and later deported to Communist Poland.

Sam Carr, chief of the Canadian Communist Party, also received a six-year sentence, although he fled Canada and was not apprehended until January 1949 in New York. U.S. authorities returned him to Canada, and he went to jail. Although the commission's final report accused Carr of playing a key role in recruiting agents, he was tried and convicted of conspiracy to commit forgery for his role in obtaining a false passport for a Soviet spy in Los Angeles, using the name of Ignacy Witczak.

Witczak, whose real name is unknown, was a long-term Soviet penetration agent. He appeared in Los Angeles in 1938, claiming to be a Canadian immigrant of Polish birth and carrying a Canadian passport identifying him as Ignacy Witczak. Enrolled in the University of Southern California, he earned a B.A. and M.A. in political science and was admitted to a Ph.D. program. He had a wife and young child. The GRU, however, had made an error in his "legend," or fake background. It had given him the passport of a real person, one Ignacy Witczak of Polish birth who had immigrated to Canada in 1930 and become a Canadian citizen in 1936. The real Witczak had also fought in Spain with the International Brigades, a body of international volunteers sponsored by the Communist International. The Comintern had collected the passports of many of its American and Canadian volunteers and turned them over to Soviet intelligence for their use. The GRU had thought that Witczak had died in Spain and their fake Witczak was free to appropriate his identity. The real Witczak, however, had survived and returned to Canada. This produced a problem in 1945 when the fake Witczak's Canadian passport expired. Renewal could trigger a discovery that there were two Witczaks. On GRU instructions, Sam Carr paid a $3,000 bribe to a Canadian official to take care of the problem. Less than a week after this successful transaction, Gouzenko defected and alerted Canadian authorities to the scheme. It was an easily proven charge, and it enabled the Canadian government to convict Carr rather than pursue a more difficult espionage case.

Informed of the fake Witczak by Canadian authorities, the FBI put him under surveillance. It discovered that although his only known employment since 1938 was as a part-time instructor at the University of Southern California with a salary of $1,700, he had banked $16,000. Witczak traveled from Los Angeles to New York and Washington in 1946, all the while under FBI surveillance. He was observed passing material to a midlevel official of the Interior Department whom he appeared to have met by prearrangement at the Library of Congress. Probably alerted about Gouzenko's defection, he appeared to have detected the surveillance and vanished in late 1945 and was presumed to have returned to the Soviet Union. Gouzenko had the impression that Witczak was establishing a deep-cover reserve espionage apparatus to be activated if a break in American-Soviet diplomatic relations or some other trauma disrupted the networks run by GRU officers operating under diplomatic cover. Witczak's wife, Bunia, who also had a fake Canadian passport and likely was also a GRU officer, and their American-born son were smuggled aboard a Soviet ship in early 1946 and returned to the USSR. Carr received a six-year jail sentence for his role in procuring Witczak's fake Canadian passport.

Five people were named in the third Canadian commission interim report, at the end of March 1946, but only one of them, Durnford Smith, an electrical engineer working for the National Research Council of Canada, was convicted of conspiring to violate the Official Secrets Act. Among Gouzenko's documents were cables indicating that Lunan had introduced Smith to Russians to whom he gave documents. He received a five-year sentence. The other four, Eric Adams, Israel Halperin, J. S. Benning, and Fred Poland, were all acquitted. Halperin, whom the Royal Commission accused of turning over top secret information on weapons systems to Lunan, was allegedly the agent code-named "Bacon" in Gouzenko's documents. A professor of mathematics at Queen's University, Halperin worked on weapons research. His address book contained contact information for many of those arrested, and he had supplied Klaus Fuchs with reading material when he was briefly interned in Canada at the beginning of World War II. Lunan had implicated Halperin in his confession but refused to testify against him in court, earning a contempt citation. The Gouzenko memos indicated that Halperin was reluctant to provide information and refused to put anything down in writing. In one document Lunan noted that "it has become very difficult to work with him" and that, as Halperin realized the full extent of Lunan's activities, "he has a particular dislike for them."

Several other individuals were named in the commission's final report, publicly released in mid-July 1946, either as potential recruits or knowing collaborators but they were not tried. The Canadian spy trials generated a very mixed reaction. There were widespread protests about the way the accused were treated, held in secret without access to lawyers, questioned in camera and forced to testify, deprived of contact with family, and threatened with contempt citations. Those who did not break down and confess when confronted with incriminating evidence were wont to win acquittals when tried. Ten defendants were convicted and imprisoned (including May in England) and sixteen others were either acquitted or released upon appeal. The Royal Commission with its special powers proved successful in eliciting a great deal of testimony from the accused and a number of confessions, and its reports constituted a powerful propaganda tool for the government, but it was far less effective in a court of law, aside from those it induced to confess.

But courts of law are not necessarily the most effective venue to learn about an espionage case. One of those accused, Matt Nightingale, was acquitted because the only direct testimony against him came from an admitted accomplice – Gouzenko. Stolen documents such as those taken by Gouzenko caused problems for prosecutors. The Canadian government was reluctant or unable to introduce some evidence into court. These procedural and legal issues undoubtedly thwarted some of the prosecutions.

The Gouzenko case, however, pushed Soviet espionage into the consciousness of not just the Canadian but also the American public. His documents demonstrated to Western intelligence services just how serious a problem Soviet espionage was. After all, the primary vehicle of the Soviet intelligence services was not the GRU, the division for which Zabotin worked, but the KGB. The involvement of several high officials of the Canadian Communist Party and the use of dedicated members of the party and sympathizers to purloin documents or provide information were also telling. Gouzenko was the first prominent post–World War II defector from Soviet intelligence to expose a widespread Communist Party–based spy network, but he would not be the last.

FURTHER READINGS

The *Amerasia* Case

Klehr, Harvey, and Ronald Radosh. *The Amerasia Spy Case: Prelude to McCarthyism*. Chapel Hill: University of North Carolina Press, 1996.

Comprehensive scholarly history of the case.

Kubek, Anthony. *The Amerasia Papers: A Clue to the Catastrophe of China*. Washington, D.C.: U.S. Government Printing Office, 1970.

Digest of documents and testimony about Amerasia *commissioned by the U.S. Senate Internal Security Subcommittee.*

Larsen, Emmanuel S. "The State Department Espionage Case." Reprinted in book 3 of *Plain Talk: An Anthology from the Leading Anti-Communist Magazine of the 40s*, edited by Isaac Don Levine. New Rochelle, N.Y.: Arlington House, 1976.

A 1946 essay from the magazine PlainTalk *by State Department official Emmanuel Larsen, who pleaded no contest to charges brought against him in the* Amerasia *case, claiming that he did not realize the links between the others in the case and the CPUSA or the extent of the theft of classified documents.*

Service, John S. *The Amerasia Papers: Some Problems in the History of US-China Relations.* Berkeley: Center for Chinese Studies, University of California, 1971.

Defense of Service's views on China.

Owen Lattimore

Lattimore, Owen. *Ordeal by Slander.* Boston: Little, Brown, 1950.

Lattimore's account of the attacks on him as a spy and Communist sympathizer by McCarthy and others.

Newman, Robert P. *Owen Lattimore and the "Loss" of China.* Berkeley: University of California Press, 1992.

Ardent defense of Lattimore and his views.

Ybarra, Michael. *Washington Gone Crazy: Senator Pat McCarran and the Great American Communist Hunt.* South Royalton, Vt.: Steerforth, 2004.

Thorough biography of McCarran that discusses his obsession with Lattimore.

Gouzenko: A Canadian Spy Case with American Repercussions

Bothwell, Robert, and J. L. Granatstein, eds. *The Gouzenko Transcripts: The Evidence Presented to the Kellock-Taschereau Royal Commission of 1946.* Ottawa, Ont.: Deneau, 1982.

Excerpts from the Canadian government investigation.

Gouzenko, Igor. *The Iron Curtain.* Edited and translated by Andy O'Brien. New York: E. P. Dutton, 1948.

Gouzenko's own account of his defection.

Knight, Amy. *How the Cold War Began: The Gouzenko Affair and the Hunt for Soviet Spies.* Toronto: McClelland & Stewart, 2005.

Taschereau, Robert, and Roy Lindsay Kellock, Royal Commissioners. *The Report of the Royal Commission Appointed under Order in Council P.C. 411 of February 5, 1946 to Investigate the Facts Relating to and the Circumstances Surrounding the Communication, by Public Officials and Other Persons in Positions of Trust, of Secret and Confidential Information to Agents of a Foreign Power. June 27, 1946.* Ottawa: E. Cloutier, printer to the King, 1946.

The publicly released report of the Canadian government investigation.

Whitaker, Reginald, and Gary Marcuse. *Cold War Canada: The Making of a National Insecurity State, 1945–1957.* Toronto: University of Toronto Press, 1994.

Discusses the Gouzenko case. Highly critical of anticommunism and Canadian government counterespionage activities.

3

Elizabeth Bentley

THE CASE OF THE BLOND SPY QUEEN

THE HEADLINE IN THE *NEW YORK WORLD TELEGRAM* ON JULY 21, 1948, "Red Ring Bared by Its Blond Queen" began one of the most important and most frustrating of the early Cold War spy cases. Its importance stems from the astounding number of Soviet spies, more than thirty, identified by Elizabeth Bentley and the impact of her revelations on shaping the attitudes of the American public toward Soviet espionage and the role American Communists played in it. What gave the Bentley affair its frustrating aspect, however, is that none of those she identified as Soviet sources were ever tried for espionage and only two were imprisoned, one, a minor figure, for perjury and another for contempt of court.

The U.S. Justice Department decided not to bring espionage charges because the cases came down to the word of a single witness, Elizabeth Bentley, a former Soviet spy and ex-Communist, against the denials of those she accused – with no documentary or other direct evidence of espionage. The FBI amassed sufficient indirect supporting evidence to convince it of Bentley's truthfulness. Federal prosecutors, however, judged that juries, even if convinced that Bentley was probably telling the truth, would be unlikely to send someone to prison without direct corroborating evidence. Because there were no trials on the central aspects of Bentley's claims, most of the evidence the FBI gathered remained secret for nearly fifty years, and the Bentley case faded from public memory. The end of the Cold War and the opening of archives both in the old Soviet bloc and in the United States, however, have brought out documentation more than sufficient to establish that Elizabeth Bentley gave accurate testimony on the important points of her story, and a dramatic story it was.

Elizabeth Bentley was born in 1908, the only child of a middle-class New England family with conventional Republican and Protestant preferences. A bright girl, she won a scholarship to Vassar College, one of the most elite women's colleges in the United States. After graduating in 1930 with a degree in languages (French and Italian), she began teaching at a select girls' finishing school in Virginia. Soon she decided to enroll in graduate school at Columbia University, an uncommon undertaking for women in that era. Her initial work was sufficiently impressive, and in 1933 she won a fellowship to the University of Florence. In Italy, however, she neglected her studies and began an active life of parties, drinking, and romances, including one with her Italian faculty adviser. She did poorly in her courses but, with her faculty adviser's aid, completed a thesis (an assistant of his likely did much of the writing) that was accepted for a master's degree by Columbia University upon her return to New York in 1934.

Back in New York, Bentley had difficulty finding employment in the midst of the Great Depression and grew increasingly frustrated with her circumstances. A neighbor introduced her to the American League against War and Fascism, a group secretly controlled by the Communist Party. She found activists of the group congenial companions, and it was soon a central part of her life. The neighbor, who also turned out to be a secret Communist, urged her to join the CPUSA. Bentley did so and quickly plunged into active party work – taking classes in Marxism-Leninism at a CPUSA school, attending several party meetings a week, joining party marches, and accepting a series of offices in her local party club. Until 1938 Bentley held a variety of short-term jobs interspersed with periods of unemployment, all the while also participating in the demanding round of Communist Party meetings, demonstrations, and literature distribution. In 1938 Columbia University's placement office, mindful of her Italian-language skills, referred her to an opening for a clerical position at the Italian Library of Information, a semiofficial cultural information and propaganda bureau for the Fascist-controlled Italian government. She got the job and immediately went to her CPUSA superiors to volunteer as a party spy inside a pro-Fascist institution. They directed her to a senior party officer named Jacob Golos.

Born in Russia in 1890, Golos joined the early Bolshevik movement as a teenager. Exiled to Siberia for political agitation by the tsarist government, he escaped via Japan and came to the United States in 1910 and was a founding member of the American Communist Party in 1919. With secret funding from the party, in the late 1920s Golos set up the "World Tourists" travel company that had a contractual relationship with

Intourist, the official Soviet travel agency. Its chief business was the selling of Intourist services on commission. These included travel tickets for transport to the USSR as well as hotel and travel services inside the Soviet Union. It also arranged parcel shipping to the USSR, a major source of business due to the large number of immigrants who had family in Russia. The Intourist contract guaranteed World Tourists steady business because almost every American visiting the Soviet Union had to make arrangements through Intourist, the only agency allowed to provide commercial tourist services inside the USSR. Further, Amtorg, the USSR's trading arm, encouraged businessmen seeking to do business with the Soviet state to make their travel arrangements through World Tourists. World Tourists, then, provided a method for the Soviet Union to subsidize the American Communist movement indirectly because the agency's covert owner was the CPUSA itself. World Tourists, however, also facilitated clandestine international travel by American Communists. When heading to the USSR or other foreign destinations on party business or assignments for the Communist International, CPUSA officials and cadre often did so using fake identification and false passports. World Tourists bought their tickets and arranged their travel and never asked embarrassing questions about the travel documents being used.

In addition to running World Tourists, Golos assisted the CPUSA's underground arm. The Communist Party had always regarded the maintenance of a secret, conspiratorial apparatus as a necessity. The CPUSA's secret apparatus, headed from the early 1930s until 1938 by Josef Peters, had several functions. Defensively, it guarded against infiltration of the party by government agents and prepared for a possible government crackdown on the Communist movement by hiding party documents, setting up facilities for secretly printing party literature, and planning for secret "safe houses" where key party cadre (officials and full-time organizers) could hide. The party underground also linked groups of secret party members who worked for U.S. government agencies to the CPUSA by providing ideological instruction and guidance as to how these members could use their government posts to assist the Communist movement. The party underground acted as an auxiliary for Soviet espionage in the United States by providing couriers and safe houses, identifying and vetting potential spies, and making available sundry other services. The CPUSA covert arm also conducted offensive operations by infiltrating rival political movements or institutions targeted by the CPUSA.

In pursuit of this last goal, the CPUSA sent Bentley to Golos after she offered to spy on the Italian Library of Information. Golos found her enthusiasm appealing and sanctioned her work. She reported regularly to him on the library's promotion of Mussolini's Fascist regime but was fired early in 1939 when library administrators became aware of her anti-Fascist views. Golos then began to use her as an assistant in his clandestine activities. For example, she became one of his "mail drops." Fearing that his mail might be under surveillance, Golos had sensitive correspondents send mail to Bentley, who then conveyed it to him. The Communist International in Moscow used the CPUSA, by the 1930s a highly disciplined and competent organization, as a conduit to the small Canadian Communist Party and the even smaller and fractious Mexican Communist Party. Bentley began receiving Golos's mail from Canadian and Mexican Communists involved in covert work for Moscow. One of his Mexican mail contacts was a leader of an armed Communist attack on the home of Communist dissident Leon Trotsky. Trotsky escaped, but the attackers took away and later murdered a guard (an American Trotskyist volunteer). At Golos's direction, Bentley also got a clerical job at McClure's news syndicate, a distributor of feature articles to newspapers and magazines. Golos suspected the head of the syndicate of links to Nazi Germany and wanted Bentley to see if she could find confirmation (she couldn't). All the while, Bentley and Golos's personal relationship grew closer. Golos had sent his wife and son to live in the USSR in the mid-1930s, and by 1940 he and Bentley had become lovers. (Golos's American-born son renounced his American citizenship, became a Soviet citizen, and fought in World War II as a Soviet sailor with its Red Navy Baltic fleet.)

Bentley's role as an aide in Golos's covert work grew after the onset of World War II. With the signing of the Nazi-Soviet Pact in August 1939, the USSR became a nonbelligerent ally of Germany. Meanwhile, while formally neutral, the United States under President Roosevelt's leadership became the chief nonbelligerent ally of Great Britain, France, and other nations fighting Hitler. The CPUSA immediately shifted from its prior anti-Fascist stance to all-out support for the Nazi-Soviet Pact and opposition to FDR's policies. The Roosevelt administration, previously indifferent to covert Communist activities, reacted with irritation and moved against the most blatant Communist illegality that had surfaced – passport fraud. Party leader Earl Browder was indicted, tried, and imprisoned for his use of false American passports in the 1930s. William Weiner, the CPUSA's national treasurer, was also convicted for use of a false passport, but the court suspended his sentence when he claimed to have a life-threatening heart condition. The government indicted party official Harry Gannes for passport fraud as well, but his case was repeatedly delayed, and he died in 1941 before trial.

The investigation of the false passports also led to World Tourists and Jacob Golos. In the spring of 1940 U.S. prosecutors indicted Golos and his company (he was officially the sole owner of its World Tourists' corporate stock) for failing to register with the U.S. government as official agents of a foreign power (the USSR). Seeking to head off further investigation and a public trial, Golos and World Tourists immediately pled guilty. He was fined $500 and given a two-year suspended prison sentence.

Golos got off remarkably lightly (Browder received a four-year term and served fourteen months in prison). But, obviously, federal authorities had developed some knowledge of his covert activities. Further, U.S. government internal security investigations, rare in 1930s, began in earnest with the coming of war. The FBI expanded rapidly and, while its chief priorities were German, Japanese, and Italian espionage, particularly covert funding of isolationist and antiwar agitation, it started to pay more attention to Soviet espionage and Communist subversion.

Concerned about more government scrutiny, Golos took steps to continue his covert work but with greater security. He created a new cover business, United States Service and Shipping Corporation, with secret CPUSA funding, to carry out the same activities that the legally tainted World Tourists had performed. Golos had no official connection to the new company and made sure that its legal relationship with Intourist and other Soviet entities was sufficiently distant to avoid falling under the legal requirement to register as a foreign agent. A socially respectable Communist sympathizer with no overt ties to the party officially headed United States Service and Shipping. Elizabeth Bentley, with the title of vice-president, effectively ran the organization.

Fearing surveillance, Golos also used Bentley, then unknown to the FBI, more frequently as his courier and go-between in his covert work. After Bentley defected, a search of FBI records showed that she had been spotted several times during FBI surveillance of Golos, but she was not identified as an assistant in his work, only as a social acquaintance. Throughout 1940 and 1941 she received mail, took phone calls, and carried messages and documents back and forth between Golos and his growing number of clandestine contacts. After Nazi Germany attacked the Soviet Union in June 1941, the pace of Golos's activity rapidly accelerated, as he and other Communists did everything they could to assist the Soviet Union by stealing American technology and government secrets.

In some cases Golos's and Bentley's contact with an espionage source was short-lived. Golos would identify a potential source, or a secret CPUSA member with access to information would volunteer his services to the Soviet cause. With Bentley's assistance, Golos would do initial checking on the source and then pass the potential spy on to professional Soviet intelligence officers who would then manage him. For example, someone known to Elizabeth Bentley only as "Julius" contacted Jacob Golos. Julius had initially asked contacts in the CPUSA to put him in touch with Soviet intelligence; he offered the services of a group of Communist engineers then working in the American defense industry to the Soviet cause. Golos checked him out and turned him over to the KGB. Bentley told the FBI about Julius in 1945, but she didn't know Julius's family name, where he lived, or where he worked, and it would take the FBI five years to figure it out. But her physical description fitted Julius Rosenberg precisely, and Bentley would testify in the trial that led to his conviction and execution for espionage. (See Chapter 5 for an account of Rosenberg's involvement in atomic espionage and his leadership of a network of engineers who stole advanced military technology.)

In 1942 and 1943, however, Golos also developed and directly managed a large number of Soviet spies himself, using Bentley as his courier and go-between to pick up the espionage "take" (copies of documents and microfilm) and deliver requests and instructions. Because Golos's sources and networks were almost all based on secret CPUSA members, Bentley also often delivered party literature and picked up party dues. Golos would then either deliver the information directly to Soviet KGB officers or via an intermediate stop with Earl Browder, chief of the CPUSA. Golos became a close associate of Browder and functioned as one of his links to Soviet intelligence after the party leader was released from prison in 1942. Browder recruited some sources himself and turned them over to the KGB through Golos.

Golos's health deteriorated in 1943, partly due to the pace and stress of his work, and he handed off more responsibility to Bentley; late that year he died of a heart attack. She immediately assumed his role as the link between his agents and networks and the KGB. Consisting of two large espionage networks (the Silvermaster group and the Perlo group), each of which had its own leader as well as a number of singleton spies that Bentley handled individually rather than through an intermediary, it was a large and impressive array of sources.

The Silvermaster Group

Nathan Gregory (Greg) Silvermaster, with the assistance of his wife and William Ludwig (Lud) Ullmann, a close family friend, headed the largest espionage apparatus. Silvermaster was a midlevel government economist who worked for the Board of Economic Warfare when Bentley dealt with him. While he had access to some useful information, it was his energy in recruiting and managing other secret Communists and Soviet sympathizers in the government that was remarkable. Silvermaster's apparatus included two of the most highly placed espionage sources the Soviets ever possessed. Harry Dexter White, a Soviet sympathizer rather than a CPUSA member, held the influential position of assistant secretary of the Treasury and had access to valuable information on high-level U.S. policies. Lauchlin Currie, like White a Soviet sympathizer, was a White House aide to President Roosevelt and assigned during the war to assist in administering the Board of Economic Warfare and its successor, the Foreign Economic Administration. In addition to providing information about high-level U.S. policy making, both men also promoted and protected the careers of midlevel officials who spied for Stalin. For example, security officials raised questions about Silvermaster's employment at the Board of Economic Warfare based on suspicions that he might be a secret Communist. Both White and Currie intervened to head off the inquiry and vouched for his loyalty and non-Communist status.

George Silverman, also an economist, was another important member of the Silvermaster apparatus working as civilian chief of analysis for an assistant chief of staff for the U.S. Army Air Force at the Pentagon. He provided information on American military aviation planning. When Lud Ullmann was drafted, Silverman arranged to get Ullmann a commission as an Army Air Force officer and assignment to a staff position at the Pentagon, where he continued both his espionage and his residence with the Silvermasters. Other valuable members of the Silvermaster network included Frank Coe, director of the Division of Monetary Research in the Treasury Department, and Solomon Adler, the Treasury Department's representative in China. Coe, Adler, and White performed a signal service for the Communist cause by using their bureaucratic authority to delay delivery of a large congressionally authorized gold loan to the Chinese Nationalist government, then fighting both Japan and a Communist insurgency led by Mao Tse-tung. Without the gold, China's currency depreciated and hyperinflation undercut public support for the Kuomintang regime. White also used his position in the U.S. Treasury to persuade the Chinese Nationalist government, heavily dependent of American aid, to hire an American-educated Chinese economist Chi Ch'ao-ting (see Chapter 2). Chi, however, was a Chinese Communist Party spy and worked to undermine the Nationalist regime from within. When the Nationalists lost the civil war to the Communists in the late 1940s, Chi emerged as a senior official of the new Communist government.

The Perlo Group

Victor Perlo headed the second large spy ring supervised by Golos and Bentley. Perlo himself was a senior economist in the War Production Board overseeing U.S. military industrial production. The Perlo group included a number of useful sources for the USSR. Harold Glasser, a senior Treasury Department economist, served as vice-chairman of the War Production Board during the war and economic adviser to U.S. military forces and occupation authorities in North Africa and Italy. Immediately after the war he was the Treasury Department adviser with the American delegation that accompanied the U.S. secretary of state to a meeting with the Soviet foreign minister. Another active spy in the Perlo group, Charles Kramer, was a lawyer and professional staff member of the U.S. Senate Subcommittee on War Mobilization, giving him considerable access to information of interest to the Soviets. Another Perlo network source was Donald Wheeler, an employee of the Research and Analysis section of the Office of Strategic Services (OSS), America's World War II foreign intelligence agency and forerunner of the CIA.

Bentley's independent single agents served in a number of sensitive positions, including four other OSS employees. One was particularly highly placed: Duncan Lee, who held OSS rank as a lieutenant colonel, served as an aide to General William Donovan, head of the OSS. Julius Joseph was deputy chief of the OSS's Far Eastern operations, and Helen Tenney was an analyst in the Spanish section of OSS. The most energetic, however, was Maurice Halperin, chief of the Research and Analysis section of OSS's Latin American division. Halperin used his position to collect U.S. State Department reports, documents, and diplomatic cables by the score and deliver them to Bentley and the USSR.

By any measure, Golos and Bentley put together and managed an astounding number of spies for the Soviet Union (only the chief ones are noted here). Their success won them considerable praise from the KGB but also a measure of concern. Golos had assembled these assets in late 1941 and 1942 when Soviet espionage in the United States expanded rapidly, and numerous secret Communists and Soviet sympathizers eagerly volunteered to deliver American military, technological, and diplomatic secrets to Stalin. The KGB welcomed the arrangement because it initially did not have enough professional intelligence officers available in the United States to manage so many sources. Further, the KGB trusted Golos. Born and raised in Russia, he had been a member of the Bolshevik movement prior to his arrest by tsarist police and his escape to the United States as a young man. Although the details are still unclear, when he returned to the Soviet Union in the 1920s, he appears to have been recruited into the OGPU, predecessor to the KGB, and possibly held officer rank. He was not, however, a trained, professional foreign intelligence officer but rather the product of an earlier era when legal (aboveground) and illegal (underground) Communist political organizing was mixed with and overlapped espionage and intelligence work.

Even before Golos died in late 1943, the KGB had been pressing to assume direct control of his networks. It was not inclined to allow Bentley any of the autonomy it had given Golos. By 1944 the KGB station in the United States had a large contingent of professional Soviet officers who had learned how to operate in America. They regarded the methods of Golos and Bentley as amateurish. The Silvermaster and Perlo networks were far too large. Too many of their members socialized with each other and were aware of the covert activities of the others. Many sources also continued to participate in the underground political activities of the Communist Party. For reasons of security, the KGB wanted its spies to cut ties with the Communist Party and cease radical political activity. It wanted the two large networks to be broken down into small cells isolated from each other. Bentley was American, not Russian like Golos, and had no status or history with the KGB. In mid-1944 the KGB began to remove Golos's sources and networks from Bentley and transfer them to its professional officers. By the fall of 1944 she was no longer in contact with any active Soviet sources. To further increase security, the following year the KGB ordered her to sever her connection with United States Service and Shipping.

To soften the blow, Bentley received a financial settlement, and the KGB assured her that she would be called upon for future work. By mid-1945, however, she was despondent. Her lover, Golos, was dead. The covert work they had shared had been taken away from her. And even her cover job of running United States Service and Shipping had been eliminated. Lonely, bored, and at times drinking to excess, she began to brood and reconsider her life. She also began to suspect that the FBI was closing in on her. It was, however, a case of "the wicked flee when no man pursueth"; the FBI did not have her under surveillance and was surprised when she showed up at its New Haven, Connecticut, office in August 1945 with a vague complaint that a man had approached her who might or might not be a federal agent of some sort. Initially, the FBI treated her report as a routine case of possible impersonation of a federal official. However, in October she contacted the New York FBI office and provided more detailed information about her role in Soviet espionage. The FBI quickly began a series of interviews and launched background investigations to confirm specifics in her story so that it could judge whether it had a genuine defector from Soviet espionage on its hands or a kook who was confessing to nonexistent crimes. By November the agency was convinced of her authenticity, she signed a detailed 115-page typed statement of her activities, and FBI investigations expanded to cover the specific individuals Bentley had identified as Soviet sources.

At FBI direction, Bentley arranged a meeting in New York with her chief Soviet contact, Anatoly Gromov, who posed as a Soviet diplomat. Gromov actually headed all KGB operations in the United States and his real name was Gorsky. The FBI followed him from Washington to New York and observed his meeting with Bentley, who told him that she wanted to get back into espionage work. The FBI hoped to use Bentley to gather direct evidence of espionage. Gromov did not bite, however, and told her she should remain on the sidelines for a time. Gromov had suspected that the meeting had been under surveillance and within a day heard from KGB headquarters in Moscow that Bentley had defected. The FBI's plan to use Bentley as a double agent had fallen victim to its close relations with the British security services, which it had informed of Bentley's defection. The news had reached Kim Philby, a senior British intelligence officer who had been a Soviet spy since the 1930s, who quickly informed his KGB contact. KGB headquarters in Moscow ordered that those sources who had contact with Bentley should be warned to cease espionage activity, destroy incriminating material, and prepare for possible FBI scrutiny. It also told its officers in the United States to inform those sources who might be compromised by Bentley that for their own protection the KGB was breaking contact with them for an indefinite period. Not knowing precisely when Bentley had defected, the KGB feared that the FBI had already arranged to observe Bentley meeting with some of her former sources, just as it had done with Gromov. To prepare for this eventuality, the KGB also recommended that these sources should not deny having known and met with Bentley; to deny what the FBI had witnessed would simply confirm their guilt. Instead, they should admit meeting Bentley but claim that the contact was innocent and benign. The KGB also withdrew from the United States Soviet officers whom Bentley had known. KGB officers under diplomatic cover were immune from arrest, but once Bentley had identified them to the FBI, they would have been under constant surveillance and their ability to carry out espionage duties drastically reduced. Those illegal Soviet officers whom Bentley knew were in even greater danger because they were not covered by diplomatic immunity; several quickly returned to Moscow.

Philby's warning was sufficiently timely to prevent the FBI from gathering any direct evidence of espionage by those Bentley had identified. The FBI did observe one source, Charles Kramer of the Perlo network, hastily removing material from his residence and disposing of it in a street-side trash can far from his home. The FBI agents following Kramer checked the trash can and found that he had been dumping his collection of Communist literature. On December 1, 1945, the FBI also observed Alexander Koral, a New York City school system maintenance engineer, visiting Gregory Silvermaster and his wife at their Washington, D.C., residence. After leaving the Silvermasters' home, Koral made a series of maneuvers to evade surveillance, which confirmed to trailing FBI agents that his visit was irregular. The agents kept him in sight and quickly identified him. FBI records showed that Koral had been observed in contact with a known KGB officer years earlier and was a secret Communist. Confronted by the FBI, he provided a partial account of his activities. Koral and his wife had been couriers carrying messages and documents between Soviet KGB officers and their American sources scattered across the United States. His visit to the Silvermasters was to deliver the warning of Bentley's defection. Koral claimed, however, that his courier job was motivated by a need for money and that he had no idea that the men for whom he carried messages and documents were Soviet spies. As long as he stuck to that story, his testimony, even if he could be pressured to testify, was only indirect evidence of espionage by those he dealt with.

The KGB's success in warning its sources presented the FBI and the Justice Department with a difficult situation. The investigation of Bentley's story produced a wealth of corroborating indirect evidence that convinced government officials she was telling the truth. But it did not yield any undeniable proof of ongoing espionage or any "smoking gun" evidence in the form of stolen documents. Nor had Bentley saved any documents or other physical evidence of her work as a spy.

As a last resort, the FBI confronted those Bentley had identified in hopes that one would break and confess. The ploy failed. The suspects either denied the charges and offered innocent explanations of their contacts with her or refused to make any statement. For example, Bentley had identified Duncan Lee, a senior officer of the Office of Strategic Services as a Soviet source she had met with on a number of occasions. Questioned by the FBI in 1947, Lee admitted that he had met with Bentley on a one-on-one basis over a two-year period during his OSS service, both in Washington and during trips to New York. Lee, claimed, however, that these meetings were innocent social contacts with a woman he had only know as "Helen." He also acknowledged to the FBI that he had met Helen's friend "John" (Jacob Golos). Bizarrely, he told the FBI that despite numerous meetings with Helen he never learned her last name (or John's) and knew nothing of her activities. That a highly placed OSS officer engaged in intelligence work in wartime would over two years meet privately with someone and never learn that person's full name or background strained credibility. Nor did Lee disclose to the FBI that he had journeyed to the USSR in the mid-1930s. In 1947 the FBI was not yet aware of his visit to Moscow, but it did know that in 1940 a neighbor had complained that Lee (then finishing Yale Law School) had accumulated a large body of Communist Party literature in his apartment and as a young lawyer had volunteered his services to the China Aid Council, a body run by secret Communists that raised money to assist the Chinese Communists. Despite testimony that taxed credulity and evidence suggesting secret Communist sympathies, a jury in a criminal case, if it had come to that, in the end would have seen the case as Duncan

Lee's word against Elizabeth Bentley's. Lee was a respected attorney with connections to influential and distinguished lawyers; Thomas Corcoran, the politically well-connected lobbyist-lawyer, who worked so effectively for John Service in the *Amerasia* case (see Chapter 2), represented Lee in various legal matters. While Lee had held high rank as an OSS officer, his accuser, Bentley, was a self-confessed Soviet spy. Without additional direct evidence, few prosecutors would have been optimistic about winning a conviction from a jury. Under those circumstances, the FBI and the Justice Department concluded that attempting criminal prosecution of Lee, or any of the others Bentley identified, was ill-advised.

Counterespionage operations, however, are not principally about winning criminal convictions. Their chief purpose is to learn about and stop loss of government secrets. Bentley's information allowed the FBI to identify a large number of persons who had spied for the Soviet Union and make it impossible for them to continue their espionage. A number of those Bentley identified left government service when military and civilian war agencies demobilized in 1945. The FBI contacted the personnel and security offices of key federal agencies to ensure that no one was rehired. Those that remained in government jobs were encouraged to resign or were fired. By the end of 1947 most were gone; the handful that resisted were ousted by 1950.

Once government officials had concluded that espionage prosecutions would likely be futile, the rationale for keeping Bentley's story secret faded. The Justice Department reluctantly (for political reasons) and the FBI with some enthusiasm allowed Bentley to go public and testify to Congress in 1948. Her testimony produced the *New York World Telegram* headline on July 21, 1948, that screamed "Red Ring Bared by Its Blond Queen." Thereafter, reporters searching for color to enliven their stories of espionage often called Bentley the "blond spy queen." Her many critics also used the sobriquet as a term of derision. Despite this lurid title, Bentley in 1948 was a brown-haired, undistinguished looking forty-year-old woman far removed from the provocative image of a seductive "Mata Hari"-style spy queen.

Despite her ordinary appearance, Bentley's testimony to various congressional committees was anything but dull. She matter-of-factly described her role in creating and managing two huge Soviet spy rings in World War II Washington and reeled off the names of scores of federal officials as secret Communists who handed over government military and diplomatic secrets to the USSR, from the Office of Strategic Services, War Production Board, Board of Economic Warfare, U.S. Senate, Foreign Economic Administration, U.S. Army and Army Air Force, Treasury Department, State Department, Office of the Coordinator of Inter-American Affairs, and the White House itself. Her testimony to the U.S. House Committee on Un-American Activities, repeated later to many civic groups as well as in a popular autobiography, had a major impact on public opinion because the breadth and depth of Soviet espionage she described appalled most people. It convinced many Americans that the government had been complacent about the Soviet espionage threat and that the American Communist Party was the instrument of a hostile foreign power. More than anyone else, Elizabeth Bentley convinced millions of Americans that the problems of secret Communists in the government and Soviet espionage were not matters of a few isolated bad apples but of a systematic and substantial assault on the integrity of the government.

The House Committee on Un-American Activities called many of those Bentley identified as Soviet spies to testify. Most invoked their right under the Fifth Amendment to the Constitution not to provide testimony that could be used against them in a criminal prosecution. For example, former War Production Board economist Victor Perlo, identified by Bentley as the leader of a large spy ring, made a brief statement describing himself as a New Deal supporter, but then cited the Fifth Amendment to questions about Communist Party membership or other matters. Years after the Bentley controversy died down, Perlo dropped his pretense of being a New Deal liberal and emerged openly as a veteran Communist and chairman of the CPUSA's economic commission. Citing the Fifth Amendment brought no legal penalty, but to most of the public, refusing to testify on those grounds suggested that truthful testimony would be tantamount to a confession of guilt.

The Trials of William Remington

A few minor court cases and prosecutions resulted from Bentley's testimony and the FBI's follow-up investigations. The one with the most serious consequences involved William Remington. Joseph North, editor of the Communist Party's cultural journal, *New Masses*, had introduced Remington, a young economist with the War Production Board, to Jacob Golos as a possible source. Golos completed the recruitment, and Bentley, along with collecting Remington's CPUSA dues, picked up War Production Board information from him on airplane production, high-octane gasoline, and synthetic rubber. When Remington entered the U.S. Navy in 1944, he ended contact with Bentley. She described him as a minor, low-level source.

The FBI interviewed Remington in 1947, and he confirmed that he had known North, who had introduced him to Golos and Bentley. Remington, however, insisted he had known them only as John and Helen with no last names (the same story that Duncan Lee had advanced). He even agreed that he had met privately with "Helen" and given her War Production Board literature. However, he had thought Bentley was a journalist and had only given her publicly available information. The FBI found it difficult to credit his story that he had met privately with a journalist to give her information she could pick up publicly. He also agreed he had paid Bentley money, but denied it was CPUSA dues, only payment for newspapers she had given him. As for North and Golos, Remington described his meetings with them as innocuous. Remington denied that he had ever been a Communist or participated in Communist activities and insisted that although he had been an active public member of the Communist Party's antiwar front group, the American Peace Mobilization, during the Nazi-Soviet Pact period, he had actually opposed its positions. This, too, strained credulity.

Why Remington made such implausible statements is unclear. When the FBI interviewed him in 1947 he was working for the Commerce Department and in the process of applying for a sensitive job with the Atomic Energy Commission. He may have tried to explain away Bentley's evidence in the hope that he could salvage his government career if he convinced the FBI of his innocence. The ploy failed and the Atomic Energy Commission turned down his application. The FBI also blocked Remington's attempt to get a job with President Truman's White House staff. Perhaps realizing that his hopes for promotion were being blocked by doubts about his loyalty, Remington contacted the FBI, stated that he had come to see Communist subversion as serious, and volunteered to become an FBI informant reporting on his fellow government bureaucrats. His offer was ignored.

Meanwhile his employment as a Commerce Department economist was put in jeopardy when the federal Civil Service Loyalty-Security Review Board set up by President Truman to review federal employees ruled in

1948 that there were grounds to question his loyalty. It cited in particular evidence that he had been an active young Communist in college and during his initial government employment when working for the Tennessee Valley Authority in the late 1930s.

Remington, however, hired a skilled legal team that appealed the loyalty board ruling. Before the civil service loyalty commission that heard his appeal, Remington presented himself as a fervent anti-Communist, repeated his claims of not knowing that Bentley was a Communist, and defended his past associations with Communists as innocent, inadvertent, or a consequence of his relationship with his radical mother-in-law. His lawyers succeeded in getting the review board to ask Elizabeth Bentley to appear, but she refused and the board had no power to compel her testimony. The appeal board in January 1949 reversed the original board's ruling, taking the view that President Truman's executive order mandated a finding about current loyalty rather than activities from the 1930s and early 1940s and that, in the absence of Bentley's testimony, it would not credit her story about his role in espionage. For the moment, his job with the Commerce Department was saved.

He had also brought a $100,000 libel suit against NBC for broadcasting Elizabeth Bentley's statements about him on *Meet the Press*. In February 1950 NBC's lawyers settled for $9,000. Remington and his supporters treated this as vindication, but Lawrence Spivak, the journalist host of *Meet the Press*, stated, "We advised against settlement because we did not believe a libel had been committed. It was settled on the basis of the legal expenses involved, and the amount of the settlement indicates that it was based on expedience." And neither NBC nor Bentley retracted anything said on the program.

The FBI and the Justice Department, however, were furious that someone they were convinced was a security risk had succeeded in keeping a government job. They regarded Bentley's allegations of his espionage as credible and Remington's disavowals of earlier Communist loyalties as falsehoods. As a practical matter, the evidence that Remington had been a spy (Bentley's testimony) was no stronger than what was available against others Bentley had named, and that was not considered sufficient to win a conviction. Remington's claim that he had never been a Communist or participated in Communist activities, however, was another matter. The FBI pursued witnesses and evidence on that matter and slowly put together a strong case. Called before a federal grand jury in 1950,

Remington chose not to invoke his right against self-incrimination when asked about his Communist background. Instead, he once again denied having taken part in Communist activities or having been a Communist. The grand jury, however, was impressed by the array of evidence the U.S. attorney presented, including testimony by people who knew Remington as an active Communist in the 1930s. What sealed Remington's fate was the testimony of his ex-wife, Ann Moos Remington. Initially, she had supported her former husband's denials of Communist ties. But the grand jury's aggressive foreman, John Brunini, pressed her hard with probing questions and told her she had no right to refuse to answer his and other jurors' skeptical questions (she did if she claimed the Fifth Amendment). After four hours of questioning she broke down and changed her story, testifying that both she and her ex-husband had been Communists and had participated in Communist activities in the late 1930s. In June 1950 the grand jury indicted Remington for perjury for denying membership in the CPUSA.

Remington's trial began in December 1950. Elizabeth Bentley testified about her espionage relationship with Remington, but the prosecution's case regarding Remington's Communist loyalties was built around the testimony of Ann Moos Remington. She stated both she and William Remington had been Communists. She also testified that he had given confidential information to Bentley, although that was not directly at issue in the perjury count. Additionally, prosecutors brought in former college classmates from Dartmouth who testified to his activities in the Young Communist League and former Communists who testified about his attendance at Communist meetings and recruitment activities when working for the Tennessee Valley Authority. Remington testified in his own defense, denied ever being a Communist, blamed his association with radicals on his former wife and her mother, and maintained that those former Communists who had identified him as a party member at the TVA were mistaken. Remington's lawyers also exposed a covert relationship between John Brunini, the foreman of the grand jury that indicted Remington, and Elizabeth Bentley. He had assisted with preparation of her autobiography, a major conflict of interest that should have disqualified him from participating in Remington's indictment. The trial jury, however, brushed that off as irrelevant and after deliberating for six hours convicted Remington on the first ballot. Judge Gregory Noonan sentenced him to five years in prison.

Remington's lawyers immediately appealed, claiming technical irregularities in the prosecution. A three-judge U.S. Appeals court agreed in part, ruling that Judge Noonan's charge to the jury had been vague about what constituted Communist Party membership. But while it voided the guilty verdict, it let the indictment stand and merely ordered a new trial. Federal prosecutors could have appealed to the Supreme Court or proceeded with a new trial. But one of the assistant prosecutors, Roy Cohn, suggested a different tactic. He argued that while the government might win reinstatement of the conviction at the Supreme Court, it also risked a ruling that expanded on the appeals court decision and might void the original indictment, particularly if the relationship of the grand jury foreman with Bentley became an issue. A new trial, however, was also a risk. Judge Noonan had essentially left it to the jury to decide on the basis of the evidence what constituted "membership" in the Communist Party. A new judge might, in light of the appeals court decision, impose a very narrow technical definition that would be difficult to prove. Cohn argued that it would be simpler to put the original indictment aside and quickly seek a new one from a different grand jury, thus eliminating the Brunini problem. Further, he pointed out, Remington in his perjury trial testimony had made even more sweeping sworn statements disavowing his earlier Communist activity, thus providing additional grounds for a perjury indictment.

The Justice Department adopted Cohn's strategy. A new federal grand jury met, heard many of the witnesses who had testified in the first trial as well as a new one the FBI had located, and on October 24, 1951, indicted Remington on five counts of perjury: when he testified that he had never knowingly attended Communist Party meetings, never paid Communist Party dues, and never asked anyone to join the Communist Party and when he denied knowing of the existence of the Young Communist League at Dartmouth and giving classified information to Elizabeth Bentley. The final count was the only one that spoke directly to the issue of espionage. These were all of sufficient specificity that they avoided the definitional question of what constituted "membership" in the CPUSA and focused on matters where the government had witnesses and evidence refuting Remington's denials.

Remington's lawyers attempted to block the new prosecution by making their own appeal to the Supreme Court of the appeals court ruling on the first trial and contesting the right of the government to put aside the first indictment pending a Supreme Court ruling on their appeal. But on

March 24, 1952, the Supreme Court rejected Remington's petition for a writ of certiorari requesting a review of the appeals court decision. This ruling left the way open for a trial of the perjury indictment issued by the second grand jury.

Remington's second perjury trial began on January 13, 1953, before U.S. Judge Vincent Leibell in New York City. Myles Lane, the chief federal prosecutor, presented fourteen witnesses. The testimony of Ann Moos Remington was again central to the case. But Elizabeth Bentley loomed larger than in the first trial because one of the counts directly dealt with her relationship to William Remington. Individually less important but cumulatively of great weight were Dartmouth classmates and TVA colleagues who testified that Remington had been knowledgeable of and active in the Young Communist League at Dartmouth and with a CPUSA unit at the TVA.

Remington again testified in his own defense and changed his story significantly. He abandoned his previous position that he had never been attracted to communism and said that during the 1930s he had supported the ideals and principles of communism. He continued, however, to deny any organizational involvement with the CPUSA or membership in or even knowledge of the Young Communist League at Dartmouth. He also modified his story of his relationship with Bentley, stating he "may have been indiscreet" in terms of material he gave her but continued to deny that he knew that Bentley and Golos were Communists and certainly had no notion that they were spies.

On January 28, after nearly twelve hours of deliberation, the jury reported that it had found Remington guilty on two counts (denying giving Bentley sensitive information and denying knowledge of the Young Communist League at Dartmouth), not guilty on one count (denying attempting to recruit someone into the CPUSA), and unable to reach a unanimous verdict on the remaining two counts (attending party meetings and paying dues).

On February 4, 1953, Judge Leibell sentenced Remington to three years' imprisonment on each count. Leibell, noting that Elizabeth Bentley had described him as a spy but not a very important one, ruled the terms would run concurrently for a combined sentence of three years. A three-judge appeals court panel rejected Remington's appeal on a two-to-one decision on November 24, 1953. The U.S. Supreme Court denied certiorari (review) on February 5, 1954. Remington, meanwhile, had entered prison and was serving his sentence. On November 22, 1954, two fellow inmates sought out and attacked Remington, and he died of his injuries on the 24th. The motives of his murderers were never clear: robbery, an ongoing prison feud, and hatred of a Communist may all have been involved.

After the collapse of the USSR, a 1948 memo surfaced from the KGB archive written by Anatoly Gorsky, former head of the KGB station in the United States. It listed William Remington as one of forty-three Soviet sources and KGB officers likely identified to American authorities by Elizabeth Bentley after her defection.

While Bentley had identified Remington as a minor source for the Soviets, two men Bentley named as major sources, William Ludwig Ullmann of the Silvermaster group and Edward Fitzgerald of the Perlo group, invoked the Fifth Amendment and refused to testify when called before congressional committees. In 1954 Congress passed and President Eisenhower signed the Immunity Act that granted authorities the option of giving immunity from criminal prosecution in order to get testimony from a witness in espionage and subversion cases. Immunity, of course, removed grounds for claiming a right not to testify. The Fifth Amendment to the Constitution states that no person "shall be compelled in any Criminal Case to be a witness against himself." If immunity from prosecution was provided, then one was not compelled to be a witness against oneself and could not refuse to testify.

Ullmann, one of the earliest affected by the new law, was called before a U.S. grand jury in 1954 and refused to testify, citing his Fifth Amendment rights. The Justice Department then gave him immunity. He continued, however, to refuse to answer any questions, and a federal judge sentenced him to six months in prison for contempt of court. Ullmann appealed, arguing that the immunity act was unconstitutional, but the U.S. Supreme Court in a seven-to-two ruling (*Ullmann v. United States*) found against him. Ullmann then withdrew his refusal and testified for five days to a grand jury in 1956. In light of his compliance, his contempt conviction was dropped. Federal grand jury testimony is normally secret and usually made public only when introduced as evidence in a criminal proceeding. For example, Alger Hiss (see Chapter 4) was tried for the crime of perjury. The perjury at issue was his testimony to a U.S. grand jury that he had not delivered U.S. State Department documents to Whittaker Chambers in 1938 and had no contact with Chambers in 1938; consequently, his grand jury testimony was made public in the course of the subsequent perjury trial. In the case of Ullmann's 1956 testimony, there were no subsequent trials of any kind, so his testimony has remained secret to this day, and he refused to make any public statements about what he had said.

Edward Fitzgerald faced the same situation as Ullmann. Called before a grand jury to answer questions about Bentley's identification of him as an active Soviet spy, he refused to testify, citing the Fifth Amendment. The government gave him immunity, he continued to refuse to answer grand jury questions, and received a six-month contempt of court sentence. Unlike Ullmann, however, Fitzgerald continued his defiance and went to prison in 1956. There is no indication in the public record indicating why government prosecutors chose Fitzgerald and Ullmann for immunity from all those implicated by Bentley.

One minor figure Bentley named, William Taylor, sued the *Washington Daily News* in 1954 for libel for its coverage of Bentley's statement that he was part of an espionage ring. Not wanting the expense of a trial, the newspaper settled the suit out of court and withdrew its statements about Taylor. Bentley was upset by the paper's retreat, and she herself never retracted her description of Taylor. Taylor's lawyers prepared a wide-ranging study that assailed Bentley as a liar and fraud and circulated it widely to the press. The FBI answered with a memo that replied point-by-point and supported Bentley's credibility.

Elizabeth Bentley enjoyed a few years of notoriety after her testimony to the House Committee on Un-American Activities in 1948. Congressional committees investigating one or another aspect of Soviet espionage or Communist infiltration of the government frequently called her to testify, and she was a witness in several trials, including the espionage trial of Julius Rosenberg (Chapter 5). For a time she also lectured to civil and political groups. With the help of a ghostwriter, she wrote a melodramatic autobiography, *Out of Bondage*, which sold well. Under constant and blistering attack as a fake, fraud, and liar by Communists, their allies, and liberals who resented the use that conservatives made of her testimony, she also endured several abusive relationships with men, drank heavily, and fell into debt. Several teaching positions at women's schools vanished amid personal scandals and irresponsibility. Her last post was as a teacher at Long Lane School in Middletown, Connecticut, a penal school for delinquent girls. She died in 1963 at the age of fifty-five from abdominal cancer, a condition often associated with chronic alcoholism.

As for those she identified as Soviet spies, a number left the United States in the late 1940s or early 1950s, probably not coincidentally with the Justice Department's decisions to prosecute Alger Hiss, Julius Rosenberg, and others on espionage-related charges. Bentley had identified Michael Greenberg as a Soviet source at the Board of Economic Warfare during World War II. He succeeded in transferring to the State Department in 1945 but resigned abruptly in 1946, probably in response to Bentley's defection. After the FBI interviewed him in 1947 (he denied all), he fled the United States for Great Britain. (Greenberg had been born in Britain but became a naturalized American citizen in 1944.) Frank Coe and Solomon Adler, Treasury Department economists whom Bentley had identified as secret Communists and spies, immigrated to Communist China, received government jobs, and became ardent, vocal followers of Communist dictator Mao Tse-tung.

Maurice Halperin, one of Bentley's spies on the Office of Strategic Services, succeeded in transferring to the U.S. State Department after the OSS dissolved in the fall of 1945. In 1946, however, after Bentley's defection, Halperin quietly resigned and took an academic post at Boston University teaching Latin American studies. When Bentley's story became public in 1948, Halperin denied any involvement in espionage and communism, but in 1954, further pressed about his activities by government officials, he abruptly moved to Mexico and refused to return. In 1958, fearing deportation to the United States, he fled to Moscow where Soviet authorities gave him a post in one of their leading scholarly institutions. Unhappy with life in the Soviet Union, however, in 1962 he moved to Cuba. But after a few years, Halperin found Cuban communism as disillusioning as the Soviet variety had been. He moved to Canada in 1967 and quietly broke with communism.

Lauchlin Currie, the White House aide Bentley identified as a Soviet source, left government service soon after Truman became president. He, too, denied Bentley's description of him as a Soviet spy but in 1950 immigrated to Colombia. Currie, born in Canada, had not become a U.S. citizen until 1934 when he began work for the federal government. American law in the 1950s required that naturalized citizens who left the United States return periodically or lose their citizenship. Currie allowed his citizenship to lapse and then became a Colombian citizen. Duncan Lee, once a senior official of the OSS, did not permanently emigrate but found employment in Bermuda and for the rest of his life lived mostly abroad. Others Bentley identified as spies went in various directions after they were forced out of government service. Most sought anonymity and found employment and new careers far from the public limelight. The leaders of Bentley's largest espionage apparatus, Gregory Silvermaster and Ludwig Ullmann, moved to Long Beach Island off the New Jersey coast and became prosperous property developers and homebuilders.

Venona and Bentley's Vindication

For decades after she told her story, Elizabeth Bentley was pilloried by historians and journalists as a neurotic, alcoholic fantasist who lied, exaggerated, and embellished her story. That none of those she accused were ever convicted, or even indicted, for espionage seemed prima facie evidence that her account lacked substance.

The Venona project was one of America's great counterespionage successes in the early Cold War and remained a secret until after the collapse of the Soviet Union in 1991. During World War II the Soviet embassy in Washington and Soviet consulates in New York and San Francisco sent and received hundreds of thousands of international cables (telegrams). Under wartime regulations American authorities received copies of all international cables (all nations followed this practice in wartime). The USSR was aware that the U.S. government received copies of its cables but did not object because it sent them in what it believed was an unbreakable code. The Soviet cipher system, called a one-time pad system, was unbreakable if used correctly. American code breakers, however, were among the best in the world. Fearing that the USSR might negotiate a separate peace with Nazi Germany on the order of the 1939 Hitler-Stalin Pact, U.S. Army commanders in 1943 ordered cryptanalysts of the Army Signals Intelligence Service to see if Soviet diplomatic cables could be deciphered. (The Army Signals Intelligence Service was the forerunner of the contemporary National Security Agency, America's high-tech electronic listening and cryptanalytic intelligence arm.)

American code breakers spotted a technical flaw in the use of the one-time pad cipher system in a limited number of Soviet cables and began a project that was eventually given the cover name "Venona." The work moved slowly, however, because the Soviet cipher system was extremely difficult, the Soviet procedural error affected only a limited number of messages, and, not surprisingly, American code breakers gave highest priority to work on German and Japanese codes during World War II. Consequently, by the time the first messages were read, in 1946, the original purpose had been superseded by events. But the first messages that were read turned out not to be about Soviet diplomacy but to and from Soviet intelligence officers of the KGB who operated out of Soviet diplomatic offices, and they dealt with Soviet infiltration of and spying on the American government. In the context of the developing Cold War the Venona project moved from the back burner of American code breaking to the front. As the project developed, the FBI joined the project to follow up on the information gleaned from often only partially deciphered messages. The General Communications Headquarters, the highly regarded British code-breaking agency, also joined the effort. The result was the breaking of nearly three thousand Soviet cables in whole or in part.

The deciphered cables were only slivers of total Soviet cable traffic. The technical flaw in Soviet use of the one-time pad cipher also limited the cables that could be broken chiefly to the period 1943 to 1945 with only a few 1946 cables broken and none sent to or from the United States after that time. Nor were the cables deciphered quickly. The first messages that could be read were broken in 1946; large sections were read in the late 1940s and during the 1950s, but a substantial number were not deciphered until the 1960s and 1970s. Nonetheless, from a counterintelligence point of view they were an immensely rich resource. American security officials were able to read back-and-forth exchanges between KGB field officers in the United States and their headquarters in Moscow discussing ongoing espionage directed at the United States. The cables indicated that more than 350 persons assisted Soviet espionage against the United States during World War II. Of these, 180 were identified by their real names or enough details were contained in the messages to allow the FBI to identify the real name of a spy hidden behind a cover name. The real persons behind the remaining cover names remained unidentified.

It was a deciphered Venona message that identified the British physicist Klaus Fuchs (cover name Charles) as a Soviet spy inside the Anglo-American atomic bomb project. His confession along with several dozen additional deciphered Venona messages led to the identification, arrest, and conviction of Harry Gold (cover name Goose), David Greenglass (cover name Bumblebee), and Julius Rosenberg (cover name Antenna).

The Venona decryptions provided overwhelming confirmation of Elizabeth Bentley's 1945 statement to the FBI regarding her espionage activities. Scores of Venona messages discuss Bentley (cover name Clever Girl), the large espionage networks run by Gregory Silvermaster (cover name Pal) and Victor Perlo (cover name Raider), and all the major and most of the minor spies identified by Bentley: Ludwig Ullmann (cover name Pilot), George Silverman (cover name Aileron), Harry Dexter White (cover name Richard), Duncan Lee (cover name Koch), Maurice Halperin (cover name Hare), Frank Coe (cover name Peak), Solomon Adler (cover name Sachs), Alexander Koral (cover name Berg), Charles Kramer (cover name Mole), Edward Fitzgerald (cover name Ted), and Lauchlin Currie (cover name Page). The Venona decryptions provided conclusive documentary evidence that supported Elizabeth Bentley's testimony. From the point of view of security officials inside the U.S. government, once Venona decryptions became available in increasing volume after 1946, it was not a matter of their believing Bentley's accusations and rejecting the denials of Perlo, Halperin, and the others who claimed innocence. Based on Venona as well as other evidence, they knew Bentley was telling the truth while the others were lying.

The Venona project and its deciphered messages, however, were secret and were never used in court. There were two reasons for this. First and foremost, the code breakers of the National Security Agency did not want the Soviet Union to know the extent to which the United States had broken into its cable traffic. The Soviets, however, did know something about the project. In 1950 several deciphered Venona messages had led the FBI to Jones York, an American aircraft engineer. Under questioning, York confessed that he had been recruited by Soviet intelligence in the mid-1930s for aviation industrial espionage and had continued in that role throughout World War II, including supplying the Soviets with technical information on advanced American military aircraft in part for money and in part due to pro-Soviet sympathies. (The three-year statute of limitation on an espionage charge precluded an espionage prosecution of York, and in view of his confession and cooperation, the government did not pursue other charges. York's espionage remained secret until Venona was made public in 1995.) York described several couriers who had periodically met with him to pick up his stolen material and deliver cash in exchange. York described one from the early 1940s in detail and remembered his given name clearly as "Bill" and, less clearly, his family name as something like "Villesbend."

Based on York's information and its follow-up investigation, the FBI suspected that York's Bill Villesbend was William Weisband, a Russian linguist who worked for the super-secret National Security Administration. Weisband claimed he had been born in Egypt, the child of Russian emigrants. (Later investigations suggest that this was a cover story, and he had been born in Russia.) He immigrated to the United States in the 1920s, became a naturalized citizen in 1938, and was drafted into the U.S. Army in 1942. His linguistic talent gained him an officer's commission in the Army Signal Corps in 1943, and he served in Italy and Great Britain and at Arlington Hall, the headquarters of the Army Signal Corps code breakers and the predecessor of the National Security Agency. After demobilization he took a civilian job in 1946 as a Russian-language linguist at Arlington Hall, where he later assisted in translating some of the deciphered Venona messages.

The FBI brought York to where he could observe a number of people entering a building and asked if he could identify any of them. He picked out one as the man he had known as Bill. It was William Weisband. The FBI repeatedly interviewed Weisband. In 1950 he denied any participation in espionage but refused to sign a statement to that effect and declined to cooperate with the FBI investigation. A federal grand jury examining his case subpoenaed him to appear and respond to questions. He could have appeared and refused to testify by invoking the Fifth Amendment, but instead refused even to appear. A federal judge then sentenced him to a year in prison for contempt of court. Not surprisingly, the NSA promptly fired him. Reinterviewed by the FBI in 1953, he admitted knowing York, but refused to explain the circumstances. This time he declined to affirm or deny involvement in espionage.

Over the years that followed, the FBI and NSA concluded that betraying the Venona project was likely among the least significant aspects of Weisband's espionage. Security officials suspected that Weisband had been recruited by the KGB in 1934 and had assisted its industrial espionage, chiefly as a courier to sources, until he was drafted. It was in this role that he had met with Jones York. He continued to assist Soviet intelligence while in the U.S. Army but lost contact in late 1945 or early 1946 when many KGB and GRU officers withdrew from North America in the wake of the Gouzenko and Bentley defections. He reestablished contact in 1948 when new KGB officers sent to the United States slowly revived agents and networks not compromised by the defections. It was likely at this time he informed the Soviets of the Venona project. More importantly, however, NSA security officials concluded that he also informed the Soviets at this time that NSA had broken into virtually every Soviet military radio cipher system. These Soviet military communication codes were much less sophisticated (and less labor intensive to use) than the "one-time pad" cipher system used by the Soviet intelligence agencies in its international cables. So thoroughly were American cryptographers reading Soviet military radio traffic that the United States had near-real-time knowledge of major Soviet troop, equipment, and supply movements.

But in 1948, over a period of few months, every one of the systems the United States had broken into "went dark," in code-breaker slang, when the Soviet military hastily implemented new and more demanding cipher systems. The consequences were extremely grave. In 1950 Stalin approved Communist North Korea's plans for an invasion of South Korea. The North Korean military depended entirely on the Soviet Union for the logistics of war, and after Stalin's decision, the Soviet military in the spring of 1950 organized a massive transfer of weapons, aircraft, artillery, tanks, trucks, ammunition, fuel, and supplies to North Korea that allowed the invasion to proceed in June. Had NSA in 1950 been able to read Soviet military communications as it had prior to the systems going dark in 1948, the United States would have been forewarned of the coming invasion and been able to use diplomatic or military action to block it. As it was, the invasion was a total surprise, and defending South Korean and American forces initially were overwhelmed by the massive North Korean attack. The resulting Korean War cost the lives of over 35,000 American military personnel as well as the deaths of several million Koreans and Chinese.

Although concluding that William Weisband had wreaked enormous damage on American electronic and cryptographic intelligence, prosecutors saw little basis for bringing a successful criminal charge against him. York's identification was not sufficient; like those named by Bentley, a court contest would have come down to the uncorroborated word of a confessed Soviet spy. Further, the early 1940s espionage York could testify to directly was exempt from prosecution under the three-year statute of limitations provision then part of the espionage statute (Congress later amended this to ten years). Given Weisband's refusal to confess or provide sworn testimony (which might have opened him to a perjury charge if he made provably false statements), the single contempt-of-court sentence of one year in prison was the only legal penalty Weisband paid for his betrayal. Weisband died in 1967, and the story of his espionage did not become public until Venona was released in 1995 and he was identified as a probable source code-named Link.

But even after realizing that Weisband had likely betrayed the Venona project to the Soviets, the National Security Agency still wanted the project kept secret and its deciphered messages kept out of legal proceedings. Weisband had been consulted on some of the translation work on the Venona project, but he only knew about the specific messages on which he had worked. Nor did he know of any of the messages decoded after his unmasking in 1950. While understanding that the Soviets knew of the Venona project, NSA wanted the USSR kept in the dark about just which messages the United States had read. Consequently, for cryptologic security reasons, NSA insisted that Venona and its messages remain secret, and they did. Not until 1995, after the collapse of the Soviet Union, were the deciphered messages made public.

Further, even if the NSA had not insisted on secrecy, it is not clear that the messages would have made good evidence in a criminal trial. In its internal discussions about using the messages, the FBI thought they would be difficult evidence to present to a jury. Code breaking is an arcane intellectual skill, and most people cannot follow the exceedingly intricate and astoundingly tedious process that allows a cryptanalyst to take an international cable that appears to be random Latin alphabet letters, convert it to apparently random numbers, then, by stripping out the one-time-pad cipher, convert it to a second set of apparently random numbers, then decode the numbers into Cyrillic Russian text, translate the text into English, and, if necessary, do further investigation to identify the real name behind a cover name. The FBI thought it likely that even if NSA allowed the Justice Department prosecutors to use Venona messages in court, a moderately clever defense lawyer would use the intellectually challenging nature of the deciphering of a one-time-pad message to cause at least one member of a jury (and one would be sufficient) to balk at sending someone to prison on the basis of a process that most people could not understand.

Venona was not the only documentary confirmation of Elizabeth Bentley's story. After the collapse of the USSR, Russian archives were partially opened. While the main archives of the Soviet intelligence services, the KGB and GRU, remain closed, other archives such as that of the Communist International were opened, and these contained some communications with these agencies dealing with Soviet espionage in the United States using the services of American Communists. The KGB's Russian successor also released selected documents from KGB archives to highlight past successes and justify its continued existence to a newly empowered Russian public. These documents also confirmed and corroborated Bentley's story.

Documents coming out of the KGB archive also underlined the enormous damage done to Soviet espionage by her defection. The KGB withdrew from the United States those Soviet intelligence officers with whom she had worked. Most had diplomatic cover and could not be arrested, but once identified as intelligence officers by the FBI, their effectiveness was severely reduced. This meant the loss of contact not only with Soviet sources Bentley had known but with many other contacts of these officers as well. KGB documents demonstrated that, in the wake of Bentley's 1945 defection, the agency had to sever contact with the majority of its American spies. So many Soviet intelligence officers were withdrawn that by 1948 the KGB station in the United States was reduced to a few inexperienced officers without adequate English-language skills. Eventually new officers with the needed skills and experience were found, but that took some years. Bentley's story of the large number of secret Communists in the government and the ease with which they had been recruited into espionage spurred President Truman and the Congress to set up a wide-ranging internal security program that within a few years eliminated most Communists from government employment. Bentley's story also contributed significantly to the development of a national anti-Communist consensus in the late 1940s that destroyed the political effectiveness of the American Communist Party.

The Bentley Case: A Conclusion

By the time of her lonely death in 1962, Elizabeth Bentley had faded from the public scene. After the Vietnam War shattered the public consensus behind America's anti-Communist Cold War policies in the 1970s, a significant segment of the public and many historians came to regard the concern about Communist subversion and Soviet espionage in the 1940s as products of hysteria and paranoia with no basis in fact. Venona was still secret, and the FBI investigative files that backed her story were closed to research as well. Elizabeth Bentley became an object of derision, ridiculed as the clownish "Blond Spy Queen" and habitually depicted in textbooks as a fantasist, fraud, or liar. Those she had identified as Soviet sources were treated as innocent victims and martyrs of sinister anti-Communist hysteria.

But in the 1990s, after the collapse of the Soviet Union and the end of the Cold War, Venona was made public and Russian archives were also partially opened. FBI files had been partially opened even earlier. Venona and these other archival evidence showed that Elizabeth Bentley had told the truth and those she identified as Soviet sources were just what she said they were: spies who had assisted Soviet espionage against the United States. It also became clearer that Bentley's defection triggered events that brought about a catastrophic collapse in Soviet espionage in the United States just as the Cold War got under way and contributed to a permanent political isolation of the American Communist Party Although it produced only a few minor court cases, the case of the "Blond Spy Queen" had a major impact on the early Cold War and on the course of American history.

FURTHER READINGS

Elizabeth Bentley

Bentley, Elizabeth. *Out of Bondage: The Story of Elizabeth Bentley.* New York: Devin-Adair, 1951.

> *A melodramatic and embellished version of events by Bentley, though in the main sticking to her original debriefing by the FBI in 1945. A ghostwriter assisted Bentley in preparing the book. The 1988 reissue of* Out of Bondage *(New York: Ivy Books) contains a detailed "afterword" (113 pages) by Hayden Peake that examines Bentley's credibility on the basis of Freedom of Information documents and published histories.*

Haynes, John Earl, and Harvey Klehr. "The Golos-Bentley Network" (chapter 3) and "Friends in High Places" (chapter 4). In *Venona: Decoding Soviet Espionage in America.* New Haven: Yale University Press, 1999.

Kessler, Lauren. *Clever Girl: Elizabeth Bentley's Life In and Out of Espionage.* New York: HarperCollins, 2003.

> *Full-length, thoroughly researched biography of Bentley, finding her story largely accurate and reliable. Treats Bentley sympathetically. Written in a*

journalistic style with light documentation and a less scholarly approach than Kathryn Olmsted's biography.

Olmsted, Kathryn S. *Red Spy Queen: A Biography of Elizabeth Bentley*. Chapel Hill: University of North Carolina Press, 2002.

Thoroughly researched and the first scholarly biography of Bentley to appear. Judges that her statement to the FBI and early testimony were accurate but that later she tended to embellish and exaggerate. Views her personally in a critical light.

Weinstein, Allen, and Alexander Vassiliev. "Love and Loyalties, II: Elizabeth Bentley and Jacob Golos" (chapter 5), "Harvest Time, I: The Silvermaster Network in Wartime Washington" (chapter 8), "Harvest Time, II: The Perlo Group" (chapter 10), "Flight from Exposure, I: The Washington Sources" (chapter 13). In *The Haunted Wood: Soviet Espionage in America–The Stalin Era*. New York: Random House, 1999.

Wilson, Veronica A. "Elizabeth Bentley and Cold War Representations: Masks Not Dropped." *Intelligence and National Security* 14, no. 2 (Summer 1999): 49–69.

Finds that Bentley's failure to fulfill traditional gender prescriptions offended some commentators, who used this failure to cast doubt on her story, and discusses Bentley's attempt to counter these doubts with a public performance of traditional femininity.

William Remington

May, Gary. *Un-American Activities: The Trials of William Remington*. New York: Oxford University Press, 1994.

Suggests that Remington lied about his Communist background and that considerable evidence backs up Bentley's story but that the government prosecution of Remington was legally flawed.

Harry Dexter White

Craig, R. Bruce. *Treasonable Doubt: The Harry Dexter White Spy Case*. Lawrence: University Press of Kansas, 2004.

A thorough and scholarly biography highly sympathetic to White that concludes, "based on the totality of evidence, there is little doubt that Harry Dexter White engaged in . . . 'a species of espionage'" but judges that those actions were consistent with White's "Rooseveltian internationalism" and that White "saw no

dichotomy in being a full-time member of the Rooseveltian progressive estab-
lishment ... while at the same time assisting the Soviet regime."

William Weisband

Benson, Robert Louis, and Michael Warner. "Who Was William Weisband?" In *Venona: Soviet Espionage and the American Response, 1939–1957*, edited by Robert Louis Benson and Michael Warner. Washington, D.C.: National Security Agency; Central Intelligence Agency, 1996.

4

The Alger Hiss–Whittaker Chambers Case

T HE HISS-CHAMBERS CASE GENERATED MORE NEWSPAPER
and media coverage and more angry debate than any of the other
early spy cases. It did so because the accused spy, Alger Hiss, was a
prominent member of the Washington foreign policy establishment that
had come to power under the leadership of Franklin Roosevelt and his New
Deal. People very quickly chose sides in the Hiss-Chambers case based
more on partisan political considerations than on the facts of the case.
To his detractors, predominately Republicans and conservatives, Hiss
showed that betrayal reached into the highest levels of the government
and that the Roosevelt and Truman administrations had been negligent or
worse in regard to the threat of Soviet espionage. To his defenders, largely
Democrats and liberals, Hiss was an innocent patriot attacked by sinister
reactionary forces (Richard Nixon and the FBI) that concocted a false
story of espionage with no goal other than discrediting the New Deal. This
bitterly angry debate not only predominated at the time but has continued
in the more than fifty years since Hiss was convicted of perjury.

The Hiss-Chambers case began as a minor episode in Elizabeth Bentley's story. In the summer of 1948 the U.S. House of Representatives
Committee on Un-American Activities called Bentley to testify about her
career as a Soviet spy in the early 1940s. One of Bentley's claims was that
the spy rings she had supervised for the Soviet KGB had been drawn from
covert networks of secret Communist Party members who were federal
government employees. To buttress her story, the committee also called
witnesses to testify about the existence of an underground Communist
Party organization in Washington in the 1930s. One of those supplemen-
tal witnesses was Whittaker Chambers. His August 3, 1948, testimony,
however, set off a chain of events that produced a spy drama that quickly
overshadowed Elizabeth Bentley's saga.

Whittaker Chambers

New York's intellectual and journalistic circles knew Whittaker Chambers as a polarizing figure. While recognizing his literary talent, many left-leaning intellectuals detested him for his fierce hostility to Stalin's regime and communism. For some the distaste was compounded because they regarded him as a traitor for having turned against the Communist movement he had once embraced. To the broader public, Chambers was an obscure figure, although many had unknowingly read his journalism. He had joined the widely read news magazine *Time* in 1939 and quickly proved himself not only an able editor of the work of *Time*'s reporters but a colorful and insightful writer in his own right. He chiefly oversaw the magazine's book and intellectual sections but also edited its foreign news for a period in World War II and had given both a combination of trenchant analysis and appealing prose. Particularly when he edited foreign affairs coverage, however, he had clashed with reporters and writers who admired Joseph Stalin and wrote of the USSR as a benign power rather than as a dictatorship temporarily allied with the United States against the more immediate menace of National Socialist Germany.

Chambers, born in 1901, had grown up on Long Island in a dysfunctional and economically pressed family. His intellectual talent got him into Columbia University, but he dropped out in 1923 after upsetting school officials with a blasphemous story about Jesus in the undergraduate literary journal. He wandered the country taking a series of temporary jobs, returned briefly to Columbia, and then joined the Communist Party, all the while also pursuing a dissolute bohemian life-style. He earned a meager living as a free-lance journalist and writer. In the late 1920s he developed a reputation as a skilled literary translator. Chambers was hired, for example, to translate from the original German the first American edition of the childhood favorite *Bambi*. By 1929 he was working as a news editor for the Communist Party's flagship journal, the *Daily Worker*, and teaching journalism in a party school. The CPUSA, however, fell into turmoil when Moscow ordered the expulsion of its leadership, and Chambers dropped out for two years. By 1931 he had been reconciled with the party after he wrote a short story, "Can You Hear Their Voices?" When it was acclaimed by Soviet critics as one of the finest examples of "proletarian literature" produced in the period, he was named to the national board of the CPUSA's literary front group, the John Reed Clubs, and given a salaried position as editor of *New Masses*, the Communist literary-intellectual journal in 1932.

Chambers did not hold his new job for very long. In 1932 the CPUSA leadership ordered him to leave open party work and join its covert arm. Using a variety of names and living in a variety of places, he worked in the party's underground until mid-1938 when he broke irreconcilably with communism. He then reentered society under his real name and in the spring of 1939 got a job at *Time* magazine where he remained until his 1948 testimony to the House Committee on Un-American Activities.

Chambers stated that he had been sent to Washington in 1934 as liaison between the Communist Party's covert arm and secret groups of Communists who worked for the U.S. government. Participants in these covert Communist units included a number of young professionals, lawyers, economists, and others, radicalized by the Great Depression of the 1930s, who had joined the rapidly expanding federal New Deal agencies set up by President Franklin D. Roosevelt. Under the civil service rules of that era, regular government employees were required to avoid membership in partisan political organizations. Federal civil service employees could vote, of course, and participate in civic and nonpartisan organizations, but holding an office in either the Democratic or Republican parties, much less the Communist Party, was a firing offense. In defiance of this rule, government employees who were secret members of the Communist Party (there were no government employees who were open Communists) maintained secret caucuses that met sometimes monthly, but more often weekly, where members discussed the latest party literature: its newspaper, the *Daily Worker*; its theoretical journal, the *Communist*; its literary journal, *New Masses*; and the multitude of special-issue pamphlets the party published. Usually one of the group's activists or a visiting party official would give a lecture on some aspect of party policy. These secret caucuses also discussed how they could use their work in the government to promote Communist goals and collected information on government plans that might assist party organizers.

Chambers called one of the groups with which he worked the "Ware Group," because Harold Ware, a CPUSA specialist in Communist agricultural policy, had first established it. Ware had initially set up a small Communist caucus around lawyers who worked for the Agricultural Adjustment Administration, a New Deal agency established to provide economic relief to farmers hard-hit by the Depression. Ware had died in an auto accident in

1935, and Josef Peters, head of the CPUSA underground, took over party contact with the group. It was Peters who put Chambers in contact with the members of the group. (Peters had been an official of the Communist regime that briefly seized power in Hungary in 1919. After its collapse, he fled to the United States and became an official of the CPUSA's Hungarian immigrant affiliate. The party sent him to Moscow for Comintern training in the early 1930s, and he returned to supervise the party's organizational work and its clandestine arm. After the Hiss-Chambers affair became public, Peters returned to his native Hungary and took a post with the post–World War II Communist regime.)

In his August 2, 1948, testimony to the House Committee on Un-American Activities, Chambers described the Ware group and similar cells formed at other government agencies, but he professed no direct knowledge of espionage by their members, stating: "The purpose of this group at that time was not primarily espionage. Its original purpose was the Communist infiltration of the American Government. But espionage was certainly one of its eventual objectives." It was this latter point that reinforced Bentley's testimony that the spy rings with which she worked in 1942–1944 were based on earlier Communist political networks.

Chambers identified a number of people whom he had known as participants in the 1930s CPUSA underground in Washington. Most were little known and had left government service years earlier. Nathan Witt, for example, had held the important post of first secretary (staff director) of the National Labor Relations Board in the late 1930s and had been in a position to influence NLRB actions that would assist Communist trade-union organizers. Witt's partiality for Communist unions was not well concealed; after irritating Roosevelt's White House, he had been forced to resign in 1940, eight years prior to Chambers's testimony. Another secret Communist lawyer Chambers named was John Abt. Abt had been chief counsel for the Civil Liberties Subcommittee (known as the La Follette committee) of the U.S. Senate Education and Labor Committee in the mid-1930s when it held highly publicized investigations of employer resistance to union-organizing campaigns. Abt's position had been a sensitive one, but, again, he had left federal employment years earlier. In 1948 he was a private attorney specializing in labor law.

Two people Chambers named were less obscure. One was Harry Dexter White, who as assistant secretary of the Treasury had been a powerful figure in Washington in the early 1940s. He left that post in early 1946 to become American representative to the newly established International Monetary Fund, a body he had helped to design. Unhappy with the Truman administration's resistance to Stalin's foreign policy, however, he had resigned in 1947 and in 1948 was a prominent supporter of Henry Wallace's bid for the presidency on the leftist Progressive Party ticket. Chambers accused White only of secretly assisting the Communist underground in the mid-1930s when he was a midlevel Treasury Department economist. In her testimony, however, Elizabeth Bentley had stated that by 1944 White had become a Soviet spy.

White demanded an opportunity to respond to Bentley and Chambers and testified to the House committee on August 13, 1948. He vehemently denied giving any assistance to the Communist Party or Soviet intelligence and insisted that he had no knowledge that any of his close associates had been Communists. He cited more than a decade of public service, and in ringing tones declared, "I believe in freedom of religion, freedom of speech, freedom of thought, freedom of the press, freedom of criticism, and freedom of movement. I believe in the goal of equality of opportunity, and the right of each individual to follow the calling of his or her own choice, and the right of every individual to an opportunity to develop his or her capacity to the fullest. I consider these principles sacred. I regard them as the basic fabric of our American way of life, and I believe in them as living realities, and not mere words on paper. That is my creed." It was a powerful statement and made more dramatic when he died of a heart attack three days later.

The deciphered Venona messages and KGB archival evidence made public in the 1990s established that Bentley told the truth and White lied. He had, in fact, been a Communist sympathizer, had knowingly assisted secret Communist economists to obtain jobs in the Treasury Department, and had cooperated with Soviet intelligence agencies during World War II. But his death in 1948 ended further public investigation at that time. There was no trial where Bentley's and Chambers's charges were tested, nor did the House Committee on Un-American Activities see any point in pursuing an investigation of a dead man. With little evidence publicly available beyond Bentley's and Chambers's claims and White's impassioned denials, it appeared to many people at the time that a loyal American and innocent man had been driven to his death by baseless accusations, an image reinforced by leading newspapers and journalists.

Alger Hiss

The other prominent figure Chambers had cited was Alger Hiss (Bentley had not discussed Alger Hiss in her testimony.) Although he had not climbed as high as White – an assistant cabinet secretary – Hiss had been a rising star in the U.S. State Department and, in the eyes of some, had been a likely candidate for future high appointment. Born in 1904, he grew up in Baltimore but also attended an elite prep school in Massachusetts before graduating from Johns Hopkins University in 1926. He finished Harvard Law School in 1929 and received a much-coveted Supreme Court clerkship with Justice Oliver Wendell Holmes. He worked briefly for two prestigious law firms, first in Boston and then in New York. In 1933, however, he abandoned private law practice and became an attorney for the Agricultural Adjustment Administration. He then worked for a time for a congressional investigative committee headed by Senator Gerald Nye. The high-profile "Nye committee" made headlines by forcing arms industry businessmen to answer harsh charges that they had manipulated the American government's entry into World War I in order to increase their profits. He then took a legal post with the U.S. Justice Department but in 1936 accepted a salary cut in order to transfer to the U.S. State Department.

Hiss initially worked in a small State Department office run by Assistant Secretary of State Francis Sayre dealing with international economic matters. He moved to the more prestigious Far Eastern Division in 1939 and in 1944 to the Office of Special Political Affairs, where he worked closely with under secretaries of state Dean Acheson and Edward Stettinius and then became director of the office in 1945. At the 1944 Dumbarton Oaks Conference of major Allied nations that planned the United Nations, Hiss served as executive secretary and held the very high-profile position of secretary-general of the United Nation's founding conference in San Francisco in April 1945. He also accompanied Stettinius, then U.S. secretary of state, to the February 1945 Yalta Conference attended by President Roosevelt, British Prime Minister Churchill, and Soviet Marshal Joseph Stalin.

Hiss's ascent in the State Department, however, halted after President Roosevelt died and President Truman appointed James Byrnes as the new secretary of state. Byrnes took seriously warnings from State Department security officers and the FBI that evidence existed suggesting that Hiss might be a security risk. Although no formal action was taken against him, Hiss understood that his career at the Department of State would go nowhere for the foreseeable future. The press, however, knew none of this, and Hiss's public standing based on his well-publicized role in the founding of the United Nations remained high. He resigned from the State Department and in early 1947 accepted the presidency of the prestigious Carnegie Endowment for International Peace.

Like White, Hiss insisted on responding to Chambers before the House Committee on Un-American Activities. He appeared on August 5, just three days later, and denied that there was any truth to Chambers's statements. Specifically he said he had not known Chambers in the mid-1930s or later, had no sympathy whatsoever for communism, and any contact he had with people later established to have been Communists was unknowing, casual, or strictly in the course of his professional duties. He emphasized his record of public service and his close relationship to many leaders of the Washington establishment.

Not only did Hiss's testimony clash with Chambers's, but also the physical contrast between the two could hardly have been greater. As a public witness Whittaker Chambers was underwhelming. Overweight, out of shape, jowly, and plain featured, he spoke with a tired voice in a barely audible monotone. Hiss, on the other hand, was slim, fit, WASP-establishment handsome, and spoke forcefully and eloquently. When Hiss's testimony ended, the audience applauded and the press swarmed around him, treating him as a hero who had put the ignorant reactionaries of the House Committee on Un-American Activities in their place. Even committee members rushed forward to share his limelight and offer their congratulations. Highly placed Washingtonians also came to Hiss's defense. Privately, Dean Acheson, under secretary of state and soon to become secretary of state, advised Hiss on how he should handle Chambers's charge. Publicly a reporter asked President Truman if he thought the "spy scare" was "a red herring" to divert public opinion from other issues. He agreed and accused the House committee of "slandering a lot of people that don't deserve it."

Part of the rush to Hiss's defense was a simple partisan reaction. The House Committee on Un-American Activities was investigating espionage and subversion, but it was also doing so in an intensely partisan context during a tightly contested presidential and congressional election campaign. The Republican majority on the committee hoped not merely to expose espionage and subversion but also to embarrass the Truman White House and demonstrate to voters that the Democratic administrations of President Roosevelt and Truman had been at best negligent and perhaps worse in dealing with the threat of Soviet espionage and Communist subversion of the government. It hoped the investigation would contribute to Truman's defeat and help Republicans maintain a majority in the Congress. For equally partisan reasons, Democrats were eager to discredit the investigation and defend prominent New Dealers like Hiss as patriotic Americans.

Dueling Testimony

In the face of Hiss's strong rebuttal, the Republican leadership of the House Committee on Un-American Activities considered dropping the matter, but several members, notably freshman Representative Richard Nixon, and the committee's investigative staff were aware that suspicions about Hiss went beyond Chambers's testimony and were shared by the FBI, some State Department security officers, and several knowledgeable private anti-Communist activists. After some hesitation, the committee majority decided to take more testimony, initially in executive (nonpublic) session, to see if the contradictions between Chambers and Hiss could be resolved. Committee investigators also searched for corroborative documentation.

During the executive hearings Chambers and his wife Esther testified in detail regarding their relationship with Alger Hiss and his wife Priscilla in the mid-1930s. The committee concentrated on Chambers's claims about this relationship because Hiss had testified without qualification that he had never known Whittaker Chambers and had had no relationship with him at all. If Hiss were right, then the reliability of Chambers's testimony about Hiss's secret political loyalties would be seriously undermined.

Chambers claimed a close friendship had developed between the two families in the mid-1930s. He said that when he first arrived in Washington and was looking for an apartment, the Hisses had two months remaining on a lease of their old apartment, which they gave to the Chamberses at no cost; the two families even briefly shared the Hisses' new residence for a few days before delivery of the Chamberses' household goods. The two families exchanged social visits from 1935 into 1938, including several after the Chamberses moved to Baltimore (visits later confirmed by a maid). The

Hisses introduced Esther Chambers to their pediatrician when she was looking for medical care for one of her children. Chambers also described social and business auto trips with the Hisses, details of the interior of their residences and Alger's personal habits, including his enthusiasm for bird watching and excitement one day when he reported having seen a rare prothonotary warbler on a walking trail along the Potomac. Chambers also testified that Hiss had advanced him $400 in cash in the fall of 1937 to purchase an automobile and that after Hiss bought a new car he insisted that his old Ford be turned over to the Communist Party for use by an organizer.

The committee then heard Hiss's testimony, also in executive session. His description of his personal life in the mid-1930s confirmed many details that Chambers had provided, including the story about the prothonotary warbler. There had been leaks of some of Chambers's detailed executive session testimony to the press, and Hiss had to account for how Chambers would have known so much about his private life. He began to shift his testimony. While insisting that his original testimony that he had not known "Whittaker Chambers" and did not recognize Chambers's photograph was precisely accurate, he indicated that he had known someone named "George Crosley," who seemed to share some of Chambers's attributes. The committee then brought the two men together in executive session. Hiss walked over to Chambers, looked closely at him and asked him to open his mouth. He then identified Chambers as the person he had known as Crosley ten years earlier, explaining that Crosley's teeth had been in poor shape at the time but subsequent dental work had contributed to Hiss's difficulty in recognizing him.

Regardless of the name, Hiss testified to a quite different relationship from the one described by Chambers. Hiss said he had known Crosley only casually as a journalist who occasionally stopped by the Nye committee in search of newsworthy material. But neither congressional staffers nor later private investigators hired by Hiss's lawyers could locate anyone associated with the Nye committee who remembered George Crosley or Whittaker Chambers as a journalist interested in the Nye committee's work; nor have news stories or articles written by Chambers/Crosley about it ever been located. Pressed by committee members about Chambers's claim that Hiss had loaned him an apartment for two months in the summer of 1935 at no cost, Hiss insisted that he had subleased, not loaned, the final months of the Hisses' old apartment to Chambers. When questioned further, Hiss admitted that he did not ask Chambers to sign a sublease agreement and did not have any receipts for rent, but claimed that Chambers failed to pay most of the rent in any case. Hiss also confirmed that the Chamberses had briefly stayed with his family at their new residence but brushed it aside as an act of generosity rather than an example of the two families' close relationship.

Hiss's response to other questions cast further doubt on his claim that his relationship to Chambers had been casual. He admitted that he had driven Chambers to New York and other places in his automobile. He denied Chambers's story about receiving a $400 car loan in the early fall of 1937, but committee investigators produced bank records that the Hisses had withdrawn $400 from their savings account at that time. Hiss then insisted the withdrawal was for purchase of furniture for a house into which they had just moved. However, the Hisses did not relocate until several months after the withdrawal and later investigation showed that the Hisses had not even rented the new residence until after the withdrawal had been made.

Hiss's least credible testimony, however, dealt with his old Ford automobile. Asked about Chambers's claim that he had given an old car to the Communist Party, Hiss explained: "I sold him [Chambers] an automobile. I had an old Ford that I threw in with the apartment. . . . I let him have it along with the rent" when he had subleased his apartment to Crosley in the summer of 1935 for two months. Committee investigators, however, located notarized auto title records showing that Hiss had never signed the title of the car over to Crosley (or Chambers); instead, in the presence of a notary he had signed the car in question over to a used car dealership in July 1936 (not mid-1935 when Hiss claimed he had given it to Chambers). On the same day the dealership transferred the car for a nominal sum to William Rosen, a Washington dry cleaner with Communist ties.

Rosen was later called to testify before the House committee, a U.S. grand jury, and at the second Hiss perjury trial and asked about the circumstances of the sale. He admitted Communist Party membership but refused to answer questions about the auto transaction, claiming his Fifth Amendment right not to provide testimony that might implicate him in a crime. Rosen's lawyer privately informed Hiss defense attorneys that Rosen had been part of a dummy transaction arranged by the CPUSA and, on party instructions, had signed over the Ford to a Communist Party official. In a memoir written decades later, the son of a photographer who worked for a different Soviet spy ring (Philip Rosenbliet's) noted that in 1937 Rosen had also been used to arrange the transfer of a used car to his father at the behest of a Soviet intelligence officer.

In response to the documentation of the car transfer, Hiss amended his testimony, saying that while he had sold the car to Chambers in 1935 as part of the apartment deal he had not actually bothered to transfer ownership legally and that in 1936 some unknown person had showed up at his door and asked him to sign the legal transfer papers, and he had done so. Committee members were understandably incredulous that Hiss, a lawyer, would be so casual about the legal status of a car. Their suspicions only grew when committee investigators showed that Hiss had paid for automobile insurance on the car from August 1935, when he claimed he gave it to his casual acquaintance Crosley, until July 1936 when he signed it over to the used car dealer. Further, Hiss in earlier testimony had said that Chambers had subleased his apartment but had failed to pay all but a portion of the rent, which made handing over the car either in 1935 or even more so in July 1936 appear absurd.

Behind the scenes, meanwhile, the executive branch was continuing a long-drawn-out investigation of Bentley's story by means of a federal grand jury. Given the lack of direct evidence beyond Bentley's testimony, Justice Department prosecutors had decided to try to obtain a confession or some statement that might lead to a perjury indictment by subpoenaing many of those Bentley had named to testify. To their frustration, however, this tactic produced little useful testimony. Hiss and Chambers were among those called, and both maintained their positions. Asked if he had knowledge of specific instances of spying, Chambers denied that he had observed any espionage.

As the House committee executive session testimony alternated with public testimony, Hiss's public credibility, strong when he first appeared in early August, began to show signs of strain. Once overwhelmingly favorable to Hiss, some reporters and newspapers became more skeptical. Still, Hiss could have waited out the ordeal. Had he done so, there might never have been a Hiss case. In the November election, not only was President Truman reelected, but also the House of Representatives shifted from a Republican to a Democratic majority, and a Democratic-led House Committee on Un-American Activities might well have dropped the Hiss matter in the face of the two conflicting stories. That outcome was not obvious, however, and Hiss had already gone on the offensive.

The Slander Suit, the Baltimore Documents, and the Pumpkin Papers

Like all official congressional testimony, Chambers's appearance before the House Committee on Un-American Activities was privileged. Immunity from suits for slander and libel protects witnesses from legal harassment and encourages candid testimony. Hiss challenged Chambers to repeat his charges outside the immunity of congressional testimony where he would be subject to a lawsuit. At this point Chambers, too, could have ignored the challenge, leaving Hiss to claim vindication. Chambers, however, repeated his charges when interviewed on the CBS radio program *Meet the Press*. The ball back in his court, Hiss did nothing for a few weeks, making some of his supporters nervous, but finally responded with a slander suit on September 27, 1948, demanding $50,000 in compensation for the injury done by what he said was a baseless charge; he followed up with a second slander suit citing other statements by Chambers a few weeks later.

If he had lost the suit ($50,000 in 1948 was the equivalent of more than $400,000 in 2005 values), Chambers and his family faced financial ruin. He responded by upping the ante himself. As a part of the suit, Hiss's lawyers routinely demanded that Chambers produce any documentation relevant to his claims (called "discovery" in legal jargon). It is unlikely that they expected any response: in his testimony Chambers had not claimed or even hinted that he possessed evidence relevant to his charges about the Communist underground in Washington. But in the face of the slander suit, Chambers needed to produce corroboration. Additionally, under trial procedures he was legally bound to respond to Hiss's attorneys' demands. At a deposition meeting in Baltimore on November 17, 1948, Chambers and his lawyers turned over a set of documents to Hiss's lawyers that Chambers had retrieved from a nephew's apartment a few days before. Chambers had placed the documents there for safekeeping in the late 1930s. These "Baltimore documents," four sheets of paper in Alger Hiss's handwriting, sixty-five typed documents from 1938, and four yellow sheets of paper in Harry Dexter White's handwriting, changed the entire nature of the Hiss-Chambers affair.

What had been at issue in the Hiss-Chambers slander suit and the broader public confrontation was Chambers's claim that in the mid-1930s Alger Hiss had been part of the Communist Party's Washington underground organization. In the context of the early Cold War of the late 1940s, this was a serious charge about a man who had become a senior U.S. diplomat and was a candidate for some future high State Department appointment. The Baltimore documents spoke indirectly to the issue of Hiss's Communist sympathies but bore directly on another issue: espionage. Until this point espionage had not been an issue between Chambers and Hiss. Indeed, in testifying to the House committee and to a U.S. grand jury, Chambers had denied knowledge of espionage. The Baltimore documents, however, were evidence of betrayal of U.S. diplomatic information to a foreign power: the Union of Soviet Socialist Republics. The attorneys for Chambers and Hiss agreed that the documents had to be turned over to the Justice Department. With that, the initiative turned to public authorities and the civil slander suit eventually was dropped.

The Justice Department was surprised and initially ill-prepared to deal with the matter. While the FBI had concluded that Alger Hiss was a security risk in 1946, it had based its suspicions about his Communist loyalties largely on earlier information from Whittaker Chambers that spoke to Hiss's participation in the Communist Party's underground but was ambiguous about espionage. After the signing of the Nazi-Soviet Pact in August 1939 and with war imminent, the anti-Communist journalist Isaac Don Levine convinced Chambers that he had to tell the U.S. government what he knew about the Communist Party's Washington underground and the threat of Soviet espionage. Levine knew that Chambers had quietly dropped out of the Communist Party's covert arm in 1938. Chambers, however, had not gone to government authorities to tell what he knew. He wanted to reenter normal life quietly. He later explained that, because the federal government had little interest in Soviet espionage in the late 1930s, he thought going to the authorities would produce little besides difficulties for himself and his family. Levine, however, convinced him that the stakes were now higher, since the Communist underground could be used to assist National Socialist (Nazi) Germany, the Soviet Union's new ally. Chambers agreed but wanted immunity from prosecution for espionage in return for telling what he knew.

Levine was unable to get an appointment with President Roosevelt, but the White House directed him to Assistant Secretary of State Adolf Berle. Although he had a vague presidential mandate to coordinate security and intelligence matters, Berle had no executive authority over the FBI or any federal agency beyond the State Department, and the latter was oriented toward foreign diplomatic relations, not internal counterintelligence. The only security staff to which Berle had access was the State Department's own tiny personnel security office whose jurisdiction was limited to current State Department employees. The White House would have been better advised to have sent Levine to the FBI.

Levine and Chambers met with Berle at his home on the evening of September 2, 1939. Chambers had not gotten the immunity from prosecution he requested and consequently, he later explained, he provided only a partial account of his activities. In particular he did not directly state that he was involved in espionage; however, he hinted strongly enough about the matter because when Berle typed up his notes of the conversation he entitled it "Underground Espionage Agent." Berle's notes show that Chambers described a Communist Party underground with a large network in Washington and that he provided the names of several dozen people who were part of this network. In the 1990s newly opened Russian archives, deciphered World War II KGB cablegrams of the Venona project (see Chapter 3), and other documentation would confirm that most of those Chambers named had spied for the Soviet Union. Among them were Alger Hiss, his wife Priscilla, and his brother Donald. The notes also suggest that Chambers gave no special emphasis to Alger Hiss; he was just one of several dozen names Chambers provided.

Berle, in any case, did very little with the information, possibly because war had broken out in Europe and he was preoccupied with more pressing diplomatic duties. He asked the FBI for a report on Chambers and was told that the bureau had only identified him as a covert Communist. Hiss was then a midlevel but rising State Department official. Without giving details Berle discussed Chambers's charge with several senior officials, who rejected the allegation based on their personal judgment of Hiss's character. By all accounts, Alger Hiss possessed an engaging and attractive personality that won him many friends and admirers. Nor did Hiss, with his WASPish background and elite education, fit the stereotype of a Communist as an Eastern European or the son of immigrants of working-class origins. Berle then dropped the matter. This character and status defense that staved off Berle's 1939 inquiry, a belief by those who knew Hiss and worked with him that he or anyone of his background could not have done what was charged, would later provide the heart of Hiss's defense against Chambers in 1948 and thereafter.

The FBI heard from one of its sources in 1942 that Chambers had information about the Communist underground in Washington and interviewed him. By then a senior editor at *Time* magazine, Chambers did not want to pursue the matter and said he had given all of his information to Berle in 1939. The FBI then contacted Berle, who agreed to hand over his notes but did not get around to doing so until June 1943. German and Japanese espionage, in any event, had higher priority in 1943 than Soviet spying, and the FBI did little to follow up until late 1945 when Elizabeth Bentley defected.

Bentley had much to tell the FBI about Soviet espionage, but only one item had any relevance to Alger Hiss. One of the members of the spy network Bentley called the "Perlo Group" was Harold Glasser. In late 1945 Bentley told the FBI:

> Referring again to Harold Glasser, I recall that after his return from his assignment in Europe, probably in Italy, for the United States Treasury Department, Victor Perlo told me that Glasser had asked him if he would be able to get back in with the Perlo group. I asked Perlo how Glasser happened to leave the group and he explained that Glasser and one or two others had been taken sometime before by some American in some governmental agency in Washington, and that this unidentified American turned Glasser and the others over to some Russian. Perlo declared he did not know the identity of this American, and said that Charley Kramer, so far as he knew, was the only person who had this information. Sometime later I was talking with Kramer in New York City, and brought up this matter to him. At this time Kramer told me that the person who had originally taken Glasser away from Perlo's group was named Hiss and that he was in the U.S. State Department.

The FBI pressed Bentley to identify Hiss further: at the time both Alger and his brother Donald worked for the State Department. Bentley, who didn't know who Hiss was, speculated that the first name might have been "Eugene," but stated that, while she was sure of "Hiss," she couldn't clearly remember the first name.

The FBI and Raymond Murphy, a Department of State specialist in Communist matters, also reinterviewed Chambers in 1946. While he remained evasive about espionage, he confirmed his 1939 statement to Berle that Hiss had been part of the Communist underground and expected to promote Communist interests in the State Department. These bits and pieces of information were sufficient to convince Secretary of State Byrnes that Hiss was a risk and to encourage his departure from the State Department in late 1946. There was, however, no direct evidence of spying, and the Justice Department had not opened an espionage investigation aimed at Hiss, so the arrival of the Baltimore documents in late 1948 was a shock.

The Grand Jury

Initially the Justice Department reacted to the Baltimore documents in a partisan fashion, seeing the evidence as an opportunity to indict Chambers for perjury and discredit someone whose testimony Republicans had used as a weapon against President Truman in the 1948 election. In early December the grand jury, the same one before which he had stated under oath in October that he had no knowledge of espionage, recalled Chambers. He now testified that part of his earlier testimony had been false. He went on to explain that in 1936–1938 a select few of the underground Communists in Washington had been separated out and made part of an espionage network that reported to Soviet intelligence and that one of them was Alger Hiss. Chambers stated that he himself was the go-between, collecting documents and reports from sources within the government and turning the material over to Soviet intelligence officers. He explained that in 1938, when he decided to drop out of espionage, he retained some of the documents his sources furnished him for insurance. He later sent word back to Soviet intelligence through a member of his espionage network that if he or his family were harmed, the documents would be turned over to the government. If he were left alone, however, they would remain unused. When Chambers was asked why he had not discussed Hiss's espionage in his earlier testimony to Congress and grand jury, he explained that in the 1930s he had regarded Hiss as a genuine friend and had not wanted to harm him.

The grand jury was angry that Chambers had deceived it in his earlier testimony. For several weeks it appeared that federal prosecutors would urge jurors to indict Chambers for perjury. In a literal sense, of course, he had committed perjury. In sworn testimony to the grand jury in October (and in August to the House Committee on Un-American Activities), he had denied knowledge of espionage. In November he produced documents that were evidence of espionage and in December he gave a detailed account of his participation in espionage against the United States in the mid-1930s. Usually, however, when a witness gives false testimony and then later comes forward and provides a truthful account, no perjury charge is brought. To charge perjury automatically in such a case would be a disincentive for a witness to provide a subsequent truthful account, which would not serve the public interest. It is particularly true that a perjury charge is rarely brought if a witness corrects false testimony in a timely fashion before any miscarriage of justice or other adverse affect on the public interest has occurred. Chambers's case fit this pattern: he had corrected his false sworn testimony within two months of his grand jury testimony and within four months of his congressional testimony, and his false testimony had not produced any miscarriage of justice.

The Justice Department's decision was also affected by the House Committee on Un-American Activities and Chambers's possession of additional documents. After the Justice Department gained control of the Baltimore documents, it ordered both sides in the slander suit to refrain from discussing the material in public. Perhaps anticipating such a turn, Chambers had retained microfilm he had also hidden in 1938. An associate of Chambers leaked to the House committee's staff the existence of the Baltimore documents, Justice's clampdown on information, and the news that Chambers possessed additional evidence. Critics had pointed to the committee's failure to produce evidence of prosecutable crimes and derided it for smearing innocent people such as Alger Hiss. While irritated that Chambers had not told the full truth earlier, the committee realized that Chambers's documents offered a measure of vindication. It issued a broadly written subpoena requiring Chambers to produce any evidence he had, and on the evening of December 2, 1948, investigators went to his farm in rural Maryland. Theatrically, Chambers led the investigators to a pumpkin patch where he had hidden the microfilm in a hollowed-out pumpkin. The film had actually been in the pumpkin only since that morning. Like the earlier Baltimore documents, the microfilm had been retrieved from his nephew's apartment in Brooklyn. Chambers explained later that he had briefly hidden the film in the pumpkin because he had feared that agents from Hiss's defense team would steal it.

Despite its melodramatically staged hiding place, the film was additional evidence of espionage. Two strips of developed film, with fifty-eight separate prints, contained photographs of 1938 U.S. Department of State documents. A number of these had come through Assistant Secretary of State Sayre's office (where Hiss worked in 1938), had Sayre's office stamp on them, and had Hiss's handwritten initials on them. The microfilm allowed the House Committee on Un-American Activities, with Representative Richard Nixon acting as the spokesman, to shift public attention to its agenda. The committee quickly made the film public, and the press termed the material the "pumpkin papers," although it was, to be precise, film. Over the years many historical accounts have merged the Baltimore documents, turned over to Hiss's attorneys on November 17 (and then delivered to the Justice Department) with the pumpkin papers microfilm, picked up by congressional investigators on December 2. The microfilm produced a media sensation and gave Representative Nixon the opportunity to emphasize that the chief issue was espionage. He argued that it made little sense to indict Chambers, the former spy who had changed sides, confessed, and given a candid account of his actions, while ignoring Hiss, the spy who had *not* changed sides, had *not* confessed, and had *not* given a truthful account.

After a few weeks reflection, common sense prevailed at the Justice Department. The grand jury recalled Chambers, Hiss, and others in the case and demanded that the House Committee on Un-American Activities turn over the microfilm. After some initial defiance to insure even greater publicity for the film and the committee, Nixon appeared before the grand jury, reiterated the view that Chambers should not be indicted, and handed over the film.

Chambers faced a disapproving and often hostile examination about why he had earlier testified falsely about espionage. In the end, however, the grand jury and prosecutors accepted his story that he had lied earlier in hopes of sparing himself and even Hiss from the personal ruin that would likely ensue. When the slander suit forced his hand, he had then concluded that his best course was to tell the full truth. Equally plausible was his explanation that he had hidden the material in 1938 as insurance to discourage retaliation against him and his family by Soviet intelligence when he dropped out of spying.

The documents and Chambers's testimony also reached beyond Hiss. Chambers underwent intensive questioning by the FBI after he turned his material over to the government. He identified one other State Department source, Julian Wadleigh, an economist specializing in international trade. Confronted by the FBI, Wadleigh confessed and testified at both Hiss trials. He agreed he had furnished State Department documents to Chambers, and that he had met with Boris Bykov, the Soviet military intelligence (GRU) officer to whom Chambers reported, and with David Carpenter, a Maryland–D.C. area Communist organizer whom Chambers had identified as one of his assistants in the espionage network. Wadleigh said that he had known there was another Department of State source in Chambers's network but not the person's identity and had no direct knowledge of Hiss's role. In view of his cooperation and with the statute of limitations in any case precluding an espionage charge, Wadleigh was not prosecuted.

Chambers discussed his work with two other sources, William Ward Pigman and Franklin Victor (Vincent) Reno. Pigman worked for the U.S. Bureau of Standards, a scientific agency that did a great deal of sophisticated research on military technology. Under questioning, Pigman denied having delivered material to Chambers but admitted he had met on several occasions in 1936–1938 with David Carpenter, Chambers's assistant. Reno was a statistician and ballistics expert at the Aberdeen Proving Grounds near Baltimore where the U.S. Army tested advanced weaponry. On the basis of Chambers's information, the FBI confronted Reno in 1949. Reno confessed that he had supplied information to Chambers's espionage apparatus in the mid-1930s, although he denied Chambers's specific claim that he had supplied technical data about the highly secret Norden high-altitude bombsight. In November 1951 a grand jury indicted Reno for concealing Communist Party membership when he worked at Aberdeen. Reno pled guilty in February 1952, admitting he had joined the CPUSA in 1935 when studying for his doctorate at the University of Virginia and had later worked as a CPUSA organizer in Maryland using the name Lance Clark. He claimed he left the party in 1938 after he went to work at Aberdeen but admitted he concealed his past Communist affiliation on government security forms. Federal Judge William Knous sentenced Reno to three years in prison.

Chambers also directed the FBI to Vladimir De Sveshnikoff, a Russian immigrant and ballistics expert who worked on artillery for the U.S. War Department. Questioned by the FBI, De Sveshnikoff admitted that he had been recruited by the Soviets, claiming Soviet intelligence had made threats against relatives living in the USSR. From 1931 to 1938 or 1939, he had received regular payments for providing the Soviets with copies of industrial and military technology patents and U.S. military journals and technical manuals. Chambers also put the FBI on the trail of an industrial spy, Morris Asimow, who confessed that in the 1930s, while working in the research laboratories of U.S. Steel, he had provided the Soviets with technical information on steel alloy processes for money.

Chambers pointed to others, such as Carpenter, as part of his espionage apparatus but not sources of documents. Felix Inslerman, whom Chambers identified as one of his photographers, held out for several years but confessed in 1954, stating that he had been sent to the USSR, trained in photography, and sent back to the United States, where he worked for the GRU and specifically functioned as a photographer of stolen government documents for Chambers. He also confirmed that when Chambers dropped out of Soviet espionage in 1938 he had given Inslerman a message to pass on to his former associates that he would expose their activities to government authorities if he or his family were threatened. Inslerman had made a copy of the warning at the time and produced it in 1954. William Crane, a California Communist active in the underground in the mid-1930s, also confirmed meeting with Boris Bykov of the GRU, photographing Treasury and State Department documents for Chambers, and carrying out courier missions for GRU operations.

Harry Dexter White (discussed in Chapter 3) was another source for Chambers. In the mid-1930s White was head of the Monetary Division of the Treasury Department and had little access to material of interest to Moscow. However, like Hiss, White was expected to rise to a much more influential position. George Silverman, a secret Communist and economist at the Railroad Retirement Board, was a good friend of White's and assisted Chambers in handling White. White needed considerable attention, Chambers claimed, because, while a Soviet sympathizer, he was not a Communist Party member, possessed a considerable ego, and needed frequent reinforcement to keep him in a cooperative mood. Decoded Venona cables later confirmed that Silverman and White continued to work for Soviet espionage in the 1940s.

The Baltimore documents included four sets of notes in Alger Hiss's handwriting. Three of the handwritten notes summarized March 1938 State Department diplomatic cables. One dealt with a cable dated March 2 from the American embassy in Paris to Secretary of State Cordell Hull about the U.S. response to the Sino-Japanese War and Chinese purchases of French aircraft. Another section of this handwritten note summarized a second U.S. embassy message from Paris, also dated March 2, reporting the views of the French ambassador to Japan about possible aggressive Japanese moves against the USSR's Far Eastern maritime provinces. Alger Hiss later claimed that he prepared handwritten summaries to assist his superior, Assistant Secretary of State Sayre. But Sayre oversaw international economic matters, and Hiss's handwritten summary left out the parts of these cables (the reaction of European governments whose nationals had loaned money to China and on Japanese plans to impose custom duties from occupied China) relevant to Sayre's work. Instead, Hiss chose to summarize in his handwritten notes those matters of greater interest to Soviet military intelligence: Japanese military activity in China and the possible Japanese threat to Soviet provinces. A second set of handwritten notes excerpted parts of a U.S. diplomatic cable of March 3 sent from London, omitted the passage that might have interested Sayre, and instead summarized the cable's report of a talk between the American naval attaché and a British admiral about British naval maneuvers and plans for new battleships and cruisers, again a matter of interest to Soviet military intelligence but irrelevant to the work of Hiss's office. A third handwritten note, dealing with a March 11 cable, summarized a U.S. consul's report on the Japanese military order of battle and movement of troops in China while omitting those parts of the cable dealing with the attitude of Japanese officials toward American economic interests in China. Once more, Hiss's handwritten notes ignored those issues of concern to his office at the State Department but included matters of interest to the Soviet GRU.

The most startling of Hiss's handwritten notes, however, was one that did not merely summarize but nearly transcribed the text of a cable from the American chargé d'affaires in Moscow, Loy Henderson, reporting on the "Robinson/Rubens" case. This matter had nothing whatsoever to do with Hiss or Sayre's work at the State Department. It was, however, a matter of concern to Soviet intelligence.

Soviet military intelligence, the GRU, ran an extensive operation in the United States in the mid-1930s obtaining false American passports for use by its agents around the world. The CPUSA underground played a central role in this operation by helping to obtain the birth certificates of persons who died at a young age. American Communists fraudulently used these birth certificates to obtain passports, which were then given to the GRU. American passports were well respected around the world by border officials and, consequently, highly valued by Soviet intelligence. Moreover, America's large polyglot immigrant population allowed Soviet agents of varying ethnicities and languages to use the fraudulent passports.

Arnold Ikal, a Soviet citizen of Latvian origin, was one of the GRU officers involved in the false passport operation. Ikal worked in the United States in the 1930s, falsely obtaining U.S. citizenship under the name Adolph Arnold Rubens by claiming he had immigrated to the United States as a child. In 1935 he also married an American Communist, Ruth Boerger. The GRU recalled Ikal to Moscow in late 1937, and he returned with his wife, traveling with another set of false American passports as Mr. and Mrs. Donald L. Robinson.

Diplomats at the U.S. embassy in Moscow first became involved in December 1937 when they heard from American newsmen that an American woman, Mrs. Donald L. Robinson, needed assistance at the nearby Hotel National. A junior diplomat visited the distraught woman, who said that her husband had disappeared. Promising to look into the matter, he went back to the embassy to fetch a senior diplomat, Loy Henderson, and both returned to the hotel, only to find the staff claiming that Mrs. Robinson had left without explanation. Henderson went to Soviet authorities and insisted that Mrs. Robinson and her husband be located and that American embassy officials be allowed to speak to her in accordance with a Soviet-American diplomatic agreement.

Meanwhile, a careful search of State Department passport records showed that the Robinsons also possessed a second set of passports, as Mr. and Mrs. Adolph A. Rubens. The wife of a former U.S. diplomat at the U.S. consulate in Latvia also recognized the photograph of Donald Robinson as a Latvian believed to have been a Soviet intelligence agent. The real Donald Robinson was born in Queens in 1905 and had died in 1909. Mrs. Robinson had used the birth certificate of Ruth Birkland, born 1909, for her passport. The real Ruth Birkland, however, died in 1915. Soviet military intelligence, not surprisingly, was concerned with how much the U.S. government had figured out about the Robinson/Rubens matter, and Alger Hiss was furnishing it copies of Henderson's cables from Moscow. The U.S. Embassy dropped interest in her husband, but in February 1938 the Soviets finally allowed Henderson to visit Mrs. Robinson/Rubens, in a Moscow prison. She stated she wanted no U.S. embassy assistance.

Hiss told the grand jury he had written the notes about the March diplomatic cables, claiming they were summaries prepared for Sayre. But this explanation did not work for the notes on Henderson's cables, which had nothing to do with Sayre's work. Hiss denied that he had written them. Handwriting experts at the FBI and hired by Hiss's defense all contradicted his denial. At the subsequent Hiss trials, neither Hiss nor his lawyers would contest the assertion that he had written all four sets of notes, including the one on the Robinson/Rubens matter.

In addition to the handwritten material, the Baltimore documents included sixty-five typed sheets of paper, all except for one sheet consisting of summaries or nearly complete copies of Department of State documents dated from January 5 to April 1, 1938. Chambers said that he understood from Hiss, from whom he had obtained the material, that most of the typed material had been prepared by either Alger Hiss or his wife Priscilla on a typewriter in their home.

Unlike today's computer-driven word processed documents, where it is difficult and in most cases impossible to tell what particular printer has produced a particular document, the mechanical typewriters of the 1930s produced documents that could often be linked to an individual typewriter. The shape, wear marks, dents, and nicks on the metal type faces of the keys of each typewriter and subtle differences in spacing of key strokes caused by slight twists or bends in the arms of the keys often allowed an experienced documents examiner to state with a high degree of accuracy if a document was typed on a particular machine. If the questioned document could be compared with documents known to have been typed on the typewriter at issue at about the same time, eliminating the problem of changes in the type produced by age and later use, the assessment could be made with greater certainty. The FBI located personal letters typed by the Hisses from 1936 and 1937. FBI technical examiners then compared these known Hiss samples with the 1938 documents that Chambers claimed had been typed by the Hisses. Ramos Feehan, the FBI's leading documents examiner and an acknowledged expert in the field, told the grand jury without qualification that the typed Baltimore documents, with the exception of a single page, had been typed on the same Woodstock typewriter used to produce the Hisses' letters. The Hisses had owned a Woodstock typewriter in the 1930s but later gave it to a maid. The typewriter itself was located by the Hiss defense team through the maid's family in 1949 and introduced into the Hiss trials as evidence.

A documents examiner assisting Chambers's legal team during the slander suit also examined the material. His findings were similar to those of the FBI, concluding that the Baltimore documents had been typed on the Hiss family typewriter. The Hiss defense team employed its own documents examiners: they, too, concluded that the documents had been done on the Hiss family typewriter. One examiner working for Hiss's lawyers even went further than the FBI's expert, concluding that on the basis of the pattern of strong and weak key stroking in the mid-1930s letters known to be typed by Priscilla Hiss, he was convinced that the Baltimore documents also had been personally typed by Priscilla Hiss. Hiss's lawyers kept this conclusion to themselves, but when the matter came to trial, they did not contest the prosecution's assertion that the typed documents were done on the family typewriter.

The sixty-five typed pages of the Baltimore documents summarized seventy-one government documents. Of these, sixty-eight were State Department cables that records showed had been routed through the office where Hiss worked. The one page not typed on the Hiss family typewriter was a report on the Sino-Japanese War prepared by the Military Intelligence Division of the War Department that had been sent to the State Department's Far Eastern Division. Chambers never remembered clearly the source for that report, suggesting it might have been Julian Wadleigh, his other source at the State Department, or perhaps Harry White at the Treasury Department.

Among the subjects discussed in the typed material were French and Italian diplomatic reaction to the German annexation of Austria, more than a dozen U.S. embassy reports on military and diplomatic aspects of the Sino-Japanese War, plans for British arms purchases in the United States, multiple reports on battlefield and home-front conditions in the Spanish Civil War, British concerns about Japanese naval expansion, French hopes for reconciliation with Germany, diplomatic maneuvering about the increasingly aggressive stance of Nazi Germany, and a Sayre memo on a conversation between Secretary of State Hull and a senior Czechoslovak official. Compared with the original State Department documents, the typed summaries gave emphasis to military information. For example, the typed summary of a State Department cable regarding the Japanese occupation of the University of Shanghai extracted one sentence about an airfield, the only part of possible military value.

The microfilm of the pumpkin papers consisted of two strips of developed film and three cans containing rolls of undeveloped film. Technical analysis and comparison with records of Kodak, which had produced the film, showed that it had been manufactured and distributed in the mid-1930s. One of the rolls of undeveloped film was light-struck and useless. The two other rolls contained photographs of low-grade technical documents from the Navy Bureau of Aeronautics. Chambers attributed this material to William Ward Pigman. The two strips of developed film contained fifty-eight separate prints of Department of State documents, all from early 1938. Chambers had identified Felix Inslerman as the photographer for his espionage network at this time. The FBI located Inslerman and found a Leica camera in his possession. A technical examination of the two filmstrips showed that Inslerman's Leica had taken them. (As with mechanical typewriters, subtle flaws in lenses and the mechanical film handling mechanism can produce patterns on film that can link photographs to a particular camera.)

Several of the filmed State Department documents dealt with trade between the United States and Germany and could have come from either Assistant Secretary of State Sayre's office, where Hiss worked, or the State Department Trade Agreements section, where Julian Wadleigh worked. There was, however, no doubt of the origins of other photographs of three January 1938 State Department cables, totaling ten pages. All had Alger Hiss's handwritten initials and the date stamp of Sayre's office, and none of these had been sent to Wadleigh's Trade Agreements section. All three cables dealt with a matter of major Soviet interest: the Chinese-Japanese War. One of the three contained a section dealing with what American diplomats understood of Chinese Communist strategy in the war, while another reported on a lengthy discussion on Chinese-Soviet relations between the outgoing Chinese ambassador to the USSR (returning to China via Paris) and U.S. Ambassador Bullitt in Paris.

In November and December of 1948 Federal investigators also followed up another point developed from Chambers's new testimony – the Bokhara rugs. Chambers explained that in late 1936 Boris Bykov, the GRU officer to whom he reported, insisted that the chief sources of the network be generously rewarded. Chambers talked Bykov out of providing cash bonuses, arguing that the ideologically motivated spies would be offended by monetary rewards. Instead, Chambers decided to use the money Bykov gave him to purchase four oriental rugs that could plausibly be presented as gifts from the Soviet people and picked Bokhara rugs, originating in the Uzbek Republic of the USSR. Not knowing the oriental rug market, he asked a friend, the New York art critic Meyer Schapiro, to buy the rugs for him. Schapiro purchased four Bokharas from a New York wholesaler for $220 each. (This 1937 price of $220 is the equivalent of more than $2,900 in 2005 dollars.) Rather than have the rugs shipped to his Maryland residence, Chambers told Schapiro to send them to George Silverman in Washington. Chambers then picked up three of the rugs, leaving one for Silverman, and had the others distributed as holiday gifts to the leading lights of his apparatus: Alger Hiss, Julian Wadleigh, and Harry Dexter White. Chambers testified that he personally delivered a rug to Hiss.

Hiss admitted that he had received an oriental rug from Chambers. He said, however, that Chambers had given him the rug as compensation for Chambers's nonpayment of rent (although he had earlier accused Chambers of not fully paying the rent). Since Hiss had claimed to have no contact with Chambers after 1935, except for a brief visit in the first half of 1936 to settle the matter of the Ford car, he also had to insist that he had received the rug in 1935, not in the holiday season of late December 1936 or early January 1937 as Chambers testified. Meyer Schapiro, though, testified that he had purchased four Bokhara rugs from the Massachusetts Importing Company in Manhattan on December 23, 1936, for $876.71, using a check and cash. Schapiro, in fact, still had the canceled check and the rug dealer had kept a copy of the bill of sale. Schapiro also testified that, on Chambers's request, he shipped the rugs to someone in Washington with the name of "Silversomething." In depositions to the FBI, Julian Wadleigh and his former wife stated that they had received a "New Year's" gift rug from Chambers in 1937 or perhaps 1938. In later statements about the rug, Wadleigh was more certain it was New Year's 1937 that he received the rug, and he thought that it had been delivered by David Carpenter, Chambers's occasional assistant.

George Silverman, who denied any involvement in espionage, had another story. Silverman, a government economist, said he had met Chambers in Washington in the mid-1930s. He testified that they had met for lunch and dinner occasionally to discuss art and literature, and he had even loaned Chambers money from time to time. He claimed that sometime between late 1936 and the fall of 1937 Chambers asked if four rugs from an importer friend could be delivered to Silverman in Washington. Silverman agreed and, on seeing the rugs, offered to buy two of the Bokharas for $300 while also wiping out $75 Chambers owed him. (If Silverman's story were true, the financially pressed Chambers had sold the two rugs to Silverman for less than he had paid for them.) Silverman explained that he kept one rug and gave the other to his friend Harry Dexter White, while Chambers took the other two rugs. Silverman's story provided an innocent explanation for himself and White in response to Chambers's claims that the rugs were gifts for spies, but did nothing for Hiss, who claimed he received his rug in 1935 while Silverman agreed with Chambers's dating of the episode. Harry White's widow still possessed the rug he had been given and backed Silverman's version. That Silverman and White were Soviet spies and Mrs. White complicit in her husband's espionage, however, is no longer in question due to the combination of Elizabeth Bentley's testimony, the documentary proof of the decoded Venona cables, and the material in White's handwriting that was included in the Baltimore documents.

All of this documentary material and accompanying evidence demolished Hiss's claim that he had no contact with Chambers at all after 1936. How could Chambers have gotten photographs of documents from Hiss's State Department office from 1938 if Hiss had had no contact with him since 1936? How could Chambers have gotten summaries of 1938 State Department cables in Hiss's own handwriting? How could Chambers have gotten summaries of 1938 State Department documents typed on the Hiss family typewriter? Chambers had a plausible explanation: he and Hiss were both Soviet spies. Hiss stole documents or typed summaries and delivered them to Chambers who then delivered them to officers of the GRU, Soviet military intelligence.

When recalled to the grand jury in December, Hiss faced a far more skeptical audience than he had earlier. Federal prosecutors, however, were not determined to bring an indictment. At several points prosecutors give Hiss an opportunity to correct his earlier testimony and provide a new account. Like Chambers, Hiss was only at risk for a charge of perjury. Chambers had confessed to spying for the Soviet Union. He could not be indicted for espionage, however, since the statute of limitations required evidence of espionage within three years of the indictment. (Congress's subsequent change to ten years was partially in response to the Hiss-Chambers case.) Had Hiss changed his testimony and admitted to spying, he could not have been charged with espionage. He would, of course, have been admitting to earlier perjury but, like Chambers, would likely have escaped prosecution since he would have corrected the false testimony in a timely fashion. His reputation and public standing would have been destroyed, however.

Hiss ignored the offers to change his testimony and repeated his earlier statements. And when questioned by the grand jury about the Baltimore documents and the pumpkin papers microfilm, he suggested that Chambers (or unknown persons in league with him) had repeatedly sneaked into the U.S. State Department in 1938 and stolen documents from his office (or even the "burn" room where confidential material was destroyed), prepared summaries, and then slipped into the Hiss family home and typed the summaries on the Hiss family typewriter, or bribed a maid, removed the typewriter to prepare the summaries, and then returned the typewriter, all the while successfully avoiding being noticed by State Department personnel or members of the Hiss household. Grand jury members then asked Hiss why Chambers, who Hiss claimed to have known only casually in 1934–1936 and not at all since then, would undertake these bizarre acts in 1938 and then hide the material and not produce it until Hiss sued him ten years later. Hiss suggested that Chambers was insane.

The grand jury concluded that Chambers was not insane but that Alger Hiss had lied. On December 15, 1948, it indicted Hiss on two counts of perjury: one for his denial that he gave documents to Chambers in 1938 and another for denying that he had seen and talked with Chambers in 1938.

Hiss's trial did not begin until May 31, 1949, and in the interim both the Hiss defense and the FBI undertook a furious search for supporting evidence. Most of what the FBI uncovered would not become public until introduced in evidence during the trial. The Hiss defense, however, sought to influence public opinion by encouraging prominent foreign policy figures and Democratic eminences to laud Hiss's work in establishing the United Nations, his selfless dedication to public service, and his flawless personal character. On the negative side, Chambers became the target of a sustained whispering campaign aimed at discrediting his character. There were two themes in the campaign to destroy Chambers: one was true in part but irrelevant to the case and another was relevant but untrue. The first, spread widely by Hiss's supporters, was that Chambers was a homosexual. In the late 1940s public disapproval of homosexuality was widespread and intense, and many people regarded homosexuals as inherently immoral and untrustworthy. The gay-baiting was aimed at undermining confidence in Chambers's testimony.

The kernel of truth in this charge was that Chambers by his own account had engaged in a number of casual homosexual episodes from 1933 to 1938, even while maintaining relations with his wife; Chambers insisted that he had ended his homosexual activity in 1938. Afraid that the Hiss defense would use the issue, Chambers contacted the FBI and gave an account of his sexual history so that the prosecution would not be blindsided if his sexuality became an issue in court.

The second theme promoted widely by Hiss partisans was that Chambers had been mentally ill and his condition was so severe that he had been treated at hospitals for the insane. If Chambers's mental illness was one that produced illusions, a lack of contact with reality, or a fixation on some individual, it might be relevant to the case. However, the charge was false. Despite a massive effort, no one found evidence that Chambers was ever admitted to a psychiatric facility or treated for a severe mental condition.

The Hiss defense team did locate some professional psychologists who had never treated Chambers or even interviewed him but who were nonetheless eager to offer an adverse psychiatric diagnosis from a distance. These psychologists often tied the homosexual theme to Chambers's alleged insanity. Chambers's older brother had killed himself when Chambers was a teenager, and they speculated that Chambers had had a homosexual or some other unhealthy relationship with his brother, felt deep guilt for his death, and was twisted for the rest of his life. (Hiss's father had killed himself, but these same psychologists did not see this as suggesting anything unhealthy in Hiss's family.) Chambers, they theorized, developed a homosexual fixation on Hiss during their acquaintance in 1934–1936. When Hiss spurned his advances, Chambers undertook a decade-long campaign to ruin him by stealing State Department material from Hiss's office, typing material on Hiss's family typewriter, leaking hints of the matter to the FBI, and then provoking the confrontation with Hiss in 1948.

The First Hiss Trial

At the first Hiss trial, prosecutors stressed two themes: first, the testimony of Whittaker Chambers and, second, the Baltimore documents and the microfilm of the pumpkin papers. Of the two, the documents proved the most effective.

The prosecution, led by Assistant U.S. Attorney Thomas Murphy, found itself hobbled from the beginning by Judge Samuel Kaufman, who restricted the scope of evidence and witnesses prosecutors could introduce while allowing the defense wider latitude. Kaufman had only one month of judicial experience before the trial began. At the beginning of the trial, prosecutors learned that the wife of the foreman of the jury had told acquaintances that her husband was pro-Hiss. They asked Judge

Kaufman to question the foreman about possible bias, but he brushed the matter aside, saying he was sure the juror would be fair. After the trial, prosecutors discovered that the foreman, even though he was related by marriage to a friend of Hiss who later actively aided his defense, had denied any links to either Chambers or Hiss during the voir dire jury selection questioning.

Whittaker Chambers testified to his first exposure to the Communist Party in the 1920s, his move into underground party work in the early 1930s, and his shift to Soviet espionage in the mid-1930s when he supervised a small group of sources in the U.S. government that included Alger Hiss. Chambers told his story in a straightforward, unemotional way, although he was so soft-spoken that occasionally he became nearly inaudible.

State Department officials testified to the authenticity of the documents on the microfilm and produced photostats of the State Department documents from which the typed and handwritten summaries had been made and explained how department procedures in the 1930s routed this material to the office where Alger Hiss worked for Assistant Secretary of State Francis Sayre. The chief secretary in Sayre's office in 1938 testified that the contents of the handwritten summaries in the Baltimore documents were from cables irrelevant to Sayre's work, casting doubt on Hiss's claim that he summarized these cables for Sayre. FBI technical experts testified that the handwritten documents were in Alger Hiss's handwriting, the typed summaries of State Department cables had been made on the Hiss family Woodstock typewriter, and the microfilm of the pumpkin papers had been filmed with Felix Inslerman's Leica camera. The Hiss defense did not seriously contest any of these points.

While largely ignoring the documents, the defense focused on character in its cross-examination, and Lloyd Stryker, the chief defense counsel, did his best to destroy Chambers's credibility. Stryker told jurors that in primitive areas of the tropics those with leprosy were required to call out "'unclean, unclean' at the approach of a leper. I say the same to you at the approach of this moral leper." He told the jury it should disregard everything Chambers had to say because, although he had left the Communist Party in 1938, he was forever morally stained by his former membership. Chambers had been a Communist and, therefore, "was a member of this low-down, nefarious, filthy conspiracy . . . [for] twelve long years . . . a voluntary conspirator against the land that I love and you love. He got his bread from the band of criminals with whom he confederated and conspired." Further, he had written a play that was "an offensive treatment of Christ" when a college undergraduate in 1922 and was "an enemy of the republic, a blasphemer of Christ, a disbeliever in God." Stryker went over every aspect of Chambers's present and past testimony to highlight inconsistencies and dwell on Chambers's past denials of espionage in contrast to his current admission of it. Chambers, however, stuck to his story and repeated his explanation for why he had avoided telling the truth about espionage until the slander suit left him no other option.

Stryker also suggested to the jury that Chambers was mentally sick. He had asked Judge Kaufman to allow him to bring a psychiatrist, Dr. Karl Binger, into the courtroom to observe Chambers's testimony and then be called as a witness to testify as to his conclusions. Binger, however, was far from a disinterested expert. He had been associated with the Hiss defense for months and avidly promoted the idea that Chambers was a twisted homosexual who had created a fantasy story of espionage with the goal of ruining Hiss. Judge Kaufman rejected the defense's request that the jurors and the press be told of Binger's presence and his purpose but nonetheless allowed the strange procedure. When Binger came into the courtroom, Stryker publicly greeted him, and the press, and likely the jury, soon knew of his purpose. Stryker later called him as a witness over repeated prosecution objections and proceeded, in the presence of the jury, to ask a thirty-five-minute hypothetical question assuming that Chambers was a mentally ill, revenge-seeking homosexual. Judge Kaufman then told Binger not to answer and bizarrely excluded Binger as a witness on the grounds that this psychiatric testimony was not relevant. But the damage to Chambers and the prosecution had been done, particularly because Kaufman would not allow Murphy to reply to Stryker's peroration, disguised as a question.

The defense made an effort to turn aside the evidence of the documents typed on the Hiss family typewriter by arguing that the Hisses had given the machine in question to their maid, Claudia Catlett, in 1937, prior to the time that the Baltimore documents, all from early 1938, were typed. The maid and her sons supported this dating of the gift, but their testimony fell apart under prosecution cross-examination. Their new testimony contradicted earlier statements they had made to the FBI placing the gift in mid-1938, and their transparent eagerness to assist the Hisses left them with little credibility. Their claims also left unanswered the question of how Chambers obtained access to the typewriter when it was in the possession of a family that was clearly attached to the Hisses or how he even knew the Catletts had the Hiss family typewriter. As for the handwritten material and the photographed State Department documents, the defense simply argued that State Department security in the 1930s was loose and it was possible that some unknown person repeatedly burgled the State Department in early 1938 and stole the material without anyone noticing.

Attacking the documentary evidence, however, was not a strong defense, and the weight of the Hiss defense remained character. In addition to a ferocious negative attack on Chambers, the defense presented a string of prestigious character witnesses lauding Alger Hiss. These included two serving Supreme Court judges: Justice Felix Frankfurter, who had known Hiss as a law student at Harvard, and Justice Stanley Reed, who had been one of Hiss's superiors when he had worked at the Justice Department in 1935–1936, and several other prominent federal judges. In an act that reinforced the standing of Hiss's character witnesses, Judge Kaufman left the bench and in front of the jurors shook the hand of the two Supreme Court justices just prior to their testifying to Hiss's good character. Others who praised Alger Hiss as a man of unquestionable integrity included John W. Davis, the 1924 Democratic Party presidential nominee and a trustee of the Carnegie Endowment that Hiss directed in 1947 and 1948; senior American diplomats Philip C. Jessup and Stanley Hornbeck; Admiral Arthur Hepburn, who had worked with Hiss in planning the initial organization of the United Nations; and Governor Adlai Stevenson of Illinois, who had worked with Hiss in the early 1930s at the Agricultural Adjustment Administration and later at the founding conference of the U.N. Stevenson, already a national figure at the time of the Hiss trial, would become the Democratic Party candidate for president in 1952. For the most part, the prosecution could do little about the character witnesses for Hiss other than to show that most only knew a sliver of Hiss's life.

Hiss also testified in his own defense. At his attorney's prompting, he discussed his distinguished career in public service, particularly his State Department posts and role in the founding of the United Nations. He repeated the chief points of his earlier testimony to the grand jury and House Committee on Un-American Activities, maintaining that his relationship with Whittaker Chambers was casual in 1934–1935 and ended entirely by mid-1936. He repeated that he had given his old Ford to Chambers, not to the Communist Party. Hiss, however, changed part of his story about the Ford by testifying that he had not actually sold the car to Chambers in 1935 as a package deal for subletting an apartment for two months (his testimony to the House committee) but had promised to do so, had allowed Chambers to borrow the car in late 1935 for long intervals, but had not actually given the Ford to Chambers until mid-1936. Hiss claimed that in the first half of 1936 Chambers had made brief visits asking for loans and that Chambers or someone else had shown up to get his signature on the automobile transfer document. When asked why he had then given the car to Chambers despite his not paying all of his rent, Hiss said he had promised the car in 1935 and was bound by the promise.

Both Esther Chambers and Priscilla Hiss also testified. Both women supported the testimony of their husbands and received a battering during cross-examination. Esther nearly broke down and then shouted out in anger on the stand as Lloyd Stryker used his cross-examination to repeat his charges that her husband was an immoral and debauched liar as well as a self-confessed traitor. Priscilla held up better but prosecutor Murphy's aggressive cross-examination forced her to admit so many contradictions between her testimony to the grand jury and her testimony in the trial that she may have hurt rather than helped her husband's credibility.

Prosecutors and defense lawyers made their closing arguments on July 6, 1949. Thomas Murphy made an unemotional appeal to the jury to focus on how the evidence of the Baltimore documents and pumpkin papers microfilm supported the testimony of Chambers. For the defense, Stryker poured emotional venom on Chambers, arguing that he had in his life committed acts that were "psychopathic," constituted "sadism," and showed that he got "enjoyment in the creation of suffering by a filthy act." Stryker contrasted him with Hiss, whom the defense attorney described as "an honest and maligned and falsely accused gentleman" whose word could not be doubted. The jury deliberated for part of the day, retired for the night, and renewed discussion the next day. It then announced itself deadlocked, and Judge Kaufman declared a mistrial. Once discharged, jurors reported that eight of them favored conviction and four had held out for acquittal.

The Second Hiss Trial

Federal prosecutors immediately announced they would retry the case, a decision reinforced by interviews with a number of the jurors. Five who had voted for conviction felt that Judge Kaufman had been biased for the defense and had contributed to confusion over evidence. Confident that they would get a different judge for a retrial and having taken the measure of the Hiss defense, prosecutors were eager for a second trial. It began on November 17, 1949, presided over by Henry W. Goddard, a senior federal judge with decades of experience. Goddard proved to be far more accommodating than Kaufman to both the prosecution and the defense in permitting evidence and witnesses to be presented to the jury. Thomas Murphy remained the chief federal prosecutor. Hiss, however, replaced Lloyd Stryker with Claude Cross as his lead advocate. The Hiss defense team had been disappointed by the eight-to-four vote for conviction in the first trial and feared that prosecutors in a retrial would be prepared to blunt Stryker's emotional rhetoric and assault on Chambers's character.

In the first trial, Murphy had emphasized how the documentary evidence corroborated the testimony of Whittaker Chambers. This tactic, however, had allowed Stryker to put Chambers on trial and shift attention away from Hiss. In the second trial, Murphy shifted the prosecution's focus to how the evidence, both the documents and testimony of Chambers and others, contradicted the testimony of Alger Hiss. The shift highlighted the charge for the jury: Hiss's perjury. Consequently, in the second trial the prosecution moved briskly through Chambers's testimony and that of others supporting his story, spotlighted the evidence of the Baltimore documents and the pumpkin papers microfilm, and then waited for Alger Hiss's testimony to unleash a withering barrage of questions that portrayed Hiss's testimony as contradictory, unreliable, and unbelievable.

Judge Goddard's more liberal attitude about what witnesses could be presented also allowed the government to present evidence excluded in the first trial. Hede Massing provided the most important. She and her husband, Paul, had been prominent German Communist activists in the late 1920s and early 1930s. After Hitler's Nazi regime came to power, they fled to the United States where Paul, an economist associated with the Marxist "Frankfurt School," obtained a post at Columbia University. Covertly, however, both Massings also worked for Soviet intelligence by recruiting new ideologically motivated American sources. Initially, they worked for Soviet military intelligence (GRU) but in the mid-1930s they shifted to the rapidly growing foreign intelligence arm of the Soviet KGB.

Hede Massing recruited a midlevel State Department official, Noel Field, a specialist in international organizations. Field's pro-Soviet sympathies were well known among his close friends, including Alger Hiss. In

1936 Hiss approached Field and tried to recruit him into his own GRU-linked network. Hiss had no idea that Field had already been recruited by Massing of the KGB. Proper espionage tradecraft held that different networks should be kept strictly separated and members of one network should not know members of another network. Under the circumstance, Field should have kept his own status as a Soviet spy secret, brushed off Hiss's recruitment effort in a way that foreclosed renewal of the offer, but reassured Hiss that Field could be trusted to keep the matter confidential. Instead, Field told Hiss that he already worked for Soviet intelligence. Field then informed Hede Massing, his KGB contact, of what had happened. Massing chided Field for having revealed to Hiss that he already worked for Soviet intelligence. She compounded Field's error, however, when she ran into Hiss at a left-wing party in Washington and chatted with him briefly about their competition for Noel Field. Field soon left the State Department for a post with the League of Nations in Switzerland.

There it might have remained but by 1938 the Massings had become frightened by Stalin's purge of his security services and, like Chambers, quietly dropped out of Soviet service. Over the years, Hede became increasingly anti-Stalinist, and in 1947 she began to cooperate with the FBI. Among other points, she related the Noel Field story and her personal knowledge that Hiss was a Soviet agent. Another member of Chambers's network, Julian Wadleigh, had testified to corroborate Chambers's story by confessing his own role as a Soviet source at the State Department, but Wadleigh did not know about Hiss. Massing's testimony provided the jury with a second eyewitness assertion that Hiss had been a Soviet agent.

Hiss's lawyers might have called Noel Field as a rebuttal witness, but Field, his wife, brother, and stepdaughter had meanwhile disappeared behind the Soviet "Iron Curtain." When a series of purge trials swept the "people's democracies" of the Soviet empire in Eastern Europe in 1949–1952, Noel Field was bizarrely identified as an American super spy. A series of defendants confessed that while working at the League of Nations in the late 1930s and running Unitarian war refugee programs in Switzerland during World War II, Field had recruited Eastern European Communist leaders, then in exile, to assist the intelligence services of the United States, Nazi Germany, and Titoist Yugoslavia. Dozens of senior officials of the new Communist regimes in Eastern Europe were executed and hundreds jailed as part of a "Fieldist" conspiracy. It was all a fraud: Field had always been a loyal Communist. When he fled to the East bloc in 1949 to avoid being called as a witness in the Hiss-Chambers case, however, his wartime contact with Eastern European Communist refugees in Switzerland made him into a handy tool for Stalin's agents to use to taint those targeted for removal by Moscow.

After Stalin's death in early 1953, the purges ended. The Eastern European Communist regimes attempted to undo some of the harm Stalin's purges had inflicted by rehabilitating those imprisoned. Field and his wife were released from a Hungarian Communist prison and, still loyal, made a public statement saying it had all been a misunderstanding. He also denied being a Soviet spy, denied that Hiss was one, and called Hede Massing a liar. The Fields remained in Hungary and were given privileged treatment. When Hungary revolted against Soviet domination in 1956, Field sided with the hard-liners and supported the Soviet Union's military suppression of the Hungarian Revolution. After the Hungarian Communist regime collapsed in 1989, its archives yielded secret statements Field and his wife gave to authorities after they were rehabilitated confirming that they had worked for Soviet intelligence, that they had known Hiss as a fellow Soviet spy, and that Hede Massing had told the truth.

Judge Goddard also allowed Hiss's defense to present its argument that Whittaker Chambers was mentally ill and had framed Hiss. Psychiatrist Carl Binger appeared as a defense witness and testified, on the basis of having read some of Chambers's writings and having observed Chambers's testimony, that he had a "psychopathic personality" and suffered from a "mental disease" that led him to engage in "pathological lying" and to "make false accusations known as pathological accusations." Elaborating, he stated that on the basis of his observations Chambers engaged in "paranoid thinking" and "fantasy," was "anti-social," and his mental state was somewhere between "the psychotic and the neurotic." Prompted by Hiss's lawyer, Binger went over Chambers's life story and depicted almost every aspect of it as pathological.

The cross-examination by Thomas Murphy was, however, devastating. Under Murphy's questioning, Binger admitted to a friendship with the Hiss family that put his professional objectivity in question. Murphy's questions also forced Binger to backtrack on his claims that Chambers suffered from personal instability and unsociability when he reluctantly conceded that Chambers's having held a professional position at *Time* magazine for ten years and rising to a senior editorial position were evidence of stability and sociability, while Chambers's successful nineteen-year marriage and two children were evidence of psychological stability. Binger also admitted that while he had based his diagnosis on Chambers's life story, he actually knew very little about Chambers's childhood and family life up to the point he graduated from high school. Binger had placed great weight on Chambers's translation of a German novel, *Class Reunion*, in 1929, suggesting that he had modeled himself on the character in the book who had ruined his more successful friend. Murphy derided the notion that a hired translator should be associated with the character and plots of a book he did not author, got Binger to admit he had not read other books Chambers had translated and had no opinion about whether Chambers had modeled himself on a character in *Bambi*, which he had also translated. By the time Murphy finished his cross-examination, Binger's credibility was in tatters.

The defense also brought in a second witness, Dr. Henry Murray, a Harvard psychologist, to reinforce Dr. Binger's testimony. Murray testified that on the basis of his analysis of Chambers's writings he suffered from a "psychopathic personality" and made many of the same points Binger had. On cross-examination Murphy got Murray to admit that he had not read anything Chambers had written in the 1930s or most of the major essays he had written for *Time* in the 1940s. By the end of his testimony, Murray admitted his analysis of Chambers's writings had been limited largely to those items Hiss's defense had given him and was neither comprehensive nor even a scientific sample. The psychological evidence provided only meager assistance to the defense.

The defense continued to place major emphasis on character witnesses. While still impressive, their impact was reduced by the prosecution's relentless focus on the Baltimore documents and the microfilm of the pumpkin papers. In response, Claude Cross, Hiss's attorney, told the jury that Julian Wadleigh, not Alger Hiss, had stolen "every one of those papers" on the pumpkin papers microfilm. Because some of the stolen material was dated after Wadleigh had left Washington on a State Department mission, Cross suggested that Chambers had yet another source in the State Department, one he had not named. As for the material in Hiss's handwriting, Cross theorized that Chambers or some agent of his had burgled Hiss's office at the State Department and stolen them. And as for the summaries of State Department documents typed on the Hiss family typewriter, Cross asserted that in some unknown fashion Chambers had gained access to Claudia Catlett's home after the maid had been given the typewriter and secretly typed the documents. He could not, however, explain how Chambers could have known that Catlett possessed the type-writer since, in Hiss's telling, there had been no contact with Chambers after 1936 and the typewriter was still in the Hiss home at that time.

Cross also had difficulty meshing the psychiatric defense with his alter-native explanation for the documents. To depict Chambers as a mentally ill pathological liar and fantasist was one thing, but the documents and the confession of Julian Wadleigh and Hede Massing's testimony were not fantasies. In his closing argument to the jury, consequently, Cross had to depict Chambers as a shrewd Soviet spy who had at least two or more sources at the State Department and was skillful enough to burgle Hiss's State Department office repeatedly but was also an unstable, antisocial, mentally ill fantasist who framed a casual acquaintance. It was a difficult argument to sell.

Thomas Murphy had an easier task. He highlighted the documentary evidence and how it corroborated the story told by Chambers, Wadleigh, and Massing. He then asked the jury to compare Hiss's testimony with the evidence on the matter of the stolen documents, the Ford car, the Bokhara rugs, the subleasing of the apartment, and the close relationship of the Hiss family with the Chamberses.

Because Judge Goddard allowed both prosecution and defense to present more witnesses and evidence than Judge Kaufman had, the sec-ond Hiss trial lasted longer, starting on November 17, 1949, with the case going to the jury on the afternoon of January 20, 1950. Later that day the jury asked for copies of the testimony of key witnesses, looked once more at the Baltimore documents, and then retired for the night. Early in the afternoon of the next day it returned and delivered a unanimous verdict of guilty on both counts of perjury. On January 25 Judge Goddard sentenced Hiss to five years in prison.

Hiss had replaced much of his legal team after the first trial and immedi-ately put together a new group of lawyers to handle his appeal. In later years they, too, would be replaced and fresh talent brought in. Altogether, Hiss had the benefit of some of the most distinguished and talented defense lawyers in the nation. All, however, was of little avail. The U.S. Court of Appeals affirmed Hiss's conviction in December 1950 and the U.S. Supreme Court denied his appeal in March 1951. In 1952 he petitioned for retrial, citing a variety of legal grounds, but federal district, appellate, and supreme courts all rejected the petition.

In 1972 Hiss gained a minor legal victory when he successfully argued in court that a federal law denying civil service pensions to persons convicted of his crime was unconstitutional. While this gained him a federal pension for his years of government work, it did not, of course, put his perjury conviction into question. Attorneys convicted of a felony are automatically disbarred in most jurisdictions, and Hiss lost his ability to practice law with his conviction in 1950. In 1975 the Massachusetts Supreme Judicial Court readmitted Hiss to the practice of law in that state, citing his blameless life after finishing his prison sentence but adding, "nothing we have said here should be construed as detracting one iota from the fact that . . . we consider him to be guilty as charged" of the perjury for which he had been convicted.

In 1978 Hiss's defense team initiated yet another major federal court action, a detailed writ asking that his perjury conviction be overturned. A federal district court reviewed the appeal and in 1982 ruled that "the jury verdict rendered in 1950 was amply supported by the evidence . . . and nothing presented in these papers . . . places that verdict under any cloud." A federal appeals court and the U.S. Supreme Court also rejected the argument. With that, Hiss's legal appeals ended.

Chambers after the Trial

Whittaker Chambers lost his job as a senior editor of *Time* magazine after he confessed to espionage. While Henry Luce, the publisher of *Time*, admired Chambers and understood that he had become a staunch anti-Communist, he regarded it as an embarrassment, nonetheless, that a senior editor had been a Soviet spy. The subsequent spell of unemployment, however, did give Chambers the time to write an autobiography. *Witness*, published in 1952, was a powerful, elegantly written book, and quickly became a best seller. Detailed and lengthy (808 pages), the autobiography emphasized Chambers's life as a Communist and Soviet spy in the 1930s and his relationship to Alger Hiss. It was also an intellectual examination of the spiritual crisis of Western civilization in the first half of the twentieth century. Chambers presented the West's rejection of its Christian heritage as the cause of the crisis and communism as a powerful but false answer. *Witness* took a darkly apocalyptic and pessimistic view of the future, and at one point Chambers stated that, in shifting from the Communist side, he felt he was "leaving the winning world for the losing world."

Except for occasional essays and articles on communism and the Soviet Union, Chambers rejected an active role in the politics of the 1950s. He rarely accepted offers, even highly paid ones, for public appearances or lectures and avoided endorsing particular politicians. When Joseph McCarthy first appeared as a highly visible public champion of anti-communism, Chambers took an interest and even cheered him on, but by 1953 Chambers had concluded that McCarthy was a self-aggrandizer interested more in using anti-Communist sentiment for his own purposes than in advancing the anti-Communist cause. Although he never publicly repudiated McCarthy, he sought to distance himself from the senator and privately warned other anti-Communists to do so as well. While Chambers received a measure of vindication from Hiss's conviction and was gratified by the strong sales of *Witness*, the 1950s were not a comfortable decade for him. Although he was a hero to many Republicans and conservatives, Democrats and liberals had a more ambivalent view. While it had been a Democratic administration that had prosecuted Hiss and most anti-Communist liberals and Truman-style Cold War Democrats accepted Hiss's guilt, many deeply resented the use that conservatives and Republicans made of his story to taint the New Deal and the Truman administration with communism. Many treated Chambers himself as a pariah with whom respectable people would not associate. Nor was Chambers entirely comfortable with Republicans and conservatives. He joined the new conservative journal *National Review* as an editor but left after a brief period because he was indifferent to the journal's conservative domestic policies and uncomfortable with its treatment of anticommunism as but one part of a broader conservative agenda.

Long overweight, Chambers suffered a series of serious heart attacks in the late 1940s and 1950s, a problem likely exacerbated by the stress of the congressional committee, grand jury, and Hiss trials of 1949 and 1950. In his final years Chambers increasingly saw himself as having sacrificed his career and privacy to rally American resistance to communism and having suffered a living martyrdom on behalf of the Christian West in what he feared would be a losing struggle with the Communist East. He died of a heart attack July 9, 1961. In 1984 President Ronald Reagan posthumously awarded Chambers the U.S. Medal of Freedom, and in 1988 the secretary of the interior designated Chambers's Maryland farm, where he had hidden the microfilm in a hollowed-out pumpkin, a National Historical Landmark.

Hiss after the Trial

After serving three years and eight months of his five-year sentence, Alger Hiss was released from prison in November 1954. He had difficulty finding employment, working briefly as an underpaid administrator in a small company and then as a stationery salesman. He separated from his wife, Priscilla, in 1958, but she refused to give him a divorce. (Hiss remarried in 1985 after Priscilla's death.)

Hiss continued to maintain his innocence, but in the 1950s and early 1960s found little support except among close friends and on the isolated pro-Soviet left. In 1957 he published *In the Court of Public Opinion*. Essentially a book-length "brief for the defense" that focused on the trial and little else, it took a legalistic approach, more concerned with the admissibility of evidence under esoteric legal rules than with the content and validity of the evidence. It was neither a popular nor critical success. In 1988 Hiss published a fuller autobiography, *Recollections of a Life*. It was noticeably restrained and spare and concentrated on Hiss's years as a New Deal lawyer and State Department official. In his treatment of the trial, Hiss described Chambers as a closet homosexual psychopath who sought revenge against Hiss for having cut off their relationship.

In the late 1960s Hiss found a broader audience for his claims. Opposition to the unpopular Vietnam War shattered the Cold War political consensus and gave credibility to Hiss's argument that he had been the victim of anti-Communist hysteria. He regained some social acceptability, began to lecture widely, maintaining his innocence and suggesting that he had been the victim of a conspiracy engineered by Whittaker Chambers in league with the FBI and reactionary congressional anti-Communists. The Watergate scandal of the mid-1970s also discredited Richard Nixon, one of Hiss's chief antagonists, and made plausible the idea that a government conspiracy had forged evidence and coerced false testimony against him.

The Historical Argument

By the mid-1970s Hiss's conviction had become a symbol to many, perhaps most, in the academic world and among journalists of anti-Communist excess and government abuse of power, which was somehow tied into the Vietnam War. A number of books appeared supporting Hiss's innocence. Some such as Earl Jowitt's *The Strange Case of Alger Hiss* (1953) developed legal points about court procedures and the admissibility of evidence and witnesses and hinted that the FBI encouraged perjured testimony against Hiss. Others presented sensationalistic conspiracy theories. Fred J. Cook's 1958 book, *The Unfinished Story of Alger Hiss*, argued for a joint FBI–Whittaker Chambers conspiracy that used a fake Woodstock typewriter to produce the damning documents, a claim for which not only was there no evidence but insurmountable technical obstacles. Ronald Seth's *The Sleeping Truth: The Hiss-Chambers Affair Reappraised* (1968) asserted the most bizarre theory, claiming that SMERSH, a counterespionage section of the KGB, had used Chambers, one of its agents, to frame Hiss in a bid to cause turmoil in the United States. The theory first advanced by Dr. Binger, that Chambers was a twisted homosexual who had imagined the espionage and faked evidence to ruin Hiss, was revived in Meyer A. Zeligs's *Friendship and Fratricide: An Analysis of Whittaker Chambers and Alger Hiss* (1967) and John Chabot Smith's *Alger Hiss: The True Story* (1977). Smith simultaneously advanced other conspiracy theories, offering readers a choice of alternatives that might convince them of Hiss's innocence. He also advanced one of his own in which he argued that Chambers had stolen the Hisses' Woodstock typewriter in 1935 or 1936 and substituted another without the Hisses ever knowing. Chambers then supposedly used the stolen Woodstock to prepare the Baltimore documents while also in 1938 gaining access to the Department of State with fake identification to steal documents with Hiss's initials on them as well as Hiss's handwritten summaries of State Department cables.

None of the books seeking to exonerate Hiss, however, attempted to reconsider comprehensively all of the evidence in the case. Allen Weinstein's *Perjury: The Hiss-Chambers Case*, the first book to do so, appeared in 1978. Weinstein was the first historian to gain comprehensive access to both the Hiss defense files and the voluminous FBI investigative files made available after a Freedom of Information Act suit. His book, a model of careful research and evaluation of the evidence, concluded that on all of the main issues in dispute Whittaker Chambers had told the truth and Alger Hiss had not. Nor did Weinstein find any evidence to support any of the conspiracy theories advanced by those seeking to vindicate Hiss. *Perjury* had a major impact on the scholarly world, convincing many people who assumed that Hiss must have been innocent that he was guilty.

Although Hiss's defenders quibbled about minor points and launched personal attacks on Weinstein, they were unable either to discredit

Perjury or point to a study of equal scholarly quality or thoroughness. A well-researched award-winning biography by Sam Tanenhaus, *Whittaker Chambers: A Biography* (1997) reached the same conclusions about the Hiss-Chambers case as had been reached in *Perjury*.

The collapse of the Communist regimes in Eastern Europe in 1989 and of the USSR itself in 1991 provided additional archival information on the case. In August 1991 John Lowenthal, a longtime member of Hiss's legal team, asked a Russian historian, former Soviet Army General Dimitri Volkogonov, to look into the Hiss case. Volkogonov responded in October 1992 with a letter to Lowenthal that said, "On his [Hiss's] and your request, I carefully studied many documents from the archives of the intelligence services of the USSR as well as various information provided for me by the archive staff. On the basis of a very careful analysis of all the information available, I can inform you that Alger Hiss was never an agent of the intelligence services of the Soviet Union." Lowenthal also recorded a video interview with Volkogonov in which he exonerated Hiss: "Positively, if he was [a] spy," according to Volkogonov, "I would have found a reflection in various files."

Volkogonov's conclusion quickly came under attack. He not only had been unable to find any documents showing that Hiss had been a spy, but he also had not found any indicating that Chambers had ever been involved in Soviet espionage either. Given Chambers's production of real documents and the confessions of numerous members of his network such as Wadleigh, Reno, and Inslerman, this was not credible. Volkogonov also admitted he had not examined the records of the GRU, the Soviet military agency to which Hiss's apparatus reported. In the face of skeptical questions, he soon modified his story, admitting he spent only two days at the enormous KGB archive (open only to researchers with the approval of the SVR, successor to the KGB), hardly enough time to make any sort of statement about what wasn't to be found. He also confessed that he had relied on archivists acting under orders of the chief of the Russian SVR to pick what files he would be allowed to see. Speaking to the *New York Times*, Volkogonov retreated completely: "I was not properly understood. . . . The Ministry of Defense also has an intelligence service [GRU], which is totally different, and many documents have been destroyed. I only looked through what the K.G.B. had. All I said was that I saw no evidence." He acknowledged that his motive in writing the letter exonerating Hiss was "primarily humanitarian," to relieve the anguish of an old man approaching death

(Hiss died in 1996). Volkogonov went on to say, "What I saw gives no basis to claim a full clarification. There's no guarantee that it was not destroyed, that it was not in other channels" and complained, "His [Hiss's] attorney, Lowenthal, pushed me hard to say things of which I was not fully convinced."

The GRU archive was not opened for research even after the collapse of the USSR. Some limited material released from KGB files was included in a 1997 edition of Weinstein's *Perjury* and also in Allen Weinstein and Alexander Vassiliev's 1999 *The Haunted Wood: Soviet Espionage in America – The Stalin Era* that documented KGB knowledge of Alger Hiss as an agent for its sister service, the GRU. One 1945 Soviet telegram decoded by the Venona project reported on a meeting between a KGB officer and a GRU source, code-named Ales, an American diplomat who was part of the U.S. delegation to the 1945 Yalta Conference between Stalin, President Roosevelt, and Prime Minister Churchill. From what the cable says of Ales, American security officials concluded that Ales likely was Alger Hiss. Other deciphered Venona messages directly or indirectly supported the credibility of testimony of Whittaker Chambers and Elizabeth Bentley. Material on Noel Field's role in Soviet espionage in the 1930s and his relationship with Alger Hiss also emerged from the newly opened archives of the security services of the Hungarian and Czechoslovak Communist regimes in the 1990s. It was symptomatic of the changed atmosphere brought about by the new evidence that the latest full-length book on the Hiss case, *Alger Hiss' Looking-Glass Wars* (2004) by the legal scholar G. Edward White, accepted Hiss's guilt as a premise and focused on the mechanisms Hiss used to convince supporters of his innocence over the many decades after his conviction.

FURTHER READINGS

Chambers, Whittaker. *Witness*. New York: Random House, 1952.

> *Powerfully written autobiography by an ex-Communist who took part in Soviet espionage and was the chief witness against Alger Hiss.* Witness *sold well at the time and continues to be highly influential in shaping perceptions of the nature of the Communist underground in the 1930s.*

Cook, Fred J. *The Unfinished Story of Alger Hiss*. New York: Morrow, 1958.

Book-length polemic arguing that Hiss was innocent of all charges. Advances the forgery-by-typewriter theory.

Hiss, Alger. *In the Court of Public Opinion.* New York: A. A. Knopf, 1957.

A brief for the defense. Takes a legalistic approach more concerned about the admissibility of evidence than the validity of the evidence. Refrains from offering a counternarrative to that of Chambers.

Hiss, Alger. *Recollections of a Life.* New York: Seaver Books/H. Holt, 1988.

An autobiography that concentrates on his role as a New Deal official. In a brief discussion of the Hiss-Chambers case, Hiss describes Chambers as psychopath and closet homosexual who sought revenge for Hiss having cut off their relationship.

Jowitt, William Allen. *The Strange Case of Alger Hiss.* Garden City, N.Y.: Doubleday, 1953.

Argues that the evidence against Hiss was perjured or faked.

Moore, William Howard. *Two Foolish Men: The True Story of the Friendship between Alger Hiss and Whittaker Chambers.* Portland, Ore.: Moorop Press, 1987.

Based on speculative analysis on the psychology of the two men.

Seth, Ronald. *The Sleeping Truth: The Hiss-Chambers Affair Reappraised.* New York: Hart, 1968.

Argues that the KGB framed Hiss and that Chambers was a KGB agent.

Smith, John Chabot. *Alger Hiss: The True Story.* New York: Penguin Books, 1977.

Maintains that Hiss was innocent. Advances a number of possible conspiracies to account for the evidence against Hiss.

Swan, Patrick, ed. *Alger Hiss, Whittaker Chambers, and the Schism in the American Soul.* Wilmington, Del.: ISI Books, 2003.

A collection of twenty-three essays on the Hiss-Chambers case with publication dates ranging from 1950 to 2001: essays by Leslie Fiedler, Diana and Lionel Trilling, William F. Buckley Jr., Rebecca West, Hugh Kenner, Sam Tanenhaus, Murray Kempton, Arthur Koestler, Sidney Hook, Irving Howe, Elmer Davis, Kingsley Martin, Mark DeWolfe Hose, David Cort, Philip Nobile, Alfred Kazin, John Judis, Eric Breindel, Ron Rosenbaum, and Hilton Kramer.

Tanenhaus, Sam. *Whittaker Chambers: A Biography.* New York: Random House, 1997.

Massively detailed scholarly biography of Chambers, including his career in the CPUSA, in Soviet espionage, and as an anti-Communist journalist and writer. Chambers "had offered himself to the nation as both sinner and savior. Some saw him as an exemplar of humble martyrdom, others as a monstrous egotist. His moral attitude at times recalled the stoic resignation of the ancient tragedians, at times the anti-heroism of Sartre or Beckett, at times the torment of the twice-born soul. 'You never changed, Whit,' Henry Zolan told him near the end, 'you just changed sides.' It was true. Each side, in the instant he joined it, seemed outnumbered, but he chose it anyway. This was his secret pride."

Weinstein, Allen. *Perjury: The Hiss-Chambers Case.* New York: Knopf, 1978.

Scholarly and highly detailed history of the Hiss-Chambers case that is essential reading for those interested in the affair. Based on FBI files, Hiss legal defense files, and a variety of other primary sources. Finds that the preponderance of the evidence suggests that Chambers's story was largely true and Hiss's was largely false.

Weinstein, Allen. *Perjury: The Hiss-Chambers Case.* New York: Random House, 1997.

New edition with new material from Russian archives on the activities of Hiss, Hede Massing, Laurence Duggan, Michael Straight, and Noel Field as Soviet intelligence contacts in the mid-1930s. The agnostic position toward whether Hiss's espionage of the 1930s continued, found in the original edition, has shifted to one of concluding that it continued well into the 1940s. Easily the most comprehensive and thorough account of the case.

White, G. Edward. *Alger Hiss' Looking-Glass Wars.* New York: Oxford University Press, 2004.

Subtle biographical-psychological study of how Hiss had a pattern of camouflaging and distorting key episodes in his life such as his participation in espionage. Examines Hiss's changing tactics over his lifetime to project an aura of innocence in the face of the evidence against him.

Zelig, Meyer A. *Friendship and Fratricide: An Analysis of Whittaker Chambers and Alger Hiss.* New York: Viking Press, 1967.

Speculative psychobiography of the Hiss-Chambers case that argues that Chambers framed Hiss out of a pathological desire for revenge for having been rejected by Hiss.

5

The Atomic Espionage Cases

I F ALGER HISS'S CONVICTION FOR LYING ABOUT HIS ESPIONAGE activities jolted many Americans because of its message that high-ranking members of the American establishment had betrayed their country, the trial and conviction of Julius and Ethel Rosenberg for helping the Soviet Union steal atomic secrets angered and frightened the public. The popular conviction that Soviet possession of a weapon that left America vulnerable to atomic incineration was the result of treachery helped inaugurate what some critics called a witch-hunt and what others called a long-overdue focus on a more rigorous counterespionage program.

By the summer of 1941 theoretical advances in nuclear physics had led British scientists to conclude that building an atomic bomb using uranium was feasible. The Maud Committee submitted a report in September 1941 detailing a three-year effort to build a bomb (cover-named Tube Alloys) that was approved by the British military. The Soviet Union learned of the report within a week from John Cairncross, a young British civil servant who had been recruited as a Soviet spy while a student at Cambridge University in the 1930s. Meanwhile, American scientists were slowly gearing up to undertake a similar effort, and once America entered the war, President Roosevelt in 1942 ordered that it be made a leading war priority. British scientists and military industrial administrators also advised Prime Minister Churchill that the atomic bomb project required a tremendous investment of industrial assets and technical manpower, but British resources were then stretched thin by the demands of conventional military production. Consequently, the United Kingdom agreed to cooperate with the United States in building an atomic bomb, and the U.S. Army assumed control of the Manhattan Project. Around the same time, the fall of 1942, Soviet intelligence launched a major new initiative to gather atomic secrets.

Klaus Fuchs: The Background

Much of the Soviets' early success was due to spies its agencies had recruited in Great Britain. One unidentified British source, cover-named Eric, provided the KGB a list of British scientists working on the atomic bomb project in early 1943 that included the name of Klaus Fuchs. To its surprise, the KGB discovered that Fuchs had been working for the GRU, Soviet military intelligence, since 1941. Born in Germany in 1911, the son of a Lutheran minister, Fuchs had secretly joined the German Communist Party as college student and, with party encouragement, had escaped to Great Britain after Hitler's rise to power. He earned a Ph.D. in physics in 1937 at the University of Bristol and went on to advanced studies at the University of Edinburgh on quantum mechanics. When World War II began he was interned and shipped to Canada as an enemy German national. The scientists who ran Britain's atomic bomb project, however, regarded Fuchs as a brilliant atomic theorist whom they needed badly, and after several months he was freed, returned to England, and began working on Tube Alloys. British security investigators gave him a clearance to work on the project despite having a record of a 1934 Gestapo report identifying Fuchs as a secret Communist that had been passed to the British late in the 1930s. Given the demands of the war, physicists of Fuchs's caliber were in short supply in Great Britain, the Gestapo was considered a suspect source, and Fuchs had largely avoided politics since leaving Germany.

In fact, as soon as he learned he was working on an atomic bomb, Fuchs got in touch with Soviet agents through refugee German Communists in Britain. Although he had become a naturalized British subject in 1942, in reality Fuchs was fervently loyal to the USSR and convinced that Great Britain wanted Germany and Russia to bleed themselves to death. He turned over information on Tube Alloys, mostly consisting of his own reports and papers, to agents of the GRU. GRU officers, however, lost contact with him for most of 1942. After reestablishing ties, he met with an agent several times in 1943. When he informed the GRU that he was being transferred to the United States, he was provided with a KGB contact in America. (By this point, the KGB had become the senior Soviet intelligence service and often took over sources first developed by GRU.)

Klaus Fuchs arrived in New York to work at Columbia University in December 1943 but was not able to meet his American contact, Harry

Gold, known to him only as Raymond, until January 5, 1944. At that time he provided a general account of the Manhattan Project, emphasizing that the major focus of his work was devising a method to separate the uranium isotopes, U-235 and U-238. U-235 is highly radioactive and best suited for achieving an atomic explosion. In nature, however, more than 99 percent of uranium is ill-suited for bomb building because it is the more stable, less radioactive U-238 isotope. The two isotopes are chemically identical, so their physical separation was difficult and constituted one of the major technical barriers to building an atomic bomb. The Manhattan Project developed several separation methods, and one worked on by Fuchs was gaseous diffusion – converting the uranium into a gaseous form and then pumping it through a porous screen through which the infinitesimally lighter U-235 isotope would diffuse faster than (and be separated from) the heavier U-238. The physics of the procedure was complex and many scientists, including those working on the USSR's secret wartime atomic project, thought this process unworkable. Manhattan Project scientists, however, solved the problem.

At subsequent meetings with Gold during the next six months, Fuchs turned over additional documents but also indicated that due to friction between British and American scientists about the extent of cooperation on the project, he expected to return to Great Britain shortly. On August 5, 1944, he failed to appear for a scheduled rendezvous. Unsure if Fuchs had returned to England or had been transferred elsewhere in the United States, the KGB sent Gold to Cambridge, Massachusetts, to see if Fuchs's sister, married to an American, had heard from him. Gold learned that Fuchs had been sent to Los Alamos. In February 1945 Fuchs arrived in Boston for a family visit and reestablished contact with Gold. At his meeting with Gold in Boston, Fuchs explained some of the scientific developments at Los Alamos. In addition to work on uranium separation, he had now gained access to the secrets about the development of plutonium as an alternative to uranium U-235 as a bomb fuel and the implosion mechanism as a way to detonate plutonium.

The Manhattan Project developed two different types of atomic bombs. The Hiroshima version was a pure uranium bomb with a "gun-type" detonator. The Nagasaki model was a plutonium bomb with an implosion detonator. With the first type, a quantity of uranium was fired down a barrel at tremendous speed to hit another piece of U-235 with such energy that the two pieces began a fission chain reaction of splitting atoms that produced an atomic explosion. The difficulty with a pure uranium atomic bomb, however, was that the uranium must be made up largely of the rare U-235 isotope. All the separation methods the Manhattan Project developed were slow and required the expenditure of tremendous industrial resources.

In face of the daunting practical problem of obtaining enough U-235, American scientists developed an alternative. A team of Berkeley scientists in 1941 had used a cyclotron to create (transmute) a new element that did not exist in nature: plutonium. Plutonium was more radioactive and fissionable than U-235 and in theory could be used as a bomb fuel. Manhattan Project scientists also found that plutonium could be created in quantity in a uranium-fueled nuclear reactor. This greatly reduced the need for laborious uranium isotope separation.

A practical plutonium bomb, however, required a different type of detonation. Plutonium was so radioactively unstable that in a gun-type bomb it would begin a premature chain reaction before the two pieces of plutonium were fully fused. The explosive blast of the premature chain reaction would destroy the rest of the plutonium before it began fission, thus producing a small nuclear explosion (a "fizzle" in Manhattan Project slang) rather than a city-destroying blast. The ingenious solution worked out was implosion. With implosion an ordinary chemical explosive was shaped in a sphere around a central core of plutonium. The explosive sphere was then set off by an array of surrounding detonators that allowed all parts of the sphere to explode simultaneously with the spherical shaping of the explosive acting as a lens to focus the explosive on the central plutonium core. The result was that the core of plutonium was simultaneously squeezed from all directions by a uniform force and all parts of the core began fission, thus avoiding a fizzle. By handing over the secret of the plutonium bomb and implosion to the Soviets, Fuchs allowed the Soviet bomb project to skip the lengthy and astoundingly expensive development stage that had led the Manhattan Project to that solution.

In June 1945 Fuchs met with Gold in Sante Fe (the closest city to the bomb project's secret site at Los Alamos), revealed that a test of the plutonium bomb was scheduled within a month, and provided details of the bomb's design. He met with Gold in Sante Fe one more time, in September, after the end of the war, to give him even more information – including precise details of the initiator used to trigger the chain reaction – about the weapon that had been used on Japan with such devastating results.

Theodore Hall: The Background

Fuchs may have been an early recruit for Soviet intelligence, but his information about Los Alamos was not the first news the Russians had about what was taking place in that top secret location. Soviet intelligence agencies had at least two other spies in place and providing vital data. The most significant was a brilliant, young physicist whose activities were not exposed publicly until the mid-1990s. Even though the FBI was aware by the late 1940s that he had been one of the Soviet Union's most productive spies, Theodore Hall was never prosecuted.

Ted Hall was a child prodigy. Born in 1925 to a middle-class New York Jewish family, he began college before he was fifteen. After two years at Queens College, he transferred to Harvard where he excelled in physics and joined the John Reed Society, a club dedicated to Marxism. One of his roommates, Saville Sax, was a fervent Communist. Just after turning eighteen years old and even before graduating from Harvard, Hall was recruited to work at Los Alamos; he arrived in late January 1944. By that fall, he had been promoted to team leader on a key implosion-related project. Seeing the world through Communist lenses, he became convinced that postwar America capitalism, armed with atomic weapons, would follow the same path to fascism as prewar Germany and Italy. In October he returned home on leave, determined to contact the Soviets and inform them about the atomic bomb.

Hall and Saville Sax tried to make contact with a Soviet official through the CPUSA and were eventually directed to Sergey Kurnakov, a military analyst for Communist newspapers who also worked for the KGB. Hall volunteered his services, insisting that only Stalin's Soviet Union could be trusted with the atomic bomb, and gave Kurnakov a report he had written and a list of the scientists working at Los Alamos. Because Hall's leave was ending and there was no time for a lengthy debriefing by a KGB officer, the Soviets agreed to allow Sax to serve as a courier after Hall returned to New Mexico. Early in November the New York station of the KGB sent its Moscow headquarters a coded telegram (later broken by the Venona project) recounting the episode, naming Hall and Sax, and giving them the cover names Mlad (Youngster) and Star (Old Timer), respectively. It was just days before Moscow learned that Fuchs, so long out of touch, had contacted his sister and revealed that he had been posted to Los Alamos.

Rosenberg and Greenglass: The Background

Still another atomic spy was just about to be activated. David Greenglass was a skilled machinist, a brash and arrogant New Yorker, and a dedicated young Communist who regarded the Soviet Union as a utopian society. He grew up in poverty on the Lower East Side of New York. An indifferent student, he dropped out of college, married his girl friend Ruth, and looked up to his sister and her husband, Ethel and Julius Rosenberg. David and Ruth were members of the Young Communist League, while the Rosenbergs were full-fledged members of the party when David was drafted into the Army in April 1943.

Julius had been a leading member of the Young Communist League when he attended engineering school at City College of New York. After graduation he got a job in 1940 as an inspector reviewing production of electronic goods for the Army Signal Corps. His position afforded him an exemption from the army, but a routine security investigation in 1941 had almost cost him his job when evidence of Communist connections surfaced. Julius approached the CPUSA about being put in touch with Soviet intelligence shortly after he went to work for the Signal Corps. According to his onetime Soviet controller, KGB officer Alexander Feklisov, Julius Rosenberg was recruited by Soviet intelligence around Labor Day 1942, after being referred by Bernard Chester (the CPUSA party name of Bernard Schuster), the CPUSA's liaison to Soviet intelligence and an associate of Jacob Golos (see Chapter 3). Motivated by his fervent communism, admiration for the Soviet Union, and desire to help it in its fight against fascism, Rosenberg quickly began supplying confidential documents and then recruited several of his friends to do the same. By 1943 Julius was overseeing an extensive network of spies, most of them former CCNY classmates working in classified military technology research, and he and Ethel had dropped out of public Communist activity, although they continued to pay party dues clandestinely through Chester.

Meanwhile the army had assigned David Greenglass to an engineering unit as a military machinist. By sheer chance in July 1944 he was picked to work as a machinist on the army-run Manhattan Project, first at Oak Ridge and then Los Alamos. Letters and phone calls to his wife alerted her and Julius to what David was doing. In one letter dated November 4, David wrote, "I most certainly will be glad to be part of the community project that Julius and friends have in mind," suggesting that he had been approached to spy and was receptive to the idea. That month, Julius told Feklisov about his brother-in-law's assignment. Eager to obtain another source at Los Alamos, Feklisov's superiors approved of David's recruitment. Ruth Greenglass met with the Rosenbergs in mid-November, just before leaving for Albuquerque for a visit with David, and agreed to ask him if he would cooperate. He leaped at the chance and gave her information about Los Alamos that she relayed to Julius after returning home.

David Greenglass returned to New York on furlough in January 1945. At Los Alamos David had been assigned to a team of machinists who manufactured physical models of the implosion detonators that scientists were sketching out in theory, and he gave Julius handwritten notes and drawings of a high-explosive lens mold being developed for the implosion plutonium bomb. He also met with Ann Sidorovich, a Communist friend of the Rosenbergs, who was to serve as a courier to the Greenglasses in New Mexico (Ruth was moving to Albuquerque). In case another courier replaced Sidorovich, Julius gave Ruth part of a panel from a Jell-O box and told her that any other courier would have the matching piece as a recognition signal. David also briefly met with Anatoly Yakovlev (real name Yatskov), a KGB officer operating out of the Soviet New York consulate with diplomatic cover. Yakovlev, who specialized in scientific intelligence, questioned Greenglass about the lens mold. David Greenglass returned to Los Alamos and was joined by Ruth in February; she rented an apartment in Albuquerque, to which David commuted on weekends.

Soviet intelligence now had three spies positioned at America's most secret locale. Los Alamos itself was a closed military base; it was out of the question to risk trying to smuggle out information since letters and phone calls were monitored. Instead, the KGB sent couriers to the nearest cities, Sante Fe and Albuquerque, where they could meet the sources when they were on weekend leaves. In December 1944 Saville Sax traveled to New Mexico and rendezvoused with Hall in Albuquerque; he received a short report containing important new information on the principles underlying the building of the bomb. When the KGB wrote a summary account of the American atomic bomb program late in February, virtually all the information in it had come from Hall and Greenglass – Gold had just reestablished contact with Fuchs days before and his report on that meeting had not made its way to Moscow. Not until April 1945 did the scientific leader of the Soviet atomic bomb project, Igor Kurchatov, receive Fuchs's report on implosion; while praising its value, he made it clear that it largely confirmed what had already been learned from Hall and Greenglass.

Sax was an unlikely and ineffective courier; not only did he dress and act unconventionally; he also had a crippled hand, which made him conspicuous. Moreover, he was a rank amateur at espionage. After his one stint as a courier, he returned to college. The Soviets enlisted a veteran agent to take his place. Lona Cohen came from a working-class Catholic family; she joined the Communist Party in 1935 and met Morris Cohen two years later. Born in 1910 into a Jewish Communist family in New York, Morris Cohen had won a football scholarship to Mississippi State University. An injury and insufficient talent ended his athletic career; he joined the CPUSA while in graduate school in Illinois and returned to New York to work as a party organizer. In 1937 he fought in the Spanish Civil War, enlisting with the Abraham Lincoln Battalion of the Comintern-sponsored International Brigades. Wounded in battle, Cohen was soon chosen to attend a special Comintern school in Spain to train spies and saboteurs for behind-the-lines operations. After the International Brigades were withdrawn from Spain in 1938, Cohen returned to America and agreed to work for the KGB. He married Lona in 1941 and quickly recruited her to help him in his then largely industrial espionage work. Morris was drafted in 1942 and Lona soon became a trade-union organizer. Early in 1945 the KGB decided to reactivate her for courier work and other duties. That spring she traveled to New Mexico to pick up information from Theodore Hall.

Around the time in May 1945 when she returned, Harry Gold's Soviet controller, KGB officer Anatoly Yakovlev, assigned him to meet with Klaus Fuchs in Sante Fe early in June. He was also ordered to meet with a second source – who turned out to be David Greenglass – on the same trip. Gold was unhappy about making two pickups on one mission; he regarded this as risky espionage "tradecraft." Yakovlev, however, was under intense pressure to verify the information Hall had supplied. On June 2, 1945, Gold picked up a long report from Fuchs in Sante Fe; the following day he met with Greenglass in Albuquerque and obtained several items. He returned east and handed over the material to his Russian contact. After Hiroshima, Lona Cohen rendezvoused with Hall in Albuquerque and received yet another report about his work at Los Alamos; Gold met again with Fuchs, who provided details about how the bomb worked; and Greenglass returned to New York in September and wrote a final report he gave to Julius Rosenberg. The presence of at least two high-level scientific sources at

Los Alamos assured the Soviets that the material they were receiving was not disinformation. Greenglass's data were far less important and scientifically detailed but still helpful, and his machinist's-eye view of the explosive lens reinforced the theoretical information about the mechanism of the implosion detonator.

J. Robert Oppenheimer and Communists at the Berkeley Radiation Laboratory

The extensive Soviet effort to penetrate the Manhattan Project had been an unqualified success. Despite the extraordinary security employed by American counterintelligence agencies, they had missed at least three spies who worked in the heart of the enterprise, the top secret desert laboratory where the bomb was built. Although American counterintelligence agencies were missing Hall, Fuchs, and Greenglass, they were not inactive. Wiretaps and physical surveillance uncovered several Soviet attempts to obtain atomic information. Several of these plots were foiled but for a variety of reasons, the perpetrators were never prosecuted. But the most worrisome issue of security revolved around the most prominent of all those at Los Alamos, J. Robert Oppenheimer. The suspicions directed at him would, years later, result in an administrative trial before the Atomic Energy Commission and the loss of his security clearance.

J. Robert Oppenheimer was one of the stars of American theoretical physics. A brilliant theoretician and inspiring teacher, he had, along with Ernest Lawrence, an extraordinary experimental physicist who received the Nobel Prize in 1939, made the University of California physics department a magnet for bright and ambitious graduate students. In the mid-1930s Oppenheimer had also become attracted to the pro-Communist left. His lover, his brother Frank and his wife, his landlady, and many friends were active members of the Communist Party. Oppenheimer joined Communist front groups, signed letters and petitions, and regularly donated large sums of money (he had considerable private means) to Communist causes through Isaac Folkoff, a veteran California Communist who also had ties to Soviet intelligence. Evidence unearthed in recent years indicates that Oppenheimer himself was likely a secret member of the Communist Party and active in a secret Communist faculty club at the University of California, Berkeley, as late as 1941. This new evidence includes the memoir of Gordon Griffiths, a fellow member of the faculty

Communist club; the journal of Barbara Chevalier about her late husband Haakon Chevalier, a professor of French literature, who had joined the U.C. Berkeley Communist club at the same time as his close friend Oppenheimer; and early 1940s KGB documents referring to Oppenheimer as a former CPUSA member. Older evidence includes a 1964 Haakon Chevalier letter to Oppenheimer indicating that in his memoir he was writing he would confirm that they had both been members of the U.C. Berkeley faculty Communist club. Oppenheimer replied at the time that he would publicly repudiate Chevalier's claim, and in his memoir Chevalier retreated by referring to their both having been members of a Marxist discussion group rather than a party unit.

In 1939 Oppenheimer met Katherine Harrison, thrice married and then the wife of a British doctor; within a year she had divorced, and they were married. Kitty Harrison's second husband, Joseph Dallet, had been a CPUSA organizer, who volunteered for the Spanish Civil War, served as the Communist political commissar of the Abraham Lincoln Battalion in Spain, and died in combat. Kitty herself had belonged to the CPUSA. One of her husband's closest friends, Steve Nelson (also a political commissar with the International Brigades), who comforted her after her husband's death, arrived in the Berkeley area in 1940 as the CPUSA's new district organizer in Oakland and quickly befriended the newly married couple. Oppenheimer was already the object of some interest to FBI agents investigating the covert operations of the Comintern apparatus on the West Coast. His connections with Nelson, suspected of being one of the key organizers of this secret network, intrigued the FBI. Wiretaps picked up mentions of Oppenheimer's associations with prominent Communists and references that he was a secret party member.

Several of Oppenheimer's graduate students were also Communist Party members – Giovanni Rossi Lomanitz, Philip Morrison, David Bohm, and Joseph Weinberg among them. Some were active in efforts of the Federation of Architects, Engineers, and Chemists and Technicians (FAECT), a small, Communist-dominated union, to organize employees of the Radiation Laboratory at Berkeley. Oppenheimer supported them, hosting talks at his home and angering his colleague and the Radiation Lab's chief administrator, Ernest Lawrence. (FAECT was regarded as such a threat to security that the Roosevelt White House later asked the Congress of Industrial Organizations, its parent body, to get FAECT to cease organizing the Radiation Laboratory. The CIO promptly ordered FAECT to withdraw its organizers.) As late as October 1942, a wiretap from Nelson's office recorded a conversation in which a Communist Party organizer mentioned a secret weapons project at the Radiation Laboratory, but the FBI, still in the dark about the Manhattan Project and unaware of the Radiation Laboratory's role in the bomb project, did not link the comment to Oppenheimer.

By September 1942 Oppenheimer was being considered to head the new remote secret weapons laboratory that would build a bomb but had faced objections from the army because of his political associations. He recognized that he needed to distance himself from his Communist friends. After being selected for the job by the newly appointed head of the Manhattan Project, General Leslie Groves, Oppenheimer began the transition from left-wing professor to scientific administrator. In March 1943 he left Berkeley to direct the newly established Los Alamos facility.

The FBI had installed a listening device ("bug") in Steve Nelson's home in early 1943. On March 30 it recorded a conversation between the party organizer and a scientist later identified as Joseph Weinberg. Complaining that Oppenheimer had cooled toward his old comrades, Weinberg indicated his own willingness to help the party. After some prodding, he discussed the effort to build an atomic bomb and offered Nelson a variety of technical information. Nelson agreed that Oppenheimer had distanced himself from his former friends, encouraged Weinberg to provide more information, and warned him to burn his party membership book before his expected transfer to one of the bomb project's remote sites. Just a week later, an FBI surveillance team watched Nelson meet with Peter Ivanov, a Soviet intelligence officer whose cover was that of a diplomat at the Soviet consulate in San Francisco.

A few days later Nelson had another late night visitor to his home, Vasili Zubilin, nominally a Soviet diplomat assigned to the Washington embassy, but actually the KGB *rezident*, that is, the chief of KGB operations in the United States. The FBI bug in place revealed that Zubilin gave Nelson a considerable stack of money and the two men discussed cooperation between the CPUSA and the Soviet espionage apparatus in America. Nelson indicated that he had been recruited for covert work late in 1942 with the approval of party leader Earl Browder.

Army security had kept the FBI out of the Manhattan Project until this point; the FBI was not even sure what it had stumbled upon when it recorded the Nelson-Weinberg conversation. But these surreptitious recordings galvanized American counterintelligence. The U.S. Army informed the FBI about the Manhattan Project, and both agencies undertook an all-out effort to identify potential spies seeking its secrets. Much of the initial concern focused on Oppenheimer and the circle of Communist graduate students around him.

It took two months for the army to identify the "Joe" who had met with Nelson as Joseph Weinberg. Not only was he a Communist, but Oppenheimer had also hired him for a job on the Manhattan Project. Two of Oppenheimer's close friends, physicist Robert Serber and his wife, Charlotte, had numerous Communist ties. Robert was at Los Alamos and Charlotte was in charge of the library there. Oppenheimer had also recently hired another Communist, David Hawkins, as his assistant and, on a June trip to Berkeley, spent the night with his former Communist lover, Jean Tatlock. Despite all their qualms about his possible role in Soviet espionage, army counterintelligence officers were unable to persuade General Groves to remove Oppenheimer, whom he deemed essential to the effort to build an atomic bomb. In July 1943 Groves ordered them to give the scientist a security clearance.

Even as Oppenheimer successfully coordinated the enormously complicated effort to construct a functional atomic bomb, security officers in both the army and the FBI remained deeply suspicious about his ultimate loyalties. Oppenheimer, however, also appeared to be going through a slow shift in his own ideological views. On another trip to Berkeley in August 1943, Oppenheimer met with several of his radical graduate students and warned them to stay out of politics. He contacted army security officials and told them that a few months earlier intermediaries in touch with an official at the Soviet consulate had approached him and at least three other scientists and had suggested passing along information to the USSR. Oppenheimer refused to name any of the other scientists or the professor who had directly approached him and was only willing to identify George Eltenton as the link to the Soviet consulate.

Oppenheimer's reluctance to identify the individual who had asked him to spy for the Russians infuriated army security officers. In addition, the fact that several of his graduate students continued to work actively, albeit covertly, in Communist causes increased suspicions that he was protecting subversives. Over the next several months, Oppenheimer resisted repeated entreaties to name the professor who had approached him. Eltenton meanwhile was investigated thoroughly. A British-born chemist, he had lived in the Soviet Union for several years. Upon relocating to California, he had become an organizer and activist for FAECT, the radical union whose efforts Oppenheimer had championed. Eltenton was acquainted with both Ivanov and Gregory Kheifets. Kheifets also posed as a diplomat at the Soviet consulate but his real job was as the KGB's resident officer in northern California.

Not until December 1943, when General Groves personally ordered him to name the man who had approached him, did Oppenheimer say that it was Haakon Chevalier, a French professor at Berkeley and one of his closest friends. Ordered to name the three scientists Chevalier had contacted, Oppenheimer admitted lying and claimed that in addition to himself the only other one was his brother Frank, a physicist and a Communist Party member. Oppenheimer denied that either he or Frank had provided any information.

Although Oppenheimer's behavior and lies fueled suspicion about his motives, General Groves continued to judge him to be far too valuable to the success of the project to fire or prosecute. There was, additionally, no direct evidence that he had passed along secret information. Any effort to prosecute Chevalier or Eltenton would require Oppenheimer's cooperation, and his time was far too valuable to waste in legal proceedings. His graduate students were another matter. Despite the shortage of qualified physicists, they were fired from their positions, drafted into the armed services, or otherwise kept away from top secret material. Weinberg, for example, was drafted and stationed in Alaska.

Such administrative ways of dealing with potential spies was not limited to suspicious scientists in California. A chemist, Clarence Hiskey, had been active in the Communist Party while a graduate student at the University of Wisconsin. In September 1943 he went to work at the Metallurgical Laboratory at the University of Chicago, part of the Manhattan Project that ran a secret atomic reactor. In 1944 an FBI surveillance of Arthur Adams, an illegal GRU agent, oversaw him meeting with Hiskey, who also put two others working on the atomic bomb project in touch with Adams. Confronted by the FBI, both denied passing on any secrets but one, John Chapin, admitted that Hiskey had told him that Adams was a Soviet agent. While the others were fired, Hiskey was abruptly drafted and assigned to routine army duty in Alaska. While he was en route, counterintelligence officers surreptitiously searched his belongings and found several pages of classified notes. On a subsequent search, however, they were gone, indicating that he had either passed them to a contact or destroyed them.

Once Oppenheimer had finally identified Chevalier as the person who had brought Eltenton's request to him, the FBI started shadowing him in New York where he was living while attempting to land a government job in Washington. In December 1943 Chevalier was observed meeting with Louise Bransten, a San Francisco heiress, Communist activist, and lover of KGB officer Gregory Kheifets. Bransten had also been meeting with Earl Browder; back in San Francisco in the spring of 1944 she introduced Kheifets to Martin Kamen, a chemist working at the Radiation Laboratory and a friend of Oppenheimer. In July Kheifets invited Kamen to dinner ostensibly to thank him for his help on a medical issue and to introduce his successor at the consulate, Gregory Kasparov (who also succeeded him as local KGB resident). Army counterintelligence and FBI agents monitored the dinner conversation, but the noise level only enabled them to hear fragments that possibly included secret information. One of the Russians left with a sheaf of papers that Kamen had brought. Confronted, Kamen claimed the Russians had only asked for his help in obtaining radiation treatments for a Soviet official suffering from leukemia. General Groves, however, ordered Kamen fired immediately; he soon obtained a job as an inspector at a shipyard.

When Oppenheimer had admitted to General Groves the nature of Chevalier's approach, he had extracted a promise that Groves would keep confidential the detail that Frank Oppenheimer was the only other person approached. Groves honored the request. Army officials continued to investigate potential spies, including anyone with a Communist past. Moreover, Groves allowed Oppenheimer to bring Frank to Los Alamos in the spring of 1945. No one suspected that, while army counterintelligence and the FBI had watched Robert Oppenheimer and his circle of Communist friends and successfully foiled several Soviet efforts to obtain information, Theodore Hall, Klaus Fuchs, and David Greenglass had passed along many of the most significant secrets of the atomic bomb.

The Red Bomb and the Postwar Trials

After World War II there were persistent rumors that the Soviet Union had attempted to ferret out atomic secrets, fueled by Gouzenko's defection and the conviction of Alan Nunn May, the British physicist implicated by his documents. Public concern became intense in September 1949 when President Truman announced that the Soviet Union had detonated an atomic bomb. Although American intelligence had always assumed that the USSR would be able to develop such a weapon at some point, the quick loss of America's atomic monopoly frightened many people and startled knowledgeable sources because it had come several years sooner than they had anticipated. It quickly became apparent that the Soviets' success was not simply due to their skilled scientists but in large measure the result of espionage.

Stalin had appointed Lavrenty Beria, chief of both the KGB internal Soviet security police and the external foreign intelligence service, to take over supervision of the hitherto small Soviet atomic program on August 7, 1945, and tasked him to produce a working Soviet bomb in the shortest time possible. Beria ordered Soviet scientists to stick as closely as possible to the proven American design that Soviet spies had supplied. After the collapse of the Soviet Union, Russian archival sources demonstrated that the first Soviet bomb exploded on August 29, 1949, was a replica of the American plutonium bomb detonated over Nagasaki, Japan, by the United States on August 9, 1945.

The Trial of Klaus Fuchs

Just days before Truman's disquieting news, a soft-spoken cryptanalyst named Meredith Gardener, working at a top secret American codebreaking installation called Arlington Hall in Virginia, informed FBI agent Robert Lamphere that he had broken a message sent from the United States to Moscow in 1944. It contained material about the gaseous diffusion process used in the Manhattan Project and made clear that the source was someone from the British contingent. This message along with other deciphered Venona cables allowed the FBI to quickly identify Klaus Fuchs as the primary suspect. Fuchs was then working at Great Britain's nuclear research center and was a key figure in Britain's now independent atomic bomb program. (Britain exploded its first atomic bomb in 1952.) The FBI informed British counterintelligence about the identification of Fuchs.

Using as a pretext the fact that Fuchs's father had accepted a position at a Communist East German university, William Skardon, an MI-5 (British internal security) investigator, began to question him in December 1949. He was unable to confront Fuchs with the decrypted cable because

American and British officials did not want to reveal that they had broken the Soviet code and were reading intelligence messages. Because Fuchs had not been caught in the act of espionage and no co-conspirators were available to implicate him, the only hope was that he would confess. Skardon slowly wore him down, until finally on January 24, 1950, Fuchs admitted spying for the Russians in Britain in 1941–1943, in the United States in 1944–1945, and in Britain after 1945. He explained that he had existed in a state of "controlled schizophrenia," living one life as a devoted Communist spy and another as a loyal British subject and normal person. He cooperated with both British and American investigators, gave detailed accounts of the material he had passed along to the Soviets, and eventually helped to identify his courier. In an effort to shield his sister, he denied ever giving the courier any documents in her Boston home. He also made it clear that, based on the questions the Russians had asked him, he was convinced that there was at least one other source at Los Alamos. After the collapse of the USSR, Russian archival information suggested that Fuchs's cooperation was less than full and that he had minimized the extent of his espionage against the British atomic program in the late 1940s.

Fuchs was charged with four counts of violating the British Official Secrets Act. None of the counts dealt with his spying while at Los Alamos; they concerned espionage while in Great Britain, New York, and Boston. He was not charged with treason, because the Soviet Union had not been at war with Great Britain. He pled guilty in February in a trial whose only witness was Skardon – who read Fuchs's confession. A month later Fuchs was sentenced to fourteen years in prison. He served nine years and was stripped of his British citizenship. When released in 1959, he left Britain for a scientific career in Communist East Germany and a position in the East German Communist elite.

Fuchs's arrest and confession caused consternation among American officials. They were enraged to discover that the British had known of Fuchs's Communist past and had not informed the FBI. And J. Edgar Hoover was infuriated that the British refused to allow his men to question Fuchs about the American courier, known to Fuchs only as "Raymond," who had picked up his information in both New York and New Mexico, until after his trial and any appeals. Because the courier appeared to have a background in chemistry or engineering, the FBI eventually became interested in a Philadelphia chemist named Harry Gold.

The Arrest of Harry Gold

Harry Gold had been born in Switzerland in 1912 to Russian Jewish parents who moved to Philadelphia when he was an infant. Forced to drop out of college because of financial difficulties, he was working as a technician for a sugar manufacturer in 1935 when a Communist friend asked him to steal industrial secrets from his employer for the Soviet Union. Although Gold was not a CPUSA member, he sympathized with the Soviet Union and admired its public condemnations of anti-Semitism from which both he and his family suffered. Gold soon became a courier, meeting with other industrial spies to pick up their information and transmit it to his Soviet contacts. He concocted an imaginary life and family with which he regaled these other spies. His real life was drab and Spartan. He finished college, and the Soviets paid for him to take more classes at Xavier University in Cincinnati.

Most of Gold's work involved industrial espionage, but not all of it was successful. In the early 1940s he met repeatedly with Benjamin Smilg, an employee of the National Aeronautics Center in Dayton, Ohio, seeking information. Smilg had accepted money for tutoring a Russian student at MIT, and the KGB threatened to expose him if he refused to cooperate. Smilg, however, kept stalling and never provided any data. Gold had better luck when he recruited Alfred Dean Slack, who worked for the Eastman Kodak Company and was later employed by an ordnance firm in Tennessee, from which he passed along a sample of RDX, a new explosive. (After the collapse of the USSR, information emerged from Russian archives that Slack had also provided information about the Manhattan Project facility at Oak Ridge, Tennessee, where he had worked for a time.)

Gold also became involved with another Soviet industrial espionage source, a chemist named Abraham Brothman, an association that contributed to his eventual exposure. Brothman, who ran his own small chemical engineering firm, had been the source of technical intelligence, chiefly industrial chemical processes, for the Soviets since the 1930s, collecting both openly available material and stealing proprietary industrial secrets from various American firms for which he worked on contract. He had been turning material over to Elizabeth Bentley and Jacob Golos in the early 1940s, but Bentley was unable to get along with the irascible and unreliable Brothman and asked to be replaced as his courier. Gold was the replacement; over the years, Brothman gave him various industrial secrets, including information about the manufacturing of synthetic rubber. In

1944, however, Gold was ordered to stop seeing his other sources and give exclusive attention to a new assignment as courier to Klaus Fuchs.

His work on atomic espionage, however, was the last of Gold's career as a courier, and when Fuchs returned to Britain, the KGB put Gold on inactive status. In December 1946, after a long hiatus, the KGB contacted him about a possible mission to Europe. When his Soviet controller learned that Gold had in the intervening period gone to work for Brothman's chemical engineering company, he was incredulous and furious. Because Elizabeth Bentley had defected and undoubtedly named Brothman, Gold, too, would fall under suspicion. The Russian was correct. The grand jury investigating Elizabeth Bentley's story called Brothman to testify in 1947. He admitted giving Bentley and Jacob Golos documents but insisted that they were not secret materials. In an effort to make his actions seem innocent, he falsely claimed that he had met Golos through Harry Gold. Gold was also called to the grand jury and likewise lied by backing Brothman's story and testifying that he had thought Golos was a legitimate businessman. Although the FBI believed both men were lying, they could not prove it at the time.

But Fuchs's information led bureau investigators in the spring of 1950 to comb their files for left-wing chemists and engineers, and Gold's name popped up because of his connections to Brothman. Based on Fuchs's description of "Raymond," the FBI considered Gold a strong suspect for the role. During questioning by the FBI, Brothman and Miriam Moskowitz, Brothman's business partner, had discussed their association with Harry Gold and what they knew of his background. The false stories Gold had told them about his imaginary family matched recollections Fuchs's sister had told the FBI about Raymond's alleged family. When agents searched Gold's home on May 22, they found a street map of Sante Fe. Although by itself not incriminating, the discovery convinced Gold that he was doomed, and he told the FBI agents, "I am the man to whom Klaus Fuchs gave the information on atomic energy." Although Fuchs had been unable or unwilling initially to identify definitively a photo of Gold as his courier, after additional questioning he agreed that Gold was the courier he had known as Raymond.

In his initial statement, Gold did not speak of meeting any espionage sources other than Fuchs. But under sustained FBI questioning, he told more and more of his career as a Soviet spy, including his own recruitment by Thomas Black, as well as his contacts with Benjamin Smilg and Alfred

Slack and his role as a courier to Abraham Brothman. Confronted by the FBI, Black also confessed to being a longtime industrial spy for the USSR but since the information he had provided did not affect national defense, he was never indicted. (Not until the Economic Espionage Act of 1996 did Congress pass a comprehensive statute clearly defining industrial espionage as a crime.)

The Trials of Brothman, Moskowitz, Smilg, and Slack

Abraham Brothman was arrested and charged with obstruction of justice for the false story he had devised in 1947. His business partner, Miriam Moskowitz, who had cooperated in the deception, was also charged with conspiracy to obstruct justice. Their trial began on November 8, 1950. Harry Gold provided detailed testimony against both of them, including his colluding with Brothman to lie to the U.S. grand jury in 1947. Elizabeth Bentley also testified to her earlier espionage contact with Brothman. Neither Brothman nor Moskowitz testified in his or her own defense, and their attorney could only attempt, with little success, to undercut the credibility of Gold and Bentley. After less than four hours of deliberation, a jury convicted them on November 22, 1950. On November 28 Federal Judge Irving R. Kaufman sentenced Brothman to seven years in prison (later reduced to two) while Moskowitz received two years. Their legal appeals failed, and both went to prison. In a minor footnote to the Brothman-Moskowitz trial, in 1952 Oscar John Vago, another business associate of Brothman, pleaded guilty to lying to a grand jury that questioned him about his relationship with Brothman. His perjury had nothing to do with espionage, however, and he received a three-year suspended sentence and was placed on probation. Although Vago presented himself at the time of his trial as an opponent of communism, when he died in 1986, his obituary revealed he had been a Communist since 1935.

The FBI arrested Alfred Slack, another Gold associate, on June 15, 1950, and on September 1, 1950, a grand jury indicted him for espionage. Faced with Gold's detailed testimony about his activities for the Soviets, Slack confessed that he had provided Gold with technical information from 1940 to 1944, receiving payment of $200 per report. Federal prosecutors, in light of Slack's quick confession, asked for a ten-year sentence. But on September 22 U.S. Judge Robert L. Taylor, noting that American soldiers in Korea were then fighting and dying in combat with Communist troops, rejected leniency and sentenced Slack to fifteen years.

Benjamin Smilg, working as a research aeronautical engineer at a government aviation laboratory at Wright-Paterson Air Force Base in Ohio, was called before government loyalty board hearings and asked about his relationship with Gold. Smilg acknowledged meeting with Gold but denied knowing that Gold was engaged in espionage. He was suspended from his job, and in 1952 a U.S. grand jury indicted Smilg for perjury for denying knowledge of Gold's status as a spy. Gold was the chief witness against Smilg at a subsequent trial in November held in Dayton, Ohio. Gold testified that, although he had approached Smilg several times, Smilg had refused to provide espionage data. Smilg testified that he had thought Gold was some sort of a radical "screwball" rather than a spy. Smilg's lawyer convinced the jury that Smilg could not have been sure that Gold was a spy and that, at any rate, he should get credit for refusing to provide espionage information. The jury acquitted Smilg on November 21, 1952.

The Arrests of the Greenglasses, the Rosenbergs, and Morton Sobell

Under additional FBI interrogation, on June 1, 1950, Gold noted he had met with an unidentified soldier in Albuquerque in June 1945. Pressed by bureau interviewers, within a few days he had provided a description and some details about this person who had given him material from Los Alamos. He did not, however, know the man's name. Based on a decrypted Venona cable, the FBI was already searching for someone cover-named Caliber, who worked at Los Alamos and had a Communist wife, cover-named Osa. They had spent time together near Los Alamos during his leave in late November 1944 and Caliber had been in New York in January 1945. Although the FBI initially thought it might be Theodore Hall, by mid-June, they had identified David Greenglass as the most likely suspect.

After his discharge from the army in 1946, Greenglass had returned to the Lower East Side of New York and gone into business with his brother-in-law, Julius Rosenberg. Their machine shop had not done well. In early 1950, after Fuchs's arrest, Julius warned David that he might have to flee the country; after Gold's arrest, Julius provided David with a large amount of cash and a plan to flee to Russia via Mexico. By this time, however, Greenglass had lost much of his earlier vision of the USSR as an ideal society. He and Ruth also now had two young children and, additionally, Ruth had recently sustained serious burns in a kitchen fire. Faced with this situation, Greenglass made no preparations for the family to flee and waited passively to see what fate handed to him. Picked up for questioning by the FBI, he confessed as soon as he was told that Harry Gold had identified him, implicating his wife, Ruth, his brother-in-law, Julius Rosenberg, and his sister, Ethel. In light of her husband's confession, Ruth also immediately confessed.

Hoping to capitalize on the momentum of Gold's and Greenglass's quick confessions, the FBI questioned Julius Rosenberg, who denied everything, asked for a lawyer, and, upon being informed that he was not under arrest, left the federal building. The only direct evidence available to the FBI was David's confession, and it was still not clear if he would cooperate fully with the government. But facing lengthy prison terms and separation from their infant children and no longer being ardent about communism, both of the Greenglasses decided to provide complete information, including about their relatives, in return for a promise that Ruth would not be prosecuted (she was named as an unindicted co-conspirator). The Korean War, meanwhile, had broken out at the end of June, and public hostility toward anyone assisting the Communist enemy quickly reached fever levels. In mid-July Ruth told the FBI that Julius had asked her to persuade David to spy at Los Alamos in Ethel Rosenberg's presence and that Harry Gold had identified himself as a courier using the recognition arranged by Julius. Julius Rosenberg was arrested and charged with conspiracy to commit espionage. The evidence against Ethel was thin; according to the Greenglasses she had been present when conversations about espionage took place. But that still left her legally vulnerable to a charge of participating in a conspiracy to commit espionage, and the government believed that charges against her might be a lever to get her husband to talk and expose the various tendrils of the far-flung network of agents he had supervised and of which he had boasted to David Greenglass. After two appearances before a grand jury, during which she relied on the Fifth Amendment to refuse to answer questions, Ethel Rosenberg was arrested.

The arrests also threw light on several of the Venona decryptions that had puzzled investigators. One fragment decoded in 1948 concerned an attempt in 1944 by a KGB agent with the cover name Antenna to recruit a man named Max Elitcher, who worked at the Navy Bureau of Ordnance, for espionage. The FBI learned that Elitcher and his close friend, Morton Sobell, had been investigated as possible Communist security risks in 1941 during the period of the Nazi-Soviet Pact. Sobell was in the process of helping Elitcher land a job at the firm where he worked on classified projects and find a home near his own in New York. The investigation did not turn up any useful information in 1948 but by 1950 it was clear that Julius Rosenberg was the Antenna who had tried to recruit Elitcher. Shaken by Rosenberg's arrest and disconcerted by the disappearance of his friend Sobell, Elitcher confessed that Julius had first contacted him about spying in 1944 and continued to make overtures for several years. Sobell had been present at several of these attempted recruitments and, on one occasion, Julius had told him that Sobell was providing information for the Soviets. Elitcher maintained that he had consistently refused to help his old classmates from CCNY.

Morton Sobell was another City College electrical engineer who had gone from the Communist Party into the service of Soviet intelligence. A close friend of Julius Rosenberg, like Elitcher he had worked for the Navy Ordnance Bureau in Washington. After obtaining an M.A. from the University of Michigan, he went to work for General Electric. Rosenberg recruited him as a spy in the summer of 1944, and he regularly turned over microfilm on sonar, infrared radiation devices, and missile guidance systems. The FBI's interest in him stemmed from his association with Elitcher, but not until the latter admitted that Julius had used Sobell's spying as a way to reassure Elitcher was there any evidence to implicate Sobell himself. Elitcher recounted several occasions when Sobell had arranged his meetings with Rosenberg. He recalled one dramatic episode about a house-hunting trip to New York just before he left his navy job in Washington. The Elitchers were planning on staying at Sobell's home but became convinced that their car was being followed. They made a detour to visit relatives and then drove to the Sobells. At first, Sobell was angry that Elitcher might have led the FBI to him, but he eventually confided that he had some important material for Julius and, rather than throw it away, he persuaded Elitcher to drive with him to Lower Manhattan, near the Rosenberg apartment. He waited in the car while Sobell delivered a canister of film. The FBI had, in fact, been tailing the Elitchers during that trip but had broken off the surveillance because it appeared that it had been detected.

As for Morton Sobell, he stopped going to work the day newspapers heralded David Greenglass's arrest and a week later vanished with his family. They flew to Mexico City, where they cashed in their return tickets and, using assumed names, attempted to book passage on ships heading to Europe. The task was complicated, however, by the family's having left the United States without passports. In mid-August all four of them were picked up by armed men (assumed to be Mexican security police), driven in a car to the Texas border, and dumped into the waiting arms of the FBI. The bureau placed Sobell under arrest on charges of conspiring to commit espionage with Julius Rosenberg. Unfortunately for Sobell, he was quickly labeled an atomic spy in the press even though his espionage had been directed to conventional military technology, and he had never had anything to do with Rosenberg's and Greenglass's atomic espionage.

The Disappearance of Joel Barr and Alfred Sarant

Another Venona message decrypted in 1948 identified Joel Barr as a Rosenberg recruit in 1944, when he had worked for a defense contractor. He too had graduated from CCNY around the same time as Sobell, Elitcher, and Rosenberg, had been a Communist Party member in 1944, and had worked on classified military research as late as 1947, before losing his job in a security investigation. In 1948 the FBI learned that he was living in Europe. Then, immediately after David Greenglass's arrest, Barr vanished from his Paris apartment, leaving behind his personal belongings.

In the course of investigating Barr, the FBI became interested in several of his friends, notably Alfred Sarant. An electrical engineer who had graduated from Cooper Union in New York, Sarant had met fellow Communist Barr when they both worked for the U.S. Army Signal Corps on military electronics at Fort Monmouth, New Jersey. Sarant was working in the physics laboratories at Cornell University and lived in a house next to Philip Morrison, a Cornell physicist and former Manhattan Project scientist who was a personal and political friend. Sarant was evasive with the FBI; after first denying that he knew Julius well, he admitted that he once thought he was being propositioned for espionage by Julius but did not bite. He held the lease on a Greenwich Village apartment that David Greenglass claimed had been used to microfilm and photograph documents. As the FBI continued its investigation, it maintained surveillance of Sarant, but with the aid of relatives, he evaded his watchers and fled the country, leaving behind his wife and young children but taking with him the wife of a neighbor, who also abandoned her children. The FBI traced the fleeing couple to Mexico, but there they disappeared. Numerous additional decrypted Venona messages established beyond any doubt that, working as a team, Barr and Sarant had been valuable sources of industrial and military secrets for the Soviets from 1942 until at least

1945 and probably later as well, supplying the USSR with technical plans for advanced American military electrical avionics and radar.

The fate of Barr and Sarant remained unknown until 1983, when a Soviet émigré linked them to two leading Soviet electronic scientists who were native speakers of English. One, Philip Staros (Sarant) died in 1979. The other, Joseph Berg (Barr) returned to the United States in 1992 after the collapse of the USSR. In 1950 the KGB had exfiltrated Barr from France and Sarant and his paramour from Mexico and relocated them to Communist Czechoslovakia with new identities. But in 1956 the Soviets relocated them to the Soviet Union and set them up as heads of a military electronics research institute that pioneered the microelectronics industry in the USSR and produced the first generation of electronic and radar guidance systems for Soviet antiaircraft missiles and submarines. Due the difficulty of gathering admissible evidence after a lapse of more than forty-five years, Barr was not prosecuted even after his return to the United States. He stayed long enough to apply for American social security benefits but returned to Russia and died there in 1998 still loyal to communism.

The Trial of William Perl

Another Rosenberg friend did not disappear but entrapped himself. William Perl was also a CCNY engineer and the most scientifically successful of the entire group. He obtained a Ph.D. from Columbia University and was working on jet propulsion (new in the mid-1940s) and supersonic air flight for the National Advisory Committee on Aeronautics (predecessor to the National Aeronautics and Space Administration) in Cleveland. At the time Perl came to the FBI's attention he was under consideration for a high-level scientific post with the Atomic Energy Commission. Perl initially interested the FBI because he had roomed with Sarant while attending graduate school. In an initial interview, he denied knowing Julius Rosenberg. Just a few days later, however, Perl telephoned the FBI and accused the agency of trying to entrap him. He recounted a story that a woman he knew slightly, Vivian Glassman, had arrived at his Cleveland apartment, signaled that she did not want to speak because the room might be bugged, indicated she knew Rosenberg, wrote out a note that someone had instructed her to fly from New York to Cleveland and give him $2,000 in cash and instructions on leaving the United States. Perl claimed that he had ordered her to leave and destroyed the note before calling the

FBI. Perl appeared to have thought he was under FBI surveillance and panicked at the possibility that his meeting with Glassman, a courier for the KGB, had been spotted. His call to the FBI was an attempt to give Glassman's meeting a benign explanation. The FBI, however, had not had Perl under surveillance, and his call only served to alert the bureau that Perl was far more deeply involved in the Rosenberg spy apparatus than it had realized.

Vivian Glassman told the FBI the same improbable story, claiming that a mystery man had approached her and explained that he had helped her former boyfriend, Joel Barr, get to Europe. On that basis she had traveled on her own money to Cleveland under an assumed name. She also said that after her return to New York, this person had come by her apartment and picked up the money Perl had refused and then disappeared. She also admitted knowing the Rosenbergs. Although it was clear to the FBI that both Perl and Glassman were lying – they knew each other well, for one thing – and that they were both up to their necks in an espionage conspiracy, there was insufficient admissible evidence to support indictments. Called before a grand jury, Glassman refused to answer any questions unless she was granted immunity. Prosecutors had her followed, called her back to testify several times, threatened her with contempt, but were unable to elicit any information. She was never indicted.

Perl was less shrewd. Called to testify before the grand jury in mid-August 1950, he did not take the Fifth Amendment but did deny knowing either Julius Rosenberg or Morton Sobell. Although there was still insufficient evidence to indict him for espionage, those egregious lies left him vulnerable to a perjury charge. The FBI was anxious to get another member of Rosenberg's spy ring to confess. David and Ruth Greenglass were peripheral parts of the apparatus, enlisted only because of David's fortuitous posting to Los Alamos. He had not been involved in the extensive military technological espionage that had characterized most of the Rosenberg group's operations. The FBI pressured the Justice Department to arrest Perl for perjury as a way to induce him to talk. Perl, by then a physics professor at Columbia University, was arrested in mid-March 1951, in the middle of the Rosenberg-Sobell trial.

The government still hoped to build an espionage case against Perl. Decrypted Venona messages made clear that he was a productive and valuable source of technical information relating to highly secret jet aircraft design beginning in 1944. His data were so important that, at the

KGB's request, Julius Rosenberg dispatched two of his Communist friends, Michael and Ann Sidorovich, to live in Cleveland in December 1944 with the sole purpose of serving as receivers and couriers for Perl's espionage. But this Venona information could not be used in court.

Shortly after Perl's arrest, a jailhouse informer who had gained Julius Rosenberg's trust told the FBI that Julius had confirmed Perl's espionage role and admitted that the Russians had arranged Glassman's visit. In subsequent conversations, the informer said Julius had mentioned a weekend during which Perl had come back to New York, removed top secret files from the office of his superior at Columbia University, and taken them to an apartment where Rosenberg, Michael Sidorovich, and an unidentified fourth man had photographed them in a marathon session lasting seventeen hours. When the FBI investigated, it learned that Perl had been in New York at the time along with Sidorovich and had checked out large amounts of classified files from the Columbia University laboratories. Although the FBI examined the returned documents for fingerprints, none turned up. Unless one of the participants confessed, the informer's information was not admissible evidence against Perl.

Prosecutors continued to hope that Julius might confess after all his appeals were denied but finally brought Perl to trial on May 19, 1953, shortly before the Rosenbergs' execution. He was charged with four counts of perjury in his grand jury testimony for denying knowing Julius Rosenberg, Morton Sobell, Helene Elitcher (wife of Max Elitcher), and the Sidoroviches. U.S. Attorney Robert Martin introduced evidence that Perl knew all four, including Perl's attendance at a dozen meetings of the electrical engineers section of the Young Communist League at City College when Julius Rosenberg was its president and Morton Sobell one of its most active members. Also testifying was a Cleveland man who stated that Perl and the Sidoroviches came to his home in 1948 and test-drove a car he was selling. Perl contended that although he was acquainted with Rosenberg and Sobell, their relationship was not deep enough for him to really "know" them and that was what he had meant when he denied knowing them in his testimony to the grand jury. He also said he simply had no memory of the Sidoroviches. As for Helene Elitcher, he said he did know her but only as Max Elitcher's wife and had not realized when he was asked about Helene Elitcher that this was Max's wife. The jury acquitted him on the counts of perjury in regard to Helene Elitcher and the Sidoroviches, convicted him on the two counts of denying knowing Rosenberg and Sobell, and urged clemency to the judge. Judge Sylvester Ryan, however, brushed aside the clemency request, calling Perl's testimony an "affront to mature minds" and stated that in his grand jury testimony Perl "had willfully and knowingly given false testimony." He imposed a five-year sentence. In February 1954 a unanimous three-judge U.S. Appeals Court affirmed Perl's conviction. The court opinion, written by Judge Harold R. Medina, stated, "It is a deplorable fact that this young man of such promise and ability should have become so enmeshed in the toils [of espionage] as to willfully testify falsely before a grand jury of the United States embarked upon an investigation of Soviet espionage; but on this record, free from any taint of error, he has justly been found guilty of that offense."

Theodore Hall and Saville Sax Avoid Arrest

In April 1950, just as the investigation into the Rosenberg ring was gathering steam, government cryptographers broke a KGB message from November 1944 reporting on Ted Hall's and Saville Sax's initial contact with Soviet intelligence. The message gave their names in plain text, describing Hall as "19 years old . . . a graduate of Harvard University . . . a talented physicist [who] . . . handed over to Bek [KGB agent Sergey Kurnakov] a report about the Camp [KGB cover name for Los Alamos] and named the key personnel employed on Enormoz [KGB cover name for the U.S. atomic bomb project]." By early May intensive FBI inquiries had established that Hall was the spy cover-named Mlad in other cables and that his movements and background perfectly matched the information in the cables.

After leaving Los Alamos in 1946, Hall had begun graduate work at the University of Chicago. He soon married, after telling his future wife about his spying. He and his wife joined the Communist Party in 1948, and Hall asked Saville Sax, now living in New York, to let the Soviets know about his decision to join the CPUSA, which he assumed would end his usefulness to the Soviet Union. Meanwhile, in March 1948, Klaus Fuchs, living in Britain, had made his second contact with Soviet intelligence since 1945 and told them that American scientists were working on a hydrogen bomb and that much of the theoretical work was being done at Chicago. On a trip to New York in August 1948, Hall heard from Sax that the Soviets wanted to reactivate him. After a clandestine meeting, he agreed and over the next eighteen months he induced two other scientists to help the Soviets and regularly traveled to New York to meet with KGB officers.

The KGB so valued this network of volunteers that it sent a new illegal officer to New York to oversee its activities. Born William Fischer to émigré Russians living in Great Britain, he became better known after his arrest as Colonel Rudolf Abel. He arrived in the United States in November 1948 and by 1949 was directing Morris and Lona Cohen, who supervised the espionage activities of Hall, his two scientist friends, and at least two other sources as yet unknown. Late that fall, Abel met with the Halls, who were once again anxious to end their ties to Soviet intelligence. Although he pleaded with them to continue, in February 1950, shortly after the birth of his daughter, Ted Hall resumed open political activities in the pro-Communist Progressive Party. Saville Sax was also publicly active in Communist affairs. Their decision to end their espionage was fortuitous, coming just a few weeks before Hall and Sax became FBI targets.

When the FBI questioned Harry Gold about the soldier he had contacted in Albuquerque, Hall and Sax were originally on the short list of suspects. But Gold did not identify a picture of either one, and David Greenglass was soon tabbed as the man who had provided him with information. That Hall and Sax were now openly involved with leftist causes suggested that they had ceased spying; the Venona messages were useless as legal evidence and, absent catching them in the act, there was no way to prove that they had done anything. Only their own confessions or the testimony of their accomplices could implicate them. Because both Hall and Sax were publicly active in Communist causes, it seemed unlikely that they would cooperate with the FBI. Their accomplices were unknown.

The FBI's investigation of Hall and Sax went on for more than a year but produced no significant leads. Finally, in March 1951, in the middle of the Rosenberg trial, both men were picked up in Chicago and questioned simultaneously. Both denied espionage, claimed to be unable to identify a photograph of their Soviet contact, and had innocent, if not convincing, explanations for any of their suspicious activities. After the first interview, Hall refused to cooperate or answer any more questions. Faced with his stonewalling, the FBI had hit a dead end. The bureau continued its surveillance. Hall and Sax meanwhile unsuccessfully tried to get in touch with the Cohens, who had been Hall's couriers for years.

In fact, what neither Hall nor the FBI knew was that Morris and Lona Cohen had already fled the country. The Cohens received word from their KGB superior to leave in late June 1950 shortly after David Greenglass had been picked up for questioning. They left New York in early July, traveled first to Mexico, and, after an odyssey through numerous countries with false passports, arrived in Moscow in November 1950. They would resume their espionage in the West within a few years.

By early 1952 Hall was able to reestablish contact with Soviet intelligence. At its suggestion, he soon moved to New York, where he held several meetings with Soviet agents over the next year and a half. Shortly before the Rosenbergs' execution in June 1953, the man who had given the KGB far more valuable atomic information than that provided by the Rosenberg ring suggested to his KGB controller that he should confess to save them from the electric chair. He was dissuaded. In the fall of 1953, no longer under investigation, the Soviet Union having exploded its own thermonuclear device, Hall told the Russians that he was ending his work for them.

The Trials of Gold, the Rosenbergs, Sobell, and Greenglass

While Ted Hall waited to see if the government would arrest him for atomic espionage, the focus of the entire nation was directed at the members of the Rosenberg ring, accused of stealing the secrets of the atomic bomb and transmitting them to the Soviet Union. The first person to be convicted was Harry Gold. The trial, before U.S. Judge James P. McGranery in Philadelphia was short: prosecutors read the charge, Gold pleaded guilty, and most of the trial was taken up with his presentencing arraignment. On December 9, 1950, Gold, despite his cooperation with the government, received a thirty-year sentence, five more years than the prosecution had recommended. Judge McGranery stated he wanted the sentence to stand as a statement of the seriousness of espionage against the United States and a deterrent for others.

The joint trial of Julius and Ethel Rosenberg and Morton Sobell opened on March 6, 1951. In an effort to put pressure on Julius Rosenberg to confess, name the other members of his spy ring (many of whom the government knew from the Venona decryptions), and provide the legal evidence that would enable their prosecution, Ethel Rosenberg had already been arrested and charged with the same crimes as her husband. That ploy had not worked. Prosecutors concluded that only the threat of death might shake Rosenberg's resolve, and they decided to ask for the death penalty. But, in order to do that, they would have to establish that the information that David Greenglass provided to Harry Gold at the behest of Julius Rosenberg was significant and had done major damage to American security interests. That raised the unwelcome prospect of government witnesses detailing classified information on the witness stand and assisting the Soviet Union's nuclear program. The Atomic Energy Commission, guardian of the secrets of the atomic bomb, did not want Greenglass to go into any detail about either the shape of the implosion lens mold or even mention the plutonium experiments about which he had told Julius. Prosecutors fretted that without details the jury might minimize the importance of the information, while the commission worried that defense attorneys would aggressively attempt to get as much classified information on the record as possible in an attempt to blackmail the government into dropping the case.

The government's original strategy was to establish the broad outlines of the Rosenberg espionage ring, demonstrating that its tentacles reached into a variety of military and industrial laboratories. The presence of Sobell in the dock along with the Rosenbergs was evidence of this tactic, as was the prosecution's list of potential witnesses – Vivian Glassman, William Perl, the Sidoroviches, and Louise Sarant (Alfred's abandoned wife), among others. None of these people had any direct involvement with Greenglass's atomic espionage, but they would place Julius Rosenberg at the center of an extensive spy ring that had its roots in the Communist Party. Shortly before trial, however, the prosecutors changed their plans. They may have been concerned that many of these potential witnesses would take the Fifth Amendment, and either confuse the jury or leave it unsure about the government's case.

Moreover, the chief prosecution witnesses added two new details to their recollections – details that strengthened the case against both of the Rosenbergs. During his initial interviews with the FBI, Harry Gold could not recall if the name of Julius Rosenberg had ever come up when he met with the Greenglasses in Albuquerque. He did allow that when he met with a contact, he usually brought "greetings" from someone as a recognition signal. At first, he thought it might have been "Ben." After a meeting with David Greenglass, he agreed that he might have identified himself as bringing "greetings from Julius." Not until the day before the trial began was he sure, and he so testified. While useful to the prosecutors, this bit of evidence only marginally strengthened their already compelling case against Julius.

More significant was new information provided by the Greenglasses that further implicated Ethel Rosenberg. Government prosecutors had long considered the evidence they could use against her in court to be weak. Ruth Greenglass had told the FBI that Ethel had been present when Julius had asked her to get David to provide information and had urged her not to discourage her husband and let him make up his own mind about the risks he would be taking. Ethel had also been present when Julius had divided the Jell-O box to be used as a recognition signal. Yet the FBI regarded Ethel simply as an accessory to her husband, and her arrest had been justified largely as a means to pressure Julius to talk.

Late in February 1951, both David and Ruth Greenglass told the FBI that in September 1945, when David, in New York on furlough, gave Julius handwritten notes and a sketch of the plutonium bomb, Julius had asked Ethel to type up the material, and she did so on a table in the Rosenbergs' living room. Ruth also claimed that Ethel had told her earlier that she typed all of Julius's material. David had previously insisted to the FBI that Ethel had never been present when he gave Julius material. Whether their memories had improved or they had invented a new story, their testimony about Ethel typing the espionage material would be the most damaging evidence presented at the trial tying her directly to espionage.

A September 1944 Venona decryption showed the KGB station in New York reporting that Ethel Rosenberg had recommended recruiting her sister-in-law, Ruth Greenglass, clearly evidence of Ethel's knowledge and involvement in her husband's espionage, but Venona could not be used in court. Another Venona decryption indicated that Ethel was aware of her husband's activities and those of other members of his espionage network, but due to her health she did not work. Ethel was also never given a cover name. While her role in Julius's espionage ring was peripheral, her knowledge of its existence and her participation in helping to recruit her brother and sister-in-law made her technically and legally a member of the conspiracy. Whether the jury would have convicted her without the Greenglasses' typing testimony is an open question, but it certainly helped the prosecution decide to present a more streamlined case.

The Rosenberg-Sobell trial began on March 6, 1951, in federal court in New York City. Judge Irving R. Kaufman, a Truman appointee, presided. U.S. Attorney Irving Saypol served as the chief prosecutor, assisted by Roy Cohn. (Cohn became well known later as a flamboyant aide to Senator Joseph McCarthy.) The first witness was Max Elitcher. He recounted how both Julius Rosenberg and Morton Sobell urged him to commit espionage. He also told the story of his trip to New York in 1948 during which he thought he had been followed and the subsequent car ride with Sobell to drop off microfilm at Rosenberg's apartment. He added that after Sobell returned to the automobile he had asked him if Elizabeth Bentley, then in the news for her revelations of Soviet espionage, had known Julius. Sobell had replied that Julius had spoken to her once on the telephone, but they had never met, so he thought she did not know who he was. On cross-examination, Elitcher admitted that he had not provided the Bentley story to the FBI in his initial statements. He also conceded that he had cooperated with the government because he was afraid of a prosecution for perjury for having lied about never being a member of the Communist Party during his security clearance by the navy.

Elizabeth Bentley later corroborated Elitcher's story. She testified that from the fall of 1942, Jacob Golos, her lover and KGB agent, had been in contact with an engineer living on the Lower East Side of Manhattan. Bentley said that she had received a half dozen phone calls from a man identifying himself as Julius who requested meetings with Golos. Although Bentley had given the FBI additional details provided by Golos about this contact that pointed to Julius Rosenberg, she was not allowed to testify to them because they were based on what Golos had told her (hearsay testimony) rather than her own observation.

Elitcher's damaging testimony against Sobell was virtually the entire case presented against him. Later in the trial, prosecutors introduced evidence that Sobell had arranged for a friend to serve as a mail drop for letters he sent to his relatives from Mexico, a story that undercut Sobell's claims that he had not fled the country after the Greenglasses' arrest but had merely gone on a family vacation. They also produced witnesses who established his use of aliases in Mexico and that he had sought ways to leave the country without proper papers.

Sobell, however, was clearly a sideshow. There were no allegations that he had anything to do with atomic espionage. He had never worked on the Manhattan Project, and no testimony linked him to David Greenglass. Neither of the Greenglasses nor Harry Gold had anything to say about him. He represented the military technology portion of the Rosenberg spy network, the one the FBI desperately wanted to crack open through Julius Rosenberg's confession. In many ways, it was Julius's more important espionage work. His involvement in atomic spying was largely accidental, due to his brother-in-law's posting to Los Alamos. And, in light of the material that Fuchs and Ted Hall had given to the Russians, it was of secondary importance, although not insignificant. Prosecutors, however, had a compelling interest in portraying the Rosenbergs as major atomic spies and were aided in their efforts by the incompetence of the defense attorneys and the classified mysteries of the atomic bomb.

The prosecution might not have been able to achieve its goals without a series of blunders by the defense. Emmanuel Bloch was a left-wing lawyer who had represented Steve Nelson during his appearance before congressional investigating committees. His father represented Ethel. The Blochs faced daunting problems. Their clients had both been Communists but to admit that might inflame the jury, given the anti-Communist fervor in the country while the Korean War raged in Asia. To deny party ties, however, would open up the danger of perjury charges. None of the attorneys possessed any technical knowledge, and the defense had no access to experts during the trial to challenge the importance of the information Greenglass claimed to have provided. Most importantly, Bloch certainly knew or suspected that his client was not innocent of espionage and that there were all sorts of hidden mines that the defense had to avoid.

The first witness after Elitcher was David Greenglass. After introducing sketches of the lens mold drawings he had given to Gold, prosecutors interrupted his testimony to have Walter Koski, an expert on high-explosive lenses from the Atomic Energy Commission, testify about their importance. Koski vouched for the general accuracy of Greenglass's sketches and declared that they would have been of great value to anyone trying to learn what was going on at Los Alamos. When Greenglass returned to the witness stand, he stated that in September 1945 he had given Julius twelve pages of description of the implosion-style bomb and sketches, one of which showed a cross section of the bomb used on Nagasaki. When one of the prosecutors, Roy Cohn, moved to introduce a duplicate copy that Greenglass had sketched the previous week, Bloch asked that it be impounded and kept confidential. And, when Cohn began to question Greenglass about the material accompanying the sketches, Bloch asked that the courtroom be cleared and offered to stipulate that Greenglass had provided information crucial to the national defense. While reporters were not excluded, Bloch's ploy, perhaps intended to demonstrate his and his clients' patriotism, backfired, confirming that Greenglass had provided Julius Rosenberg with crucial and significant information about how to construct an atomic bomb. The prosecutors never had to argue that his material was far from trivial or that it enabled the Russians to build a weapon. The Atomic Energy Commission did not have to worry that a vigorous cross-examination of Koski or Greenglass would put any secret information on the public record and make it available to America's foreign foes.

The Greenglasses were both vulnerable to challenge. David had pled guilty to espionage charges, but his sentencing had been deferred until after the Rosenberg trial. Ruth had been named as an unindicted co-conspirator. They had strong incentives to cooperate with the government. Still, on cross-examination, Greenglass remained composed, and Bloch was unable to shake his story of how Julius had recruited him to spy or how he had directly given him information. Ruth Greenglass confirmed her husband's story. Both husband and wife were adamant that Julius had given them several thousand dollars early in 1950 to prepare to flee to Mexico as the net around the espionage ring began to tighten. The defense suggested that the money was repayment of debts from the business in which Julius and David were partners and tried to hint that financial disagreements and disputes lay behind this family quarrel. Neither explanation had much purchase. When he testified, Julius flatly denied ever giving the Greenglasses large sums of money. But, if Julius had not given them the cash, there was no other explanation for its origins.

Harry Gold had already been sentenced to thirty years in prison for espionage when he appeared in court so that he could hardly be accused of pandering to the government for leniency. Inexplicably, Bloch objected when he described himself as a Soviet spy and demanded proof. That gave prosecutors an opening to have Gold detail his long espionage career and the techniques he had used as a courier, including the combined use of a verbal recognition signal, such as "I come from Julius," and some paper sign, like the cut-up Jell-O box. He described the dual mission he had received from Anatoly Yakovlev in 1945 to obtain data from both Klaus Fuchs in Sante Fe and a new contact in Albuquerque. When he arrived at the apartment on a Sunday morning, the material was not ready and Greenglass asked him to come back later in the day. Both David and Ruth mentioned Julius to Gold at the time. Gold checked into the Hilton Hotel to rest, returned to pick up an envelope and left that evening. He turned over all his material to Yakovlev on June 5, 1945, and later heard from him that Greenglass's material "was extremely excellent and very valuable." Gold then described his final meeting with Yakovlev when his business association with Brothman ended his relationship with Soviet intelligence.

Although Gold had connected the spy ring with an actual Russian agent, the defense chose not to ask him any questions. In his summation Bloch accepted the truth of Gold's testimony but brushed it aside, claiming that this major conspirator had never met Julius Rosenberg and thus had not connected him to espionage. (Gold, in fact, had told prosecutors that, after Fuchs had been arrested, the Soviets had gotten in touch with him and asked him to meet a man in Queens. The meeting did not come off, but Gold believed that Julius resembled the man he was supposed to talk with. Julius may have been afraid that, if pressed, Gold would identify him.) He had, however, linked David Greenglass to Soviet espionage and buttressed the accounts of David and Ruth that Julius was an integral part of the spy network.

Julius Rosenberg was the first defense witness. He described the modest circumstances in which his family lived, strongly denied the Greenglasses' stories about the money he had provided for espionage contacts and expenses, and insisted he had never put David in touch with Russian agents or couriers. He described David as a troublesome individual who had concocted schemes to defraud the army and was an unreliable business partner constantly in need of money. Just before his arrest, David had threatened to make trouble for Julius if he did not provide him with $4,000. While his testimony provided an alternative motive for David's charges – a family feud over money inaugurated by a shiftless troublemaker – the defense did not offer any other witnesses or evidence to buttress it. And Julius's characterization of David's threat as blackmail raised the question of what information David might have that would endanger Julius.

The most significant damage Rosenberg did to his own case stemmed from the issue of communism. In response to a series of questions from his lawyer, Julius fervently avowed his loyalty to the United States and his willingness to fight on its behalf. He insisted that every people had the right to choose its own form of government. But, when Judge Irving Kaufman asked if he had belonged to any group that discussed the Russian form of government, Julius took the Fifth Amendment rather than admit that he had been a member of the Communist Party. On cross-examination, he compounded his difficulties by refusing to answer several challenging questions, including one about whether he knew William Perl, whose arrest for perjury – denying he knew Rosenberg – had just been in the newspapers.

While Rosenberg was testifying, prosecutors also located another witness, a photographer who had taken passport photos of the Rosenberg family in May or June 1950. Julius could not remember such an occasion but conceded it might have occurred. He adamantly denied telling the photographer that the family was planning a trip to France. During rebuttal, the photographer testified that he had made photos in June and that Rosenberg said they were going to France where they had inherited property. His testimony supported David Greenglass's claim that Julius had encouraged him to flee to Mexico and indicated he was preparing to leave the country as well.

Ethel Rosenberg supported her husband's story and denied the tale of espionage recruitment and typing of materials told by the Greenglasses. Like Julius, she claimed the Fifth Amendment when asked about the Communist Party membership of her brother, David. Her own credibility with the jury was seriously wounded, however, when prosecutor Irving Saypol pointed out the contrast between the forthright denials she had made in her testimony about talking to Ruth Greenglass about David's work at Los Alamos and her use of the Fifth Amendment in response to the same questions before the grand jury. Her explanation that she had been frightened before was most certainly true but likely helped convince the jury that she had something to hide.

Not only did Morton Sobell never take the witness stand, but his lawyers presented no defense witnesses. In part, his decision not to testify was based on the fact that the only substantive evidence against him had come from Elitcher. There had been no evidence about what information he had turned over to Julius Rosenberg, and Elitcher had never actually seen him pass anything on. However, if he did take the stand, Sobell would have been confronted with the same dilemma as the Rosenbergs about taking the Fifth Amendment or admitting his Communist ties. And his claim to have gone to Mexico on a family vacation would have been savaged since prosecutors had rebuttal witnesses available to testify that he had left his job unexpectedly and with little advance warning.

The defense struck two themes in its cross-examinations, testimony, and summations. David and Ruth Greenglass were repellent people who were falsely accusing their relatives in order to wriggle out of their own troubles. Max Elitcher was a perjurer, and the government had twisted and shaped innocent behavior to make it seem suspicious. On the other hand, the defense conceded that Harry Gold had told the truth. His testimony, it insisted however, had nothing to do with any of the defendants.

It did not take the jury long to reach a decision. After only a few hours of deliberation, all three defendants were found guilty of conspiring to commit espionage. On April 5, 1951, Judge Kaufman pronounced sentence. He justified the harsh punishments he was imposing by the enormity of the crimes: at a time when the United States was engaged in "a life and death struggle," the Rosenbergs, by "putting into the hands of the Russians" an atom bomb they would not have developed for several years, had caused "the Communist aggression in Korea" and "altered the course of history to the disadvantage of our country." He labeled their crime "worse than murder," judged Ethel an "equal partner," and sentenced both Rosenbergs to be executed. He then gave Morton Sobell thirty years in prison with a recommendation of no parole.

Judge Kaufman was also the sentencing judge in David Greenglass's trial. He had been named a codefendant with the Rosenbergs and Sobell in an October 1950 indictment. Because Greenglass was cooperating with the government, he promptly entered a guilty plea, but sentencing had been deferred until after the Rosenberg-Sobell trial. On April 6, 1951, Kaufman imposed a fifteen-year sentence on David Greenglass despite his lawyer's plea that a heavy penalty would discourage any other conspirators from cooperating with the government.

Years after the case ended, convincing evidence emerged that Judge Kaufman had discussed potential punishments with executive branch officials even while the trial was in progress, a judicial impropriety. There was disagreement within the government about imposing the death penalty on Ethel. She had been indicted largely to coerce her husband and was far less involved in the conspiracy than he was. FBI chief J. Edgar Hoover, for one, was afraid that executing the mother of small children would generate public sympathy and backfire on the government. Judge Kaufman, however, was determined to impose the most stringent penalties. Whether he was motivated by genuine anger at their crime, a desire to curry public favor and publicity for a future appointment to the Supreme Court, or a need to demonstrate that American Jews were disgusted by the activities of Jewish Communists like the defendants, his decision meant that the Rosenbergs would be the only Americans convicted of spying on behalf of a wartime ally to be put to death.

The verdict and sentences were appealed to the Second Circuit Court of Appeals. The Rosenbergs' lawyers charged that the government had not proved that they intended to harm the United States, that much of the case rested on the testimony of accomplices with motives to get leniency, and that Judge Kaufman had been prejudicial. A three-judge panel consisting of Judges Thomas Swan, Harrie Chase, and Jerome Frank, all respected senior judges, heard the appeal on January 10, 1952. Judge Frank, in particular, was known as an outspoken civil libertarian and scholar of the law of evidence in criminal cases. He wrote the opinion in a unanimous decision that confirmed the trial court verdict and rejected the legal arguments of the Rosenbergs' lawyers. Frank's opinion let the death sentences stand but did express concern about the severity of the punishment. In October 1952 the Supreme Court refused to grant certiorari. Later appeals on grounds that Irving Saypol had prejudiced the case with comments he made when William Perl was arrested were also denied. President Eisenhower denied clemency. An independent attorney persuaded Supreme Court Justice William Douglas that the Rosenbergs might have been charged under the wrong law; he claimed that the Atomic Energy Act of 1946 had superseded the Espionage Act of 1917 and that the former law had no provision for a death penalty. While Douglas issued a stay of execution on June 17, 1953, just hours before the Rosenbergs were scheduled to die, the full Supreme Court vacated his order on a six-to-three vote on June 19.

While the legal case made its way through the court system, however, a band of activists and left-wing reporters began a campaign to paint the Rosenbergs as victims of a gigantic government frame-up. At first the Communist Party kept its distance from the Rosenbergs, presumably afraid that they might confess and wary of being further tarred with the brush of espionage. After all, Bernard Chester, the party's liaison to the KGB, who also continued to collect party dues from him after he dropped his open party ties, had introduced Julius to the Russians. Should he decide to save his life by telling the truth, the CPUSA would be in even deeper trouble than it was in the early 1950s.

Once it was clear that the Rosenbergs were willing to be martyrs, Communist support for their cause mushroomed. The Rosenberg case became a worldwide issue, with protests throughout Europe, orchestrated by local Communist parties. This upsurge coincided with the execution of ten prominent leaders of the Czechoslovak Communist Party, most prominently Rudolf Slánský, as American and Zionist spies. Eight of the ten people executed were Jews and, to deflect charges of anti-Semitism, Communists around the world were ordered to emphasize that the Rosenberg trial was an exercise in American anti-Semitism. The Rosenbergs were depicted as two ordinary, nonpolitical Jews being railroaded to their deaths as a warning to anyone thinking of working on behalf of world peace.

The FBI believed that only a confession by Julius Rosenberg would crack open the rest of the espionage network. Up until the evening of their execution, agents were ready to stop the process in return for that confession. Julius and Ethel Rosenberg chose, however, to go to their deaths rather than to tell what they knew about Soviet espionage. They were executed in the electric chair at Sing-Sing Prison in New York on June 19, 1953.

From August 1951 until the present, Rosenberg partisans have attempted to explain away or mitigate the evidence produced in court. Several Rosenberg defenders, notably Walter and Miriam Schneir, argued that David Greenglass's entire story was a fraud, that Harry Gold was a fantasist, and that no espionage had ever taken place. Investigators tried to prove that Greenglass could not have had access to information he claimed or that his data were fabricated or filled with errors. While Greenglass, a practical machinist and not a scientist, did make a variety of technical errors on the witness stand, the Venona decryptions make crystal clear that he was part of spy ring run by Julius Rosenberg on behalf of the Soviet Union. While the claims of the prosecutors, echoed by the judge, that the Rosenbergs had supplied the Soviets with "the secret" of the atom bomb were clearly exaggerated, the information supplied by Greenglass was nevertheless valuable and useful corroboration of what scientists Fuchs and Hall had already provided.

The only issues on which Rosenberg defenders developed a potentially compelling refutation revolved around the issue of Ethel's typing David Greenglass's espionage reports. The release of the FBI's files on the case showed that neither David nor Ruth raised this issue until just before the trial. Moreover, in an interview for a biography published in 2001 David admitted that he didn't remember whether or not he saw Ethel do the typing, but backed up the story that his wife had told. The released files and the Venona decryptions further supported the argument that Ethel had been a minor participant in the espionage ring run by Julius, but a participant nonetheless.

J. Robert Oppenheimer after the Manhattan Project

By the end of World War II, Oppenheimer had traveled far, both politically and organizationally, from the radical professor active in far-left causes in California. His success at Los Alamos had made him a celebrity known to most Americans and a major voice in the formulation of public policy on issues of atomic weaponry and science. He became director of the Institute for Advanced Study at Princeton and a leading adviser to the Atomic Energy Commission. Disillusioned with Soviet Cold War policies, Oppenheimer became identified with liberal anticommunism, although he continued to support efforts to broaden international controls on atomic weapons. Also, for several years he opposed American efforts to develop a thermonuclear hydrogen fusion bomb many times more powerful than the uranium-plutonium fission bomb.

The FBI had continued to investigate Oppenheimer's past, trying to determine the truth behind the Chevalier-Eltenton-Oppenheimer conversations about providing information to the Russians during the war. The FBI questioned George Eltenton in 1946. He admitted that, at the request of the Soviet diplomat Peter Ivanov, he had asked Chevalier to approach Oppenheimer and urge him to give the Soviets information about his scientific work. Chevalier later reported that Oppenheimer had refused and Eltenton so informed Ivanov. Chevalier confirmed the story. As leaks about his role began to circulate in 1947, Eltenton moved to England and refused to discuss the matter for the rest of his life. Although there was no convincing evidence that Oppenheimer was involved in espionage, there was plenty of circumstantial evidence that he had not been forthright with security officials about his own actions and clear and unequivocal evidence that he had lied about the Chevalier incident. In the glow of his successful administration of Los Alamos, the matter did not go any further.

By 1948 the House Committee on Un-American Activities had begun to investigate espionage at the Radiation Laboratory at Berkeley. One of the prime targets was Joseph Weinberg, who had been bugged during the war discussing atomic secrets with Steve Nelson. After the Japanese surrender, the FBI tried to construct a legal case of espionage against Weinberg, but the prime evidence, secretly recorded conversation from bugs and wiretaps, could not be used in court. There was no actual incriminating written material. The army was also reluctant to involve Oppenheimer and Lawrence in a potentially embarrassing case.

Weinberg was called to testify before an executive session of the House Committee on Un-American Activities in 1948, and he denied ever meeting with or talking to Steve Nelson. In a report it released on atomic espionage, the committee identified Weinberg only as Scientist X because of the possibility that he would be indicted for perjury. In public testimony in 1949 Weinberg denied ever belonging to the Communist Party or meeting with Nelson. Several of his graduate school friends refused to answer questions; although they were indicted for contempt of Congress, both Rossi Lomanitz and David Bohm were acquitted.

Weinberg was finally indicted for perjury in 1952. Unable to locate any credible witnesses to testify to his party membership, the government was forced to rely on Paul Crouch, a former Communist organizer turned professional informer whose reputation for truthfulness was shaky. It never introduced the surreptitious recording of Weinberg's conversation with Nelson, since it had been obtained without a warrant. He was found not guilty, even though the full spectrum of evidence shows that he had clearly lied. Weinberg may not have suffered any legal penalty, but he was fired from his teaching job at the University of Minnesota and left academia for a job at an optics firm.

CPUSA official Steve Nelson, who took the Fifth Amendment when questioned about his role in Soviet espionage, was convicted and imprisoned for violating both state and federal sedition acts in the 1950s. The Supreme Court overturned his state conviction on the grounds that federal sedition legislation had superseded state law and overturned his federal conviction on the grounds that the federal law was unconstitutionally broad. To the end of his life, even after leaving the Communist Party at the end of the 1950s, he denied any involvement in espionage. Louise Bransten likewise refused to answer any questions on the grounds of self-incrimination. Martin Kamen denied passing any classified information to the Soviets; there was not enough evidence to indict him.

When the Soviet Union successfully tested an atomic bomb in August 1949, the U.S. government came under intense pressure to begin development of a more powerful thermonuclear bomb. Oppenheimer was opposed for technical, tactical, and moral reasons. His position enraged Lewis Strauss, one of the commissioners of the Atomic Energy Commission. Revelations about Soviet espionage at Los Alamos that soon implicated Klaus Fuchs increased Strauss's concerns and launched him on a campaign to determine if Oppenheimer had facilitated these efforts and was continuing to serve Soviet interests by attempting to prevent America from developing a new weapon. He was aided by persistent unanswered questions about Oppenheimer's associations and actions, most notably the Chevalier incident. When President Eisenhower nominated Strauss as chairman of the Atomic Energy Commission in January 1953, he launched his effort to discredit the man whose policies he despised and whose loyalties he doubted.

By late 1953 with the aid of a staff member of the congressional Joint Committee on Atomic Energy, who wrote a report based on previously obtained FBI material that concluded that "more probably than not J. Robert Oppenheimer is an agent of the Soviet Union," Strauss orchestrated an order from the president directing that Oppenheimer be denied access to classified information. In mid-December Strauss informed Oppenheimer that his security clearance had been suspended based on a number of charges. Strauss offered him the option of resigning as a consultant to the Atomic Energy Commission, obviating the need for an investigation. Oppenheimer, insulted by the implication that he was not fit to serve the government, refused. In response, the commission proffered a statement of charges that rehashed Oppenheimer's associations with Communists and support for Communist causes and the Chevalier incident, and also added his opposition to the development of the hydrogen bomb.

Although he was never indicted or tried by a jury, Oppenheimer faced a security hearing to consider whether he was a loyalty or security risk to the U.S. government. The members of the three-person tribunal that heard the case against him were selected by Strauss, the hearings were held in executive session, his lawyers were never given security clearances and hence were unable to see the raw FBI files to which the hearing board would have access, and the FBI continued to bug his conversations and wiretap his phone calls throughout the process, supplying the information to the Atomic Energy Commission.

The hearing board began its proceedings on April 12, 1954, and took testimony for nearly a month. Although the hearings were conducted in secret, the press reported they were taking place the day after they commenced. In his letter responding to the charges, Oppenheimer admitted to a series of friendships with left-wingers, membership in a variety of Communist-inspired organizations, and making contributions to their causes in the 1930s. He insisted there was nothing sinister or disloyal in these activities and, further, that he had long since changed his views. He adamantly denied ever being a secret member of the Communist Party. While admitting that he should have reported the overture made to him by Chevalier immediately to security personnel, Oppenheimer insisted that it was a casual conversation and that he was sure that Chevalier was not trying to recruit him.

In his testimony, Oppenheimer repeated these claims. On cross-examination, however, he did not fare so well. The Atomic Energy Commission had located a recording of the first time Oppenheimer had told the Chevalier story to army security. It was quite different from the story he had told to the FBI in 1946. Oppenheimer was forced to admit that he had lied, referring to himself as "an idiot" for saying that Chevalier had approached three people working on the Manhattan Project. He acknowledged telling army security that Eltenton had a contact in the Soviet consulate and mentioning microfilm. Oppenheimer now claimed that virtually everything he had recounted in these earlier conversations – except the name of Eltenton – was a lie. Later, Oppenheimer suggested that he might have embroidered the story. In either case, it was not a tale calculated to leave someone with confidence in his judgment. His wife, Kitty, also testified, and disavowed any lingering affection for communism. Numerous eminent scientists, politicians, and businessmen swore to Oppenheimer's good character, including key Manhattan Project scientists, such as Hans Bethe, later to win the Nobel Prize in physics in 1955.

A number of key figures from the Manhattan Project, however, gave testimony that presented Oppenheimer's conduct in an ambiguous light or which reflected resentment or suspicion of Oppenheimer's resistance to developing the hydrogen bomb. General Leslie Groves vouched for Oppenheimer's loyalty and praised his accomplishments at Los Alamos. He explained Oppenheimer's reluctance to name Chevalier as a desire to protect a friend and not to "snitch," but then added his own belief that he had also been trying to protect his brother, Frank. When Groves had extracted Chevalier's name from Oppenheimer in 1943, he had promised to keep confidential the information he had received that Chevalier had approached both Frank and Robert. Although there is both confusion and disagreement about whether Frank was involved, in 1953 Groves believed he had been. While he insisted that he had no second thoughts about granting Robert Oppenheimer a security clearance in 1943, Groves admitted that he "would not clear Dr. Oppenheimer today if I were a member of the Commission."

Nobel Prize winner Ernest Lawrence, formerly Oppenheimer's close colleague at the Berkeley Radiation Laboratory, was too ill to testify. But the hearing board saw an interview with an Atomic Energy Commission investigator in which Lawrence concluded that Oppenheimer had been so wrong about key postwar atomic development issues that he should never have anything to do with making policy. Oppenheimer's lawyers, however, were not allowed to see Lawrence's statement and could not respond to it. Edward Teller, another towering figure in American nuclear physics but a demanding and difficult personality with whom Oppenheimer had had profound political and scientific disagreements, also appeared. Teller denied that Oppenheimer was disloyal but added that "I would like to see the vital interests of this country in hands which I understand better and therefore trust more." Both Lawrence and Teller had been deeply angered by Oppenheimer's opposition to development of the hydrogen fusion bomb.

At the end of May, the board found by a two-to-one vote that Oppenheimer was a security risk. The majority cited its lack of confidence in his judgments and a lack of candor in his testimony. By a four-to-one vote, the commissioners of the Atomic Energy Commission agreed, although they dropped any discussion of his opposition to an H-bomb and focused on the Chevalier incident and his associations with his Communist graduate students. While careful to deny that they were imputing disloyalty to Oppenheimer, their decision, coming just a day before his security clearance would have expired anyway, was clearly a punishment imposed less to protect American security than to humiliate someone who had been less than candid about his associations over the years and had become entrapped in his own falsehoods. Unlike those convicted of crimes, Oppenheimer faced no legal penalties after his hearing. He returned to the prestigious Institute for Advanced Study, remained an honored and prominent scientist, and received the Fermi Prize from President Lyndon Johnson in 1964, just four years before his death from cancer.

Although new evidence has emerged from Russian archives, once-confidential FBI files, and memoirs of former friends making clear that Oppenheimer was quite probably a secret member of the Communist Party, there has been no "smoking gun" indicating that he spied for the Soviet Union. He may well have talked incautiously to Communist friends, including Steve Nelson, prior to his appointment to oversee work at Los Alamos, but there is no indication that he turned over material about what was going on there. Although he hired some scientists with Communist connections, there is likewise no evidence that he had anything to do with the employment of Fuchs and Hall, much less Greenglass, whose cooperation with the KGB enabled the Russians to make dramatic advances in building their own atomic bomb.

While the archives of the Soviet intelligence agencies remain closed to research, the Russian government in the 1990s released a number of documents dealing with the content of the atomic intelligence delivered to the Soviet atomic bomb project. These documents do not provide much in the way of direct clues about who gave the information to the USSR but do show that the KGB and GRU sources provided the Soviets with rich and highly valuable information. However, Oppenheimer did not just know the secrets of some parts of the atomic bomb project. As scientific director at Los Alamos he knew all of the secrets, and knew all of them nearly as soon as they were created. Had Oppenheimer been an active Soviet source, the quality and quantity of what the Soviet Union learned most likely would have been greater that it actually was. Further, even in regard to what secrets the USSR did learn, if Oppenheimer had been a source, the Soviets would have learned them significantly sooner than they actually appeared to have done. But neither can it be ruled out that early in the Manhattan Project, prior to his going to security officials in 1943, he may have assisted the entrance into the project of younger colleagues whom he had good reason to suspect might be involved in or would attempt espionage.

The Trials of Rudolf Abel and Morris and Lona Cohen

The FBI began an investigation of Morris and Lona Cohen in October 1953, on the basis of a tip that they were Communists. Although they could not be found, the bureau had no suspicion that they were involved in espionage and closed the case in the fall of 1956. One year later, they were once again of interest to the FBI because of their ties to Rudolf Abel, the KGB illegal officer who had entered the United States in 1948 to oversee Ted Hall's work and lived quietly in New York under a variety of aliases, including Emil Goldfus, posing as a photographer and painter, before he was uncovered.

Abel's chief assistant, Reino Hayhanen, a KGB lieutenant colonel of Finnish background, had been sent to the United States in October 1952 using false papers identifying him as an American of Finnish ancestry. He quickly established his cover, living with a Finnish woman he had married who had no idea her husband was a spy. Hayhanen worked as a KGB courier and field man, servicing "dead drops" around the New York area where sources left information or picked up KGB material. In 1954 the KGB assigned Hayhanen to work as Abel's assistant, but the two did not get along. Abel regarded his assistant's work as bordering on the incompetent. Hayhanen began to drink heavily and after several of his miscues frustrated missions Abel had undertaken, Hayhanen was recalled to Moscow in 1957. Hayhanen, however, had acquired a taste for life in the West and suspected that Abel's reports on his performance would cripple his career prospects in Moscow. On the way back to Moscow via France, he defected, walking into the American embassy in Paris and offering to tell all in exchange for a new life in the United States. The offer was accepted.

On the basis of Hayhanen's information and after weeks of intensive surveillance of Abel's photographic studio in Brooklyn, the FBI followed him to a hotel he was using and arranged his arrest by the Immigration and Naturalization Service on June 21, 1957. In his possession were cipher pads, recognition signals, and other spy paraphernalia. Agents also found money and pictures of a couple Abel said were friends. Within a few weeks, the couple was identified as Morris and Lona Cohen. A safe-deposit box Abel used contained $15,000 in small bills and a recognition signal for use in meeting another spy. A witness told the FBI that Abel had been present at a dinner party given by the Cohens in 1950. Now convinced that the missing couple was linked to Soviet espionage but still unaware that they had supervised Ted Hall, the FBI sent their fingerprints to friendly intelligence services around the world.

Abel himself had been arrested by the Immigration and Naturalization Service as an illegal alien and held in Texas on deportation charges in the hope that he would decide to cooperate with the government and become a double agent. That ploy failed, however. While he admitted that he had entered the country illegally and was willing to accept deportation, the material found in his rooms and safe-deposit box incriminated him, and he was charged with conspiracy to gather and transmit national security information to the Soviet Union and living in the United States without registering as a foreign agent. On August 7, newspaper headlines trumpeted the arrest of a KGB colonel.

Abel's court-appointed lawyer, James Donovan, was himself a former intelligence officer, a veteran of the OSS. His one hope for freeing his client was to get the evidence of Abel's espionage seized by the government ruled inadmissible and not allowed to be presented in court. Because the Immigration and Naturalization Service had originally arrested Abel, Donovan argued that without a search warrant or an indictment for espionage, the FBI had no right to search his room and seize any espionage material. The only things it could legally have taken were items demonstrating that Abel was in the United States illegally. Government agents had also not read Abel his rights, inasmuch as they were anxious to get him to cooperate. Judge Mortimer W. Byers didn't agree with the argument, however, and Donovan's motion was denied and Abel was ordered to stand trial.

The trial began on October 14, 1957. Abel faced the death penalty. The most damaging testimony came from his former assistant, Hayhanen, who identified him as the man he knew as "Mark," a KGB colonel and his superior officer. Although Hayhanen told a complicated story of numerous meetings, drop locations, hidden messages, and assignments, he was not aware of any specific national defense or atomic information gathered by any of Abel's sources. Among the items he turned over to the government were "a short wave radio, earphones, a lens and copper plate for making microdots, a box of spectroscopic film," and hollowed coins used to hide microdots. (In one of the odder aspects of the case, even before Hayhanen defected, the FBI had been alerted to the presence of a spy in Brooklyn when a newsboy found a hollowed nickel in change he collected along his newspaper route in 1953. The nickel contained microfilm, and the newspaper boy promptly turned it in to the police, who contacted the FBI. The microfilm was a photograph of a cipher pad. Only after the FBI arrested Abel was it able to link the hollow nickel to him. What act of carelessness or accident had allowed the nickel to get away from Abel was never determined.) The FBI had also seized false birth certificates, hollowed tie clasps and cuff links, a block of wood inside of which were 250 pages of a "one-time pad" (a sophisticated cipher system), a hollowed-out pencil containing eighteen microfilms that included radio schedules, and letters from Abel's wife and daughter in the USSR.

Hayhanen may not have been aware of any particular secrets obtained by Abel's agents but did testify about an unsuccessful effort to locate a U.S. Army sergeant named Roy Rhodes, cover-named Quebec. Rhodes later testified that while serving at the American embassy in Moscow in 1952 he had been sexually compromised (a tactic known in the espionage trade as a "honey trap") while drunk and blackmailed into serving as a Soviet source. After returning to the United States, he had broken off contact with the Soviets; Abel and Hayhanen had been attempting to reestablish ties. Hayhanen also testified that the two KGB officers had buried $5,000 in Bear Mountain Park in New York to be given to Helen Sobell, wife of the Rosenbergs' convicted codefendant. After the trial, the FBI located a tiny piece of microfilm among some of Abel's possessions; it confirmed Hayhanen's claim, although he was forced to admit that he had embezzled the money rather than turn it over to her.

The only hope for the defense was to discredit Hayhanen. Donovan established that he had been married in Russia prior to his cover marriage and had never received a divorce. He went over the various domestic disputes and alcoholic episodes that characterized Hayhanen's life and emphasized his often inept and sloppy work on behalf of the Soviet Union. When one prosecution witness, an artist who had known Abel as Emil Goldfus, testified, the defense elicited a testimonial that Abel's reputation for honesty and integrity was "beyond reproach." During his summation, James Donovan contrasted Abel with Hayhanen, "a bum, a renegade, a liar, a thief," and asserted that there was no evidence that Abel had obtained secret information from the United States or transmitted it to the Soviet Union.

In the face of the physical evidence of Abel's espionage activities, however, Donovan's ad hominem argument had little impact on the jury, which quickly convicted Abel on all three counts of the indictment. In November 1957 Judge Byers sentenced Abel to thirty years in prison. The following year Sergeant Rhodes was court-martialed, given a dishonorable discharge, and five years at hard labor. Abel's conviction was upheld by the court of appeals. While Abel served his sentence in Atlanta Federal Penitentiary, Donovan appealed his conviction to the Supreme Court, claiming that the evidence seized during Abel's arrest by the Immigration and Naturalization Service should be suppressed due to the FBI's failure to obtain a search warrant or an indictment. Finally, in March 1960 the Supreme Court upheld the conviction by a five-to-four vote.

Abel, however, only served a few years of his thirty-year sentence. After months of secret negotiations between the United States and the USSR, he was exchanged for Francis Gary Powers, an American imprisoned in the USSR. Powers, the pilot of an American U-2 aircraft, had been shot down over Russia in 1960 while on a secret reconnaissance mission for the CIA. He had parachuted from his aircraft, been captured by Soviet authorities, and sentenced to ten years in prison. On February 10, 1962, starting from opposite ends, the two men simultaneously walked across the Glienicke Bridge spanning the River Havel between West Berlin and Communist East Berlin. Not until 1965 did the Soviet Union openly acknowledge that Abel had been an intelligence officer.

Abel was not the only Soviet agent to be repatriated in the 1960s. In 1959 Michael Goleniewski, an intelligence officer defecting from Communist Poland, had informed the CIA that the KGB had developed a source within the British navy. The CIA informed the British, and with Goleniewski's information the British had identified the spy as Harry Houghton, an admiralty civilian clerk at the top security Underwater Weapons Establishment in Portland, England. British security also tracked down the man to whom he gave material, Gordon Lonsdale, the alias of Konon Molody, the KGB's chief illegal officer in England. A surreptitious search of his safe-deposit box turned up spy paraphernalia, and he was observed visiting a home in a London suburb, belonging to a New Zealand couple, Peter and Helen Kroger. Peter Kroger was an antiquarian bookseller. In January 1961 British authorities arrested the participants in this espionage ring and found a cache of espionage material hidden in the Kroger home. After fingerprinting, the Krogers turned out to be the long lost Cohens, Morris and Lona.

At their trial, neither Lonsdale nor the Cohens testified. Lonsdale did make an unsworn statement taking responsibility and claiming that the Krogers were innocent friends who had agreed to hold his belongings for safekeeping and had no part in his activities. That ploy failed and all three were found guilty of espionage. Lonsdale received a twenty-five-year sentence and the Cohens got twenty years apiece. Both American and British intelligence offered the Cohens a reduction in their sentence for their cooperation, hoping that they would finally provide the evidence necessary to charge Theodore Hall with espionage. The Cohens, however, were hard-core Communists and refused any cooperation. British authorities exchanged Lonsdale for a British citizen being held by the Russians in 1964. In the fall of 1969 the British freed the Cohens in return for the release of several Britons imprisoned in Moscow. They traveled to Poland and then to the Soviet Union, where, on KGB pensions, they remained until they both died after the collapse of communism.

Ted Hall never faced trial for his atomic espionage. His research interests had turned to radiobiology and the medical uses of x-rays, and in 1962 he moved to Great Britain to take a position as a biophysicist at the Cavendish Laboratories at Cambridge University. After the release of the Venona decryptions in the mid-1990s made his espionage for the Soviet Union public, he released a statement reaffirming his distrust of the United States and expressing no regret for his actions. He died in 1999 at the age of seventy-four.

FURTHER READINGS

Holloway, David. *Stalin and the Bomb: The Soviet Union and Atomic Energy, 1939–1956*. New Haven: Yale University Press, 1994.

Judges that Soviet espionage (Fuchs, Greenglass of the Rosenberg ring) saved the Soviets at least two years and considerable resources.

Hyde, H. Montgomery. *The Atom Bomb Spies*. New York: Atheneum, 1980.

Survey.

Reuben, William A. *The Atom Spy Hoax*. New York: Action Books, 1955.

Argues that there was no atomic secret and no espionage took place. Treats the various charges of Soviet spying as manufactured by a malign American government.

Rhodes, Richard. *The Making of the Atomic Bomb*. New York: Simon and Schuster, 1986.

Comprehensive history of the Manhattan Project.

West, Nigel. *Mortal Crimes: The Greatest Theft in History; Soviet Penetration of the Manhattan Project*. New York: Enigma Books, 2004.

Klaus Fuchs

Moss, Norman. *Klaus Fuchs: The Man Who Stole the Atom Bomb*. New York: St. Martin's Press, 1987.

Discusses how Fuchs's confession to British authorities led to the Rosenberg ring.

Werner, Ruth [Ursula Kuczynski]. *Sonya's Report*. London: Chatto & Windus (Random Century Group), 1991.

Account by Werner/Kuczynski, a refugee German Communist who was a Soviet GRU agent and espionage liaison with Klaus Fuchs in Great Britain until he went to the United States in 1943.

Williams, Robert Chadwell. *Klaus Fuchs, Atom Spy*. Cambridge, Mass.: Harvard University Press, 1987.

Thorough biography.

The Rosenberg Apparatus

Feklisov, Alexander, and Sergei Kostin. *The Man Behind the Rosenbergs*. Translated by Catherine Dop. New York: Enigma Books, 2001.

Memoir by a career KGB officer who served as the case officer for Klaus Fuchs (in the United States and in the United Kingdom) and Julius Rosenberg. Treats the Rosenbergs as heroic Soviet patriots loyal to international communism and asserts his own continued support for that ideology. Also discusses in detail the espionage activities of others he worked with either directly or though Julius Rosenberg: David Greenglass, Harry Gold, Morton Sobell, William Perl, Alfred Sarant, Joel Barr, and other American Communists.

Meeropol, Robert, and Michael Meeropol. *We Are Your Sons: The Legacy of Ethel and Julius Rosenberg*. Boston: Houghton, Mifflin, 1975.

Emotional and melodramatic defense of the Rosenbergs by their two sons.

Meeropol, Robert. *An Execution in the Family: One Son's Journey*. New York: St. Martin's Press, 2003.

Nizer, Louis. *The Implosion Conspiracy*. Garden City, N.Y.: Doubleday, 1973.

Account by a leading lawyer who finds the evidence against the Rosenbergs to be ample and the trial and review fair, though he deplores use of the death penalty.

Radosh, Ronald, and Joyce Milton. *The Rosenberg File: A Search for the Truth*. New York: Holt, Rinehart, and Winston, 1983.

Detailed and extremely well researched scholarly examination of the Rosenberg case and easily the most thorough and complete historical examination. Finds that Julius Rosenberg was guilty of spying and that Ethel may have participated in her husband's activities but was not a principal; however, the government included Ethel in the indictment in an unsuccessful attempt to pressure Julius into confessing and informing on other members of his espionage apparatus. Suggests significant nonatomic espionage by those associated with Julius, including Alfred Sarant, Joel Barr, William Perl, and Morton Sobell. A new edition, The Rosenberg File *(New Haven: Yale University Press, 1997), includes a new introduction bringing in evidence that has appeared since the original publication in 1983.*

Schneir, Walter, and Miriam Schneir. *Invitation to an Inquest*. Garden City, N.Y.: Doubleday, 1965.

Argues that the Rosenbergs were innocent of any involvement in espionage, the evidence against them was faked, David Greenglass and Harry Gold gave false testimony against them, and their trial was unfair. Somewhat expanded in later editions, the Schneirs' book has long been the standard Rosenberg defense. In a short essay, "Cryptic Answers," published in the Nation *(August 14–21, 1995), the Schneirs' comment on the release of the deciphered KGB cables of the Venona project: "What these messages show, briefly, is that Julius Rosenberg was the head of a spy ring gathering and passing on nonatomic defense information. But the messages do not confirm key elements of the atomic spying charges against him. They indicate that Ethel Rosenberg was not a Soviet agent. And they implicate the American Communist Party in recruitment of party members for espionage."*

Sobell, Morton. *On Doing Time*. New York: Scribner, 1974.

Autobiography that denies any participation in espionage.

Usdin, Steven. *Engineering Communism*. New Haven: Yale University Press, 2005.

Detailed and carefully researched reexamination of the history of the Rosenberg network in light of evidence that has appeared since the collapse of the USSR. Thorough study of the role of Joel Barr and Alfred Sarant, American Communist electrical engineers, as major sources in Julius Rosenberg's espionage apparatus and their important contributions to Soviet computer and high-technology weaponry development after they secretly fled to the USSR after Rosenberg's arrest.

Theodore Hall, Morris and Lona Cohen

Albright, Joseph, and Marcia Kunstel. *Bombshell: The Secret Story of America's Unknown Atomic Spy Conspiracy*. New York: Times Books, 1997.

Well-researched journalistic examination focusing on Theodore Hall's espionage but also discussing at length Saville Sax, Morris Cohen, and Lona Cohen.

Rudolf Abel

Bernikow, Louise. *Abel*. New York: Trident Press, 1970.

Journalistic account of the case.

J. Robert Oppenheimer and the Berkeley Radiation Laboratory

Bernstein, Jeremy. *Oppenheimer: Portrait of an Enigma*. Chicago: Ivan R. Dee, 2004.

Bird, Kai, and Martin J. Sherwin. *American Prometheus: The Triumph and Tragedy of J. Robert Oppenheimer*. New York: A. A. Knopf, 2005.

> *A detailed and thorough biography. Highly sympathetic to Oppenheimer and indignantly rejects any association of Oppenheimer with espionage and dismisses or explains away evidence of his secret participation in the CPUSA.*

Chevalier, Haakon. *Oppenheimer: The Story of a Friendship*. New York: Braziller, 1965.

> *A bitter and ambiguously written book by a scholar of French literature and a friend of Oppenheimer in the 1930s and early 1940s that denies all participation in Soviet espionage or Communist activities, as well as Oppenheimer's statement that Chevalier had approached him about sharing Manhattan Project information with the Soviets, while also painting a picture of a thriving University of California, Berkeley, Communist faculty group thinly disguised as a Marxist discussion group, in which both Chevalier and Oppenheimer participated. Treats Oppenheimer as a betrayer of the progressive cause.*

Curtis, Charles P. *The Oppenheimer Case: The Trial of a Security System*. New York: Simon and Schuster, 1955.

> *Contains key documents and testimony.*

Herken, Gregg. *Brotherhood of the Bomb: The Tangled Lives and Loyalties of Robert Oppenheimer, Ernest Lawrence, and Edward Teller*. New York: Henry Holt, 2002.

> *Thorough and scholarly joint study of the role of Oppenheimer, Lawrence, and Teller in the Manhattan Project that focuses on Oppenheimer. Judges that the evidence shows that Oppenheimer was a secret member of the CPUSA for several years but did not participate in Soviet espionage. A website, "The Brotherhood of the Bomb" (http://www.brotherhoodofthebomb.com/) contains a more detailed set of footnotes than in the printed book version and also a "new evidence" section about documentation available subsequent to publication of the book about Oppenheimer's membership in the CPUSA, particularly the unpublished journal of Barbara Chevalier, Haakon Chevalier's widow, and the unpublished memoir of Gordon Griffiths, a member of the Communist faculty club at U.C. Berkeley.*

Holloway, Rachel L. *In the Matter of J. Robert Oppenheimer: Politics, Rhetoric, and Self-Defense*. Westport, Conn.: Praeger, 1993.

> *Focuses on the security clearance hearing.*

Kamen, Martin David. *Radiant Science, Dark Politics: A Memoir of the Nuclear Age*. Berkeley: University of California Press, 1985.

Autobiography of a nuclear chemist who was fired from the Berkeley Radiation Lab after FBI agents overheard him discussing the atomic bomb project with two Soviet diplomats, Kheifets and Kasparov, who were KGB officers. He maintained his conversation was innocent and largely dealt with cultural matters.

Major, John. *The Oppenheimer Hearing*. New York: Stein and Day, 1971.

McMillan, Priscilla Johnson. *The Ruin of J. Robert Oppenheimer*. New York: Viking, 2005.

Concentrates on the Atomic Energy Commission's security hearing on Oppenheimer and presents him as a martyred secular saint.

Pais, Abraham. *J. Robert Oppenheimer: A Life*. With Robert P. Crease. New York: Oxford University Press, 2005.

Polenberg, Richard, ed. *In the Matter of J. Robert Oppenheimer: The Security Clearance Hearing*. Ithaca: Cornell University Press, 2002.

Excerpts from the relevant transcripts and documents.

Peat, F. David. *Infinite Potential: The Life and Times of David Bohm*. Reading, Mass.: Addison Wesley, 1997.

Discusses the attachment to the CPUSA and suspicions, which Peat rejects, that the theoretical quantum physicist David Bohm, an Oppenheimer protégé, participated in espionage while associated with the Radiation Laboratory at Berkeley during atomic bomb project.

6

Judith Coplon

THE SPY WHO GOT AWAY WITH IT

FBI AGENTS ARRESTED JUDITH COPLON IN THE ACT OF
handing over secret government documents to a Soviet intelligence
agent yet the intricacies of the American judicial system allowed her
to escape justice. Indeed, her case highlights the difficulties American
law, designed to deal with ordinary criminality, often has with espionage
cases.

The daughter of a small New York toy manufacturer, Judith Coplon
did well in high school and enjoyed academic success at Barnard College in New York. As an undergraduate she also participated in student
groups aligned with the Communist Party and actively promoted Soviet
causes. After graduation in 1943 she got a job with the New York office
of the Economic Warfare section of the U.S. Justice Department. (The
Economic Warfare section dealt with legal issues arising from American policies to intervene in international trade to insure a supply of
strategically important commodities to the United States and its allies
and to deny those goods to enemy nations.) A routine personnel security check at the time she was hired noted her undergraduate Communist
activities, but personnel security offices were looking for Nazi sympathizers, and in 1943 Coplon's Communist links neither disqualified her
nor even earned a flag on her file for future reference in this case. It
should be noted that the attitudes of security officials toward Communists varied widely in World War II. There was no uniform policy: some,
particularly military security officers, regarded Communist association as
prima facie evidence of a security risk while others ignored it. In retrospect, if her Communist associations had been noted at the time, a
great deal of later damage to American counterespionage would have been
avoided.

Coplon's Recruitment into Espionage

Among Coplon's Barnard college friends was another young Communist, Flora Don Wovschin. Wovschin's mother, Maria Wicher, and her stepfather, Enos Regnet Wicher, were secret Communists. Enos Wicher had even worked for a period as a CPUSA organizer under a pseudonym in the state of Wisconsin in the 1930s. By 1944, however, Enos Wicher was a physicist working on American military electronic projects for Columbia University's Division of War Research. He was also a spy for the KGB. His stepdaughter, Flora Wovschin, also became a KGB source, reporting to the Soviets on her work at the U.S. Office of War Information. Wovschin was an energetic recruiter, drawing a number of young Communists into Soviet espionage. One of her recruits was her friend Judith Coplon, whose new job had obvious espionage interests to the USSR.

Wovschin sounded Coplon out and reported to the KGB that she was an excellent prospect. The KGB's New York station agreed, and a July 1944 cable deciphered by the Venona project requested Moscow's permission to recruit Coplon as an agent. The KGB's Moscow headquarters did not get around to Coplon's case for several months. Not until October did it send an inquiry to the Communist International asking if it had any background information on Coplon due to her CPUSA ties. Wovschin reported in November that Coplon was impatient for direct contact with Soviet intelligence. In December the New York KGB office reported Coplon's espionage potential had greatly increased since she had obtained a transfer from New York to the Foreign Agents Registration section of the Justice Department in Washington.

American law provided that everyone promoting the views of, disseminating propaganda for, or similarly acting on behalf of a foreign government had to register their status with the U.S. government and provide certain basic information about their activities and expenditures. Those who legitimately worked for foreign governments as lobbyists, publicists, and similar tasks routinely registered but, obviously, those engaged in espionage-related activities did not do so. While other statutes also criminalized espionage against the United States, the Foreign Agents Registration Act played a key legal role in American counterespionage operations by providing a simple statutory basis for federal investigation of spies working for foreign powers. Consequently, the Foreign Agents Registration section of the Justice Department worked extremely closely with the FBI on investigations of suspected foreign espionage. The FBI furnished the section with periodic reports of espionage investigations so that its staff could determine when evidence had mounted to a level that would support arrest and prosecution under the Foreign Agents Registration Act. From the point of view of Soviet intelligence, recruiting a source in this office would give the Soviets notice when one of its operations was under investigation and, consequently, an opportunity to warn its spies to cease activity and destroy incriminating evidence.

Vladimir Pravdin, a KGB officer who worked under the cover of a journalist for the USSR's TASS news agency, met with Coplon in January 1945 and reported to Moscow that she was a "serious person who is politically well developed and there is no doubt of her sincere desire to help us. She had no doubts about whom she is working for." Other deciphered Venona messages about Coplon reported that in 1945 she was cooperating fully and the KGB had advised her initially to refrain from stealing documents until she was confident that she had consolidated her position in the Justice Department. Coplon was bright, hardworking, and genial and quickly won approval and promotion from her Justice Department supervisors. In one Venona cable, the New York KGB reported that she was studying Russian to improve her chances of getting assigned to work on Soviet-related matters at the Foreign Agents Registration section. This gambit succeeded, and she gained access to files on FBI operations directed at possible Soviet agents. It is likely that Coplon gave the KGB early warning of many FBI counterintelligence operations from 1945 until she was identified in late 1948. Her alerts allowed the KGB to warn its sources to cease activity and break contact. Consequently, by the time a suspected incident of espionage got to the point of the FBI instituting surveillance and other measures in order to produce evidence sufficient to bring a criminal charge, the spies had been forewarned, surveillance produced little, and the extent of espionage was left in doubt.

Venona, however, put an end to Coplon's betrayal of the United States. In late 1948 several deciphered Venona messages indicated that the KGB in 1945 had a source, cover-named "Sima," working in the Foreign Agents Registration section at the Justice Department in Washington and that Sima in 1944 had been in New York working for the Economic Warfare section of the Department of Justice. The FBI launched an immediate investigation and quickly established that only one staff member of the

Foreign Agents Registration section had previously worked at the New York office of the Economic Warfare section: Judith Coplon.

To limit the damage to its counterespionage operations, the FBI had her supervisor divert her to less sensitive assignments. Coplon did not sense that she was under suspicion and continued to seek out Soviet-related matters. Only a few key supervisors knew of the FBI's investigation, and other staff members continued to furnish Coplon with Justice Department material on investigations of Soviet spying. Meanwhile, the FBI also instituted surveillance of her movements, tapped both her home telephone and her parents' phone in New York, and placed a listening device in her office.

The telephone taps would later cause the FBI enormous problems when she was tried. As interpreted by federal courts, U.S. law at the time made it illegal to secretly record (wiretap) telephone calls. President Roosevelt, however, had issued a directive in 1940 that the FBI could tap telephone conversations for reasons of national security, a directive renewed by later presidents and supported by their attorney generals. U.S. courts, however, took the view that disclosure of telephone tap information was illegal and any evidence gained in this way could not be presented as evidence in a criminal trial. For much counterespionage work, this attitude of the courts was not a serious problem. The chief priority of counterintelligence was to stop the loss of American secrets by identifying Soviet sources and thereby neutralizing their ability to get access to sensitive information; criminal prosecution was a much lower priority. Consequently, the FBI and other security agencies frequently made use of telephone taps. When a case did get to court, however, this gap between American law and the practices of counterintelligence agencies such as the FBI caused major difficulties, as was demonstrated in the earlier *Amerasia* case (Chapter 2).

FBI surveillance soon established that Coplon made trips to New York ostensibly to meet with her family but also to meet privately with a Soviet citizen, Valentine Gubitchev. The conduct of Coplon and Gubitchev prior to their meetings confirmed to trailing FBI agents that they were observing espionage. The two separately took roundabout routes and made evasive maneuvers designed to shake off surveillance before finally meeting, a pattern that confirmed for the FBI that Gubitchev was Coplon's espionage contact. Gubitchev was a Soviet engineer working for the United Nations. Even after the USSR collapsed, information on his exact status remained unclear. One veteran KGB officer has referred to Gubitchev as "cadre," a term usually meaning a career professional intelligence officer. But several other post-Soviet Russian sources identify Gubitchev as a Soviet diplomatic officer who had been co-opted by the KGB for the purpose of liaison with Coplon. It was not unusual for Soviet intelligence services to call on Soviet diplomats to perform occasional espionage tasks when their professional intelligence officers were overworked or concerned that they were under surveillance. This likely was the case at the time. After the defections of GRU officer Igor Gouzenko and KGB agent Elizabeth Bentley in late 1945, Soviet intelligence agencies in 1946 had withdrawn most of their professional officers from North America, concerned that the defectors had identified them to the FBI. They were replaced, but it took a number of years to bring the staffs of the Washington and New York KGB and GRU stations up to full strength with experienced English-speaking officers. In the meantime Soviet diplomatic personnel were now and then required to augment the ranks of the professional spies.

Due to Coplon's access to counterespionage information, the FBI was anxious to bring her case to a speedy conclusion. Moreover, senior officials in the Justice Department pressed for a rapid arrest and trial to demonstrate the government's diligence in the spring of 1949. Elizabeth Bentley's testimony the previous summer and the approaching Hiss trial had raised public concern that the Roosevelt and the Truman administrations had tolerated Soviet espionage. A quick arrest and conviction of an obviously guilty Coplon would demonstrate the administration's resolve on the matter and reassure the public. This haste, however, also played a role in the later frustrating outcomes of Coplon's trials.

Seeking to provide an occasion for an arrest with "smoking gun" evidence that would allow for an easy conviction, the FBI decided to offer Coplon some bait. It prepared a fake FBI report on Amtorg, the USSR's agency for conducting trade with the United States. Amtorg had also been used as a cover for Soviet espionage operations. The report covered a variety of matters regarding Amtorg but the "bait" was a section stating that the FBI had recruited a senior official in Amtorg's New York office as an informant and identifying him by his real name. The FBI then had one of Coplon's supervisors at the Foreign Agents Registration section show Coplon the report on March 3, 1949, and ask her views on the FBI's analysis of Amtorg operations. Investigators were sure that Coplon would quickly meet with Gubitchev to report the explosive and potentially dangerous news.

Coplon took the bait. The next day she left for New York ostensibly on a family visit. After a stop at her parents' residence, she began a convoluted trip across New York, jumping on and off subway cars, entering a restroom that allowed her to quickly exit at a different level, and darting in and out of stores. Gubitchev, meanwhile, began a similar journey across the city. More than two-dozen FBI agents were involved in attempting to keep the two under surveillance without themselves being seen. The FBI assumed that at some point Coplon would pass Gubitchev a report on the faked Amtorg report. If they could then arrest the two with the report in Gubitchev's possession, conviction in a trial would likely be a simple matter. Coplon and Gubitchev, however, did not make it easy. The two passed each other on the street but showed no signs of recognition and proceeded in different directions. Both then separately boarded the same bus and sat in seats several rows apart without making contact. They then separately left the bus, proceeded to the same subway station and boarded the same subway car. For about twenty minutes the trailing FBI agents lost contact with them. When agents reestablished their surveillance, they observed the two walking together on a sidewalk. Had the material been passed during the interval when the FBI had lost contact? If it had, Coplon and Gubitchev would soon separate for good and the opportunity to arrest them together would be lost. FBI supervisors ordered an immediate arrest.

When taken into custody, Coplon and Gubitchev pretended they did not know each other. Coplon refused to make any statement, while Gubitchev claimed diplomatic immunity from arrest. Both were searched and, to the FBI's disappointment, Coplon's report on the Amtorg memo was still in her purse. She had not actually completed the act of passing confidential government information to a representative of a foreign power. On the other hand, her actions prior to the arrest seemed to offer solid evidence of *intent* to do so. Government prosecutors would just have to provide more context and supporting evidence to convince a jury that the only reasonable explanation for Coplon having the report and meeting with Gubitchev was an intent to hand it over to the Soviet Union.

The other material found in Coplon's purse provided more than enough corroboration to make the prosecutor's task easier. Not only did her purse have an extract from the FBI "bait" material; it contained thirty pages of notes, reports and copies of government documents. Included were extracts from Foreign Agents Registration section "data slips" that summarized FBI reports on thirty-four specific espionage investigations as well as reports on her attempts to obtain an FBI survey of its anti-Soviet counterintelligence operations and other tasks given her by the Soviets.

Justice Department prosecutors thought that conviction was likely despite not finding any FBI material in Gubitchev's possession because of the sheer magnitude of the evidence found in Coplon's purse. On March 10 prosecutors procured a four-count indictment from a U.S. grand jury sitting in New York. The first count charged both Coplon and Gubitchev with conspiring to defraud the United States by obstructing the work of the Department of Justice. Count two charged Coplon with illegally attempting to transmit secret government documents to Gubitchev. The third count charged Gubitchev with attempting to obtain American national defense secrets. Count four charged Coplon with attempting to deliver defense and counterespionage secrets to Gubitchev.

Prosecutors, however, soon realized that Gubitchev's status complicated the prosecution of Coplon. While in a broad sense he was a diplomat, he was not an accredited diplomat with the Soviet UN delegation. Instead, he was on the staff of the United Nations, and it was unclear if a post of that sort qualified for diplomatic immunity. The Department of Justice, believing that he lacked immunity, wanted to proceed with prosecution. The Soviet government insisted that Gubitchev had diplomatic immunity and that he be allowed to leave the United States immediately. The U.S. Department of State did not want to make an issue of the matter and recommended deporting Gubitchev without trial. Prosecutors realized that if this issue were resolved with Gubitchev departing the United States without trial, then its prosecution of Coplon would become complicated because the counts under which Coplon was indicted specifically mentioned Gubitchev. If Gubitchev left before a trial, Coplon's attorney could demand that the indictments against her be dismissed because his departure had deprived Coplon of her right to call Gubitchev as a witness.

As a backup strategy prosecutors went to a U.S. grand jury in Washington and procured a two-count indictment against Coplon on March 18, 1949, that did not mention Gubitchev. The first count charged Coplon with obtaining national defense information with the intent to injure the United States and to benefit a foreign nation. The second count charged her with violating a statute forbidding unauthorized copying or removal of government documents, specifically documents related to counterespionage activities.

The Washington Trial

With the New York trial delayed by wrangling over Gubitchev's status, the Washington trial began first, on April 25, 1949, before Judge Albert L. Reeves. Justice Department prosecutors, John Kelley and Raymond Whearty, planned a straightforward case, emphasizing the evidence in Coplon's purse and her surreptitious meetings with a Soviet diplomat. The prosecution's case was a powerful one, with the material in Coplon's purse obvious evidence of her guilt. Coplon's defense attorney, Archibald Palmer, attempted to blunt the evidence in three ways.

First, he attempted to convince Judge Reeves that the evidence in Coplon's purse should not be shown to the jury. If he succeeded, the prosecutors would be forced to drop the case given the centrality of the documents in the purse to the government's case. Palmer maintained that the FBI had no just cause to arrest Coplon and seize her purse and, even if they did have cause, they had failed to get an arrest warrant. Although a warrantless arrest is permissible if time does not permit obtaining one, he maintained that the FBI had ample time to get a warrant. Consequently, the arrest was illegal and the evidence resulting from it could not be presented to the jury. Judge Reeves, however, ruled that given the circumstances of Coplon's meeting with Gubitchev, the FBI decision to arrest without a warrant was permissible.

Palmer also pressed FBI witnesses to learn the basis of the FBI's suspicions about Coplon and its knowledge that she would be meeting with Gubitchev. He suspected that the basis for their surveillance was that the FBI had been tapping Coplon's telephone conversations. If he were able to confirm that the FBI had used telephone taps, then he had grounds to argue that Coplon's arrest stemmed from illegal wiretaps and was the "fruit of a poisoned tree." Under the rules of the federal court system, the evidence gained from an illegal arrest, no matter how relevant to guilt or innocence, would not be able to be used in court.

In fact, the FBI had used wiretaps in its investigation of Coplon. To hide this, FBI agents who testified at the Washington trial denied *personal* knowledge of telephone tapping; in many cases these statements were true but were also a way of avoiding the broader issue of whether other FBI agents had listened in on Coplon's telephone. In retrospect, in at least one case, it is clear that an FBI agent simply lied under oath. He had taken part in the wiretapping but denied any knowledge of it. However,

Palmer was frustrated at the time. He could not find clear evidence of FBI wiretapping, and Judge Reeves allowed the evidence found in Coplon's purse to be presented to the jury. Nevertheless, Palmer succeeded in getting enough evasive and equivocal FBI testimony on the record that he had the basis for a later appeal.

Actually, the FBI was hiding something other than illegal wiretapping. Deciphered Venona cables, not wiretaps, had pointed the FBI to Judith Coplon and led to her arrest. While there was nothing illegal about the FBI's use of the Venona cables (Chapter 3), the very existence of Venona was a closely held government secret. The FBI had no intention of allowing the Soviet Union to learn anything about the Venona project by disclosing it in open court.

Unable to get the arrest ruled illegal or the evidence in Coplon's purse suppressed by Judge Reeves, Palmer then attempted to blackmail the government to force it to withdraw the evidence voluntarily. This tactic, sometimes termed "graymail" and often used by attorneys defending spies and terrorists, was based on using the procedures of the American criminal justice system (i.e., the procedure known as "discovery") to demand the disclosure of sensitive national security information connected to the case.

Prosecutors Kelley and Whearty had told the jury that Coplon's purse contained thirty-four FBI data slips, extracts from FBI investigations, chiefly about Soviet espionage, and they introduced twenty-two of the slips into evidence. Prosecutors withheld twelve data slips on grounds that their disclosure would compromise American security. Immediately responding, "There's no such thing as security when you go into a courtroom," Palmer demanded that the contents of the twelve withheld data slips be disclosed in open court. Government prosecutors argued vehemently that national security was at stake and the demand was unreasonable. Judge Reeves considered the matter and ruled that under existing criminal law, national security information that was evidence in a criminal case was not protected from public disclosure. Nor would he use his own discretion as a federal judge to shield it, stating: "I am not charged with the responsibility of protecting the security of the government." He concluded that the Department of Justice could protect the government's secrets in question only by dropping its prosecution of Judith Coplon and allowing her to go free.

Faced with this choice, FBI counterespionage agents argued for dropping the case. In their view, the damage to national security from the disclosure of the twelve data slips outweighed the importance of sending Judith Coplon to jail. The data slips revealed the methods the FBI was using to penetrate several Soviet espionage networks and included information about one informant that it feared would allow the Soviets to identify and kill him. Justice Department officials, however, overruled the FBI. The Truman administration had faced severe criticism from Republicans over its prior passivity toward Soviet espionage and desperately wanted to convict Coplon as an answer to public unease about Soviet spying.

Prosecutors then introduced the twelve sensitive data slips into evidence. One referred to a source inside the Soviet embassy in Washington, although it was unclear if it was a human being or a successful FBI bugging operation. In either case, the information would likely have helped Soviet security officers in the embassy hunt down and remove the source. A Washington businessman and lawyer, Morton Kent, killed himself several days prior to being identified in one of the newly produced data slips as having had contact with a Soviet bloc official suspected of being an intelligence officer. The circumstances were murky, and on its face the data slip was simply a routine report of who met a Bulgarian diplomat; most such contacts would be entirely benign. Kent's suicide likely was motivated by business difficulties, but possibly he had received advance word that his identity would be disclosed in court.

Palmer's attempt to force the government to withdraw its most valuable evidence against Coplon had failed. The twelve data slips, in fact, reinforced the seriousness of her espionage to the jury and made her conviction more likely. However, Palmer's ploy, the political needs of the Truman administration, and the inappropriateness of American criminal law when applied to espionage had allowed Coplon to complete her last mission. The information she had stolen from the Justice Department and attempted to deliver to the Soviet Union via Valentine Gubitchev was delivered to the Soviet Union via a flawed American legal system.

In addition to the data slips, prosecutors introduced her summary of the "bait" about an FBI informant inside Amtorg that was in Coplon's own handwriting. Also in her purse were appraisals written by Coplon on three individuals, all described as pro-Soviet and "progressive," that appeared to be background checks Soviet intelligence required on possible recruits for espionage. In a resealed package of women's stockings FBI agents had found an incriminating report of her attempt to obtain access to a secret FBI report on Soviet espionage. It read: "I have not been able (and don't think I will) to get the top secret FBI report which I described to Michael [presumed to be a Soviet contact] on Soviet and Communist Intelligence Activities in the United States. When the moment was favorable, I asked Foley [Coplon's supervisor] where the report was (he'd previously remarked that he'd had such a report); he said that some departmental official had it and he didn't expect to get it back. Foley remarked there was nothing 'new' in it. When I saw the report, for a minute, I breezed through it rapidly, remember very little. It was about 115 pages in length; summarized first Soviet 'intelligence' activities, including Martens, Lore, Poyntz, Altschuler, Silvermaster, et al. [all known Soviet agents]. It had heading on Soviet UN delegation but that was all I remember. The rest of the report I think was on Polish, Yugo, etc. activities and possibly some information on the CP, USA."

Realizing that the material in her purse was powerful evidence, Coplon and her lawyer put forward benign explanations for all of it. She testified she was carrying the extracts of thirty-four FBI reports on espionage investigations in order to study them and improve her analytic skills for a possible future civil service examination for promotion. She had made the notes about the Amtorg material because her supervisor had asked her for an opinion on the FBI report. The three character sketches were just harmless jottings about people she knew. Her report on her attempt to gain access to the top secret FBI summary of its counterintelligence operations was, literally, pure fiction. Coplon explained that she was writing a "romance novel" about a young woman working for the government and what appeared to be a report to a Soviet intelligence officer was just a passage for her book. She had stuffed it into a package of stockings simply because she didn't have the right size envelope to carry it in her purse. Asked why a copy of a book manuscript had not turned up during a post-arrest search of her office and residence, she explained that she had discarded all of the early drafts and was starting over.

Coplon also had an explanation for meeting with Valentine Gubitchev. He was her secret love. She had met him at an art gallery in New York and had been totally smitten. Subsequently she had gone to New York on nine occasions to meet him, was deeply in love, and wanted to marry him. Adopting the pose of a romance-stuck young damsel, she claimed bewilderment that anyone should think it untoward that a Justice Department analyst working on Soviet espionage investigations would be conducting a secret romance with a Soviet diplomat. Coplon also had an explanation for the circuitous route she had taken to meet with Gubitchev. He had told her that he was married (he was) and feared that his wife had hired private detectives to find evidence of his infidelity or that possibly Soviet security officers assigned to the Soviet UN delegation were checking up on him. Consequently, Coplon explained, Gubitchev had instructed her to use evasive techniques when meeting with him.

Palmer also adopted a theatrical defense and attempted to turn the trial into a farce and divert the jury's attention from the evidence. He played the clown, making repeated dramatic physical and oratorical interruptions of the prosecution's case: he loudly chewed scores of Lifesavers and candies, offering them to the jury and other persons in the court. When prosecutors addressed the jury, he stood up, danced around the courtroom to distract the jury, and even physically placed himself between the prosecutor and the jury when the former was speaking to them. Judge Reeves remonstrated repeatedly with Palmer to conduct himself correctly, but Palmer ignored him and Reeves failed to take effective disciplinary action.

In the end, Palmer's clown act failed, and Coplon's own testimony in her defense was a disaster. On cross-examination, prosecutors had little trouble shredding her explanations about why the FBI documents were in her purse. Coplon's story of Valentine Gubitchev as her one true love suffered a fatal blow when prosecutors produced evidence that during the months when she was meeting Gubitchev at various New York restaurants she was checking into hotel rooms with a Justice Department lawyer whom she was dating. In response to the cross-examination, Coplon went into a tirade, claiming she had been set up, implying that the FBI had planted the incriminating documents in her purse (which contradicted her earlier explanation), and asserting that the boyfriend with whom she had gone to a hotel was part of an FBI plot as well.

The case went to the jury late in the morning of June 29, 1949. Early in the afternoon of the next day it convicted Coplon on both counts. Judge Reeves sentenced her to a minimum of three years and four months to ten years on the first count and one to three years on the second count with the sentences to be served concurrently.

The New York Trial

The Washington trial dealt with the charges brought against Coplon by the federal grand jury in Washington. But there remained the separate set of charges the federal grand jury in New York had brought against both Coplon and Valentine Gubitchev. The New York trial, delayed by the dispute over Gubitchev's diplomatic status, did not begin until months later, with pretrial hearings starting on November 14, 1949, under Judge Sylvester J. Ryan. Ryan agreed with Palmer that the issue of FBI telephone tapping needed vigorous examination in pretrial proceedings. Under pointed questioning not only from Palmer but from Judge Ryan as well, the FBI admitted extensive wiretapping of Coplon, including conversations between Coplon and her legal advisers. Further, Ryan forced FBI disclosure that it had destroyed much of the documentation of its wiretapping in what appeared to be an effort to conceal its activities. In response to the trial disclosures, President Truman's attorney general, J. Howard McGrath, pointedly announced that FBI wiretapping in internal security cases was done with his authorization and would continue. Absent statutory authorization, however, Ryan, like most U.S. judges, held that evidence stemming from wiretaps could not be used in court. Judge Ryan ruled, though, that the FBI had developed sufficient reason for surveillance of Coplon independent of its wiretaps and refused Palmer's motion to have her arrest ruled illegal and the evidence in her purse suppressed. Nonetheless, by establishing that wiretapping had occurred, Palmer laid the basis to argue the matter further on appeal.

These pretrial proceedings were extensive and the trial itself did not begin until January 26, 1950, with the same cast of prosecutors and defense lawyers as in Washington. Valentine Gubitchev had been added to the dock; Abraham L. Pomerantz, an experienced trial lawyer, represented him.

The government's case was largely the same as in the Washington trial, recast only to give more emphasis to Gubitchev. The documents found in Coplon's purse and the circumstances of the clandestine meetings between Coplon and Gubitchev got the most emphasis. Palmer attempted to reprise the clown act that he had played in Washington, but Judge Ryan sternly enforced discipline, threatened him with disbarment, and kept him under control. Coplon then dropped Palmer as her representative and brought in lawyers from a firm that specialized in representing Communists and other radicals. With the disaster of Coplon's cross-examination in the Washington trial in mind, they chose not to have her testify or to present any defense, preferring to place their bets on a legal appeal to get the government's evidence ruled inadmissible.

On March 6, 1950, the jury returned its verdict. On the first count charging both Coplon and Gubitchev of conspiring to defraud the United States by obstructing work of the Department of Justice, it found both guilty. She was acquitted on the second count, charging her with illegally attempting to transmit secret government documents to Gubitchev. He was convicted of attempting to obtain national defense secrets, and Coplon was likewise found guilty of attempting to deliver defense and counterespionage secrets to him. Judge Ryan sentenced Coplon to five years on count one and fifteen years on count four, to be served concurrently but also consecutively with her earlier Washington sentences. This produced a combined sentence for Coplon of up to twenty-five years in prison.

Gubitchev received a five-year sentence on one count and ten years on the second. After imposing his punishment, however, the judge announced that the attorney general and secretary of state had jointly requested that Gubitchev's sentence be suspended contingent on his immediate deportation. From the beginning of the Coplon case, the State Department had wanted to deport Gubitchev to avoid a dispute with the USSR over diplomatic immunity. The Justice Department, however, needed him as a defendant in order to prosecute the New York indictments against Coplon. Their compromise, kept secret until the New York trial ended, was to try him and then deport him. Judge Ryan suspended Gubitchev's sentence, and he immediately left for Moscow.

On Appeal: Justice Frustrated

Coplon had been convicted of two counts of espionage-related crimes by a federal jury in Washington and found guilty of two similar counts by a federal jury in New York. The legal battle then moved to two different U.S. appeals courts. The outcomes frustrated and enraged much of the public and brought home the dilemmas presented under America's criminal justice system that at the time had little provision for the special circumstances of espionage cases in peacetime.

A three-judge federal appeals court panel handed down a judgment on Coplon's New York convictions on December 5, 1950. The decision, written by Learned Hand, a senior federal judge and highly regarded legal scholar, held that Coplon's "guilt was plain." Nonetheless, the appeals court overturned her conviction. It ruled that the government wiretapping and the denial of defense access to wiretap records had been improper and the government had not presented acceptable grounds for arresting her. Therefore, the search of her purse and the seizure of evidence of her espionage were illegal and could not be used in court. The appeals court did not vacate Coplon's indictment, so retrial was possible if prosecutors could present some acceptable basis for her arrest without a warrant that was not tainted by wiretapping evidence. As a practical matter, the only other evidence to justify Coplon's arrest that might have been presented were the deciphered Venona cables, and for reasons of national security those could not be disclosed in court.

A U.S. Court of Appeals three-judge panel ruled on Coplon's Washington conviction on June 1, 1951. It found that Coplon's arrest, and therefore the evidence found in her purse, had been legal on the basis of the evidence presented to the trial court in Washington. However, whether there might have been FBI wiretapping and whether such wiretapping might have tainted Coplon's arrest was unclear. Consequently, while not overturning Coplon's conviction, the appeals court ordered that it be held in abeyance pending a new hearing by a trial court on the wiretapping issue. If the court found that no wiretapping had tainted the arrest, her conviction would stand. If it had, then the conviction would be overturned, leaving a retrial a theoretical possibility. As a practical matter, however, there was no point in having a hearing. On the basis of the evidence presented in the pretrial hearings in New York, there clearly had been wiretapping and FBI witnesses at the Washington trial had misled the court. A hearing would very likely have resulted in the overturning of Coplon's conviction. Given the decision not to produce the decoded Venona cables in court, the likelihood of prosecutors being able to establish an acceptable basis for Coplon's arrest that was not tainted by wiretapping was negligible.

Hoping new evidence would turn up from somewhere or somehow and perhaps seeking to punish Coplon in at least a minor way, the Justice Department kept the indictments and her conviction (in abeyance) alive, forcing Coplon to stay within a defined federal jurisdiction and confine her travels to New York. In 1967 U.S. Attorney General Ramsey Clark ordered the dismissal of the two cases on the grounds that too much time had passed. Coplon, meanwhile, married a young attorney with the law firm who took over her defense in her second trial and opened a trendy restaurant in New York. The Soviet spy whose "guilt was plain" had gotten away with it.

FURTHER READINGS

Lamphere, Robert J. "The Spy Next Door" (chapter 7). In *The FBI-KGB War: A Special Agent's Story*, by Robert J. Lamphere and Tom Shachtman. New York: Random House, 1986.

Mitchell, Marcia, and Thomas Mitchell. *The Spy Who Seduced America: Lies and Betrayal in the Heat of the Cold War; The Judith Coplon Story.* Montpelier, Vt.: Invisible Cities Press, 2002.

An account of the case sympathetic to Coplon, critical of the FBI, and indifferent to Soviet espionage against the United States.

7

The Soble-Soblen Case

LAST OF THE EARLY COLD WAR SPY TRIALS

THE SPY TRIALS OF THE LATE 1940S AND EARLY 1950S FO-
cused on the theft of sensitive government information. Top secret
documents, atomic espionage, and military technology had been stolen.
The accused had held important government positions with knowledge
of internal U.S. policy deliberations or had access to highly sensitive
technological and military secrets, and the public was transfixed by the
trials and their aftermath. The spy cases of the latter half of the 1950s drew
less attention. The defendants had little to do with stealing significant
government secrets, although that was not for lack of trying and in part
reflected successful American counterespionage. Instead, the spies in
the last cases had chiefly participated in the Soviet Union's clandestine
campaign to suppress or discredit exiled Russian dissidents and other
ideological enemies of the USSR. In many cases their actions were not
strictly illegal under American law of that day but several of those involved
had the blood of dissident Russians on their hands. And like the Rosenberg
case, the Soble-Soblen spy trials featured siblings turning on each other.

Jack Soble, Robert Soblen, and their confederates were tried for espionage against the United States, but the history of their apparatus goes
back to Europe and Joseph Stalin's rivalry with Leon Trotsky. A brilliant
writer and Marxist theoretician, Trotsky became one of the Bolshevik
heroes of the Russian Revolution by organizing the Red Army into an
efficiently merciless military force and leading it to victory in the Russian
Civil War. He also took a leading role in ruthlessly suppressing not only
the new Communist regime's tsarist enemies on the right but also democratic socialists, independent trade unionists, anarchists, and peasant-
based social revolutionaries on the left. Trotsky, however, was no match
for Stalin in the brutal struggle inside the Soviet Communist Party that
followed Lenin's 1924 death. By the end of the 1920s, Stalin was the

unquestioned leader of the USSR, "Trotskyism" a political crime, and Trotsky's supporters either in prison or, like Trotsky himself, in exile. Trotsky set up a small international organization that claimed to be the only authentic Marxist-Leninist revolutionary movement and called on Communists to repudiate Stalin. Tiny groups of revolutionaries split away from the established Communist parties and announced their adherence to Trotsky, but their numbers were few, their resources small, and they presented little threat to the Soviet dictator's hegemony over the international Communist movement. Stalin, however, took no chances: he set out to obliterate Trotsky and Trotskyism in both an ideological and physical sense.

Infiltrating the Trotskyist Movement

As Trotsky struggled to establish a network of supporters in exile early in the 1930s, the KGB infiltrated its agents into the Trotskyist movement to disrupt it from within. Among the earliest were two Lithuanian Communist brothers: Abromas Sobolevicius (Jack Soble) and Ruvelis Sobolevicius (Robert Soblen). Jack was born in 1903, attended college in Germany, and joined the German Communist Party in the 1920s. He also spent time in the Soviet Union, married there, but then returned to Germany for additional university work. In 1929 he was expelled from the German Communist Party for Trotskyism. At his brother's espionage trial in 1961, Jack Soble claimed that in 1931 his wife returned to the USSR to see her sick mother, he was summoned to the Soviet embassy, and KGB officers coerced him into espionage with threats against his wife. The truth of this claim is unclear, however, and there is evidence that he was working for the KGB as early as 1927 and his adherence to Trotskyism in 1929 was a sham from the beginning.

Using the name Abraham Senin, Jack Soble met with Trotsky twice, first in Turkey and later in Denmark. Meanwhile his brother, adopting the name Roman Weil, also became a KGB agent, and both were active figures in the early German Trotskyist movement. But by 1932 Trotsky grew suspicious that they were disrupting his nascent German organization and ousted them. Robert Soblen/Roman Weil then openly emerged as a Stalinist and joined the German Communist Party in 1933. Jack Soble/Abraham Senin returned to the USSR in 1933 and worked for the Red International of Labor Union (Profintern) as an open Stalin loyalist.

The KGB reactivated the two brothers as covert agents in 1941 and sent them along with their families to Canada, from which they entered the United States, adopting the names Jack Soble and Robert Soblen and becoming naturalized American citizens. Jack Soble was a full-time KGB operative and supervised an extensive intelligence network that specialized in infiltration of Trotskyist organizations and other bodies of Russian exiles and anti-Stalin dissidents in the United States. Robert Soblen, a graduate of the University of Berne medical school, practiced psychiatry while also assisting his brother. In numerous KGB messages deciphered by the Venona project, the brothers are referred to by cover names derived from the identities they had used while operating inside the European Trotskyist movement: Jack was Abram (from Abraham Senin) and Robert was Roman (from Roman Weil).

Soble's network included the most successful agent the KGB ever inserted into the American Trotskyist movement, Sylvia Callen. An enthusiastic young Communist in Chicago, she was spotted and recruited by a senior CPUSA official in 1937 for covert work and turned over to the KGB. Using the name Sylvia Caldwell she joined the Socialist Workers Party (SWP), the chief Trotskyist body in the United States. She then moved to New York, assiduously undertook volunteer clerical tasks for the SWP and was rewarded by appointment as secretary to the SWP's founder and central figure, James Cannon. From that post she fed the KGB and the CPUSA with inside information on the activities of American Trotskyists.

Callen quietly left the SWP in 1947 and by 1954 was living in Chicago using the name Sylvia Doxsee, when called before a federal grand jury. Citing the Fifth Amendment, she refused to answer questions about her membership in the SWP or her relationship to the KGB. She was called back by another grand jury in 1958. The FBI had gathered more evidence of her links to the KGB, and she decided to cooperate to avoid prosecution. She testified that she met regularly with Jack Soble and other KGB agents to pass on confidential Trotskyist material. Callen was named as an unindicted co-conspirator when Robert Soblen was charged with espionage in 1960 but was never called as a witness in his 1961 trial. Because she had spied against private American citizens (not then a federal crime) and not the government, convicting her would have been difficult.

Another American Communist recruited to infiltrate the Socialist Workers Party was Floyd Cleveland Miller, known in the SWP as Mike Cort.

He confessed his activities to the FBI in 1954 and appeared as a witness in Robert Soblen's espionage trial in 1961. The story he told government investigators and a jury is confirmed by numerous decrypted Venona documents. Born in South Bend, Indiana, Miller went to school in Michigan and came to New York in 1934 where he found a job writing soap operas for radio station WMCA. He joined the CPUSA in 1936. Only a few months later a KGB officer recruited him to do "opposition work," as the CPUSA called covert action against rival political organizations. Miller's first assignment, which lasted for a year, was to listen to a wiretap the KGB had arranged on the phone in the home of SWP leader James Cannon. Next he joined the SWP and became one of its activists, while writing up reports for the CPUSA and KGB. The Trotskyists assigned him to work with the Sailors Union of the Pacific (which belonged to the AFL) in 1941, and he became editor of the union's journal. Led by firm anti-Communists, the Sailors Union of the Pacific challenged the Communist-led International Longshoremens and Warehousemens Union (part of the CIO) for leadership of maritime labor on the West Coast. Miller/Cort's position gave Communists a spy in the upper ranks of one of their chief trade-union rivals.

The Socialist Workers Party sent Miller to Mexico in 1944 to meet with Natalia Trotsky and show her page proofs of her late husband's biography of Stalin that the SWP was arranging to have published. (Stalin's campaign to obliterate Trotsky and Trotskyism achieved one of its chief goals in 1940 when a KGB agent posing as a young Trotsky supporter met privately with Trotsky at his heavily guarded exile home in Mexico. Once alone with Trotsky, the assassin grabbed a mountain climbing ax used as a fireplace poker and killed him by smashing in Trotsky's head.) Miller met in New York with Jack Soble before leaving to enable him to copy the manuscript for the KGB. Three Venona messages from that spring deal with the preparations for his trip and how he could best extract information of interest to the KGB about Trotskyist activity in Mexico.

Miller testified at Robert Soblen's trial in 1961 about his relationship with the two brothers. Jack Soble informed Miller in 1945 that he was being transferred to another KGB controller and introduced him to Robert Soblen. A Venona message from May 1945 confirms that Jack Soble had handed over his infiltrators in the "Polecats" and "Rats" to Soblen. "Polecats" was the KGB cover term for Trotskyists, while "Rats" was its code name for Zionists.

Mark Zborowski

Mark Zborowski was another Soble ring agent assigned to watch Trotskyists and Russian exiles. Zborowski had been born in Russia in 1908 and moved to Poland in 1921. He joined the Communist Party in the late 1920s, was arrested, and fled to France where he soon went to work for Soviet intelligence. He pretended to convert to Trotskyism and fed information to his Soviet masters. Close to Trotsky's son, Lev Sedov, Zborowski, using the pseudonym Étienne, took a prominent role at the founding conference of Trotsky's new international group, the Fourth International. He was later implicated in the death of Sedov and other leading Trotskyists and the theft of part of Trotsky's archive by Soviet operatives. Sedov developed appendicitis, and Zborowski persuaded him to go to a private hospital run by Russian émigrés, one infiltrated by the KGB, rather than to a French public hospital. Sedov died after the operation, and a medical murder was suspected. (Decades later Zborowski confessed that he had persuaded Sedov to go to the hospital in order to facilitate a KGB kidnapping, and Sedov's death was a surprise to him.) KGB officer and defector Alexander Orlov had written an anonymous letter to Trotsky in 1938 pointing to Zborowski as a Soviet agent, but the warning was not believed.

After the German invasion of France, Zborowski fled south and enlisted the aid of Lola Dallin, a onetime Trotskyist, who had married a well-known Russian exile and scholar, David Dallin, to immigrate to New York, where he lived in the same apartment building as the Dallins. Mrs. Dallin had helped persuade Trotsky that Orlov's letter was likely a KGB provocation. Although Zborowski later testified that he broke with Soviet intelligence in 1938 before coming to the United States, deciphered KGB cables and other testimony demonstrate that he continued to assist Soviet intelligence throughout the war. The Venona cables document his frequent meetings with his KGB superior, Jack Soble, and show that he provided details about Trotskyist and exiled anti-Stalinist activists in the United States that he had obtained through his contacts with the too-trusting Dallins.

The Kravchenko Affair
One day in March 1944 Zborowski saw and spoke briefly to a Russian looking for the Dallins' apartment. Later, the Dallins told Zborowski about a potential Soviet defector whom they had met but they did not

reveal his name. Zborowski passed the news along to his Soviet contacts, but the man in question defected before the KGB could figure out who he was.

His name was Victor Kravchenko, a Soviet engineer and midlevel bureaucrat who had arrived in the United States in 1943 as a member of the Soviet Government Purchasing Commission. The United States provided the USSR with aid of more than $11 billion during World War II. Most aid went to the Soviet Union in the form of American dollar credits given to the Soviet commission. The commission's staff then used the credits to purchase American weapons, trucks (more than 100,000), ships, aircraft (more than 7,000), food, industrial machinery, and raw material needed to assist the Soviet war effort against Nazi Germany. After placing the orders, the commission's staff then inspected the goods supplied by American manufacturers and supervised their shipment to the USSR.

The KGB carefully vetted all Soviet personnel assigned to the Soviet Government Purchasing Commission before they arrived in the United States and used a network of secret informants on the commission's staff to spot potential defectors once they arrived. Indications of disaffection or preparation for defection triggered immediate placement under KGB escort on a Soviet ship returning to the USSR. Victor Kravchenko had been disillusioned with communism since Stalin's Great Terror of the 1930s swept millions of Soviets into the labor camps of the Gulag and hundreds of thousands of others in front of KGB executioners. He had, however, kept his rage at Stalin's rule very much a secret, passed the KGB's background checks, and reached the United States. While the KGB security network watching the staff of the Soviet Government Purchasing Commission did not prevent Kravchenko's defection, Zborowski's warning almost allowed it to do so.

Kravchenko's chief concern had been what the reaction of the U.S. government would be to his defection. The USSR was an American military ally against Nazi Germany. The official government policy of friendship toward the USSR meant turning a blind eye to its oppressive totalitarian regime. When he defected, the Soviet government denounced him as a traitor and demanded that he be returned to face Soviet justice. To deal with this risk, Kravchenko contacted two prominent anti-Stalinist journalists, Eugene Lyons and Joseph Shaplen, for advice and assistance. Lyons had been United Press correspondent in Moscow in the 1930s, had observed Stalin's Terror at first hand, and returned to the United States a dedicated enemy of the Soviet Union. Shaplen, a senior journalist with the *New York Times*, spoke and read Russian and loathed the Stalin regime. They both advised against a quiet defection, arguing that Kravchenko's only chance to avoid being handed back to the Soviets was to make himself into a cause célèbre: the U.S. government would leave him alone rather than risk the bad publicity of handing him over to Soviet police. Consequently, on April 3, 1944, Kravchenko held a well-attended news conference, denounced the USSR, and placed his life "under the protection of American public opinion." The publicity worked: the U.S. government stalled and eventually turned aside Soviet demands that he be returned to the USSR. Nonetheless, the Soviet government and the CPUSA continued a multiyear assault on Kravchenko. He was followed, harassed, and threatened.

As part of its campaign, the KGB assigned Zborowski, cover-named Tulip in the Venona cables, to befriend Kravchenko, cover-named Gnat. A few weeks later, despite his best efforts, Zborowski had still not been able to meet him, and he was afraid to push the Dallins too hard for information lest they become suspicious, but he did learn that Kravchenko claimed to be "well informed about the Krivitsky case." Although Kravchenko never published anything about Krivitsky (the KGB defector who had died under suspicious circumstances in 1940; see Chapter 2), such an assertion would have been deeply alarming to Zborowski. When Krivitsky had defected in France in 1937, he met with leaders of the Trotskyist movement. In his pretended identity as the Trotskyist Étienne, Zborowski had been assigned by Lev Sedov to be Krivitsky's bodyguard during these meetings and had passed on information to the KGB about the defector's activities. Shortly before Krivitsky defected, his boyhood friend and fellow Soviet intelligence officer, Ignace Reiss, had also broken with Stalin's regime. Reiss had defiantly sent a letter to the Central Committee of the CPSU denouncing Joseph Stalin for betraying the Bolshevik Revolution. The KGB had caught up with him in Switzerland and murdered him in 1937. Among Zborowski's close friends in New York was Elisabeth Poretsky, Reiss's widow. Zborowski may have been concerned that Kravchenko knew enough about the Krivitsky case to point to a Soviet agent close to Lev Sedov, which would have led to his own unmasking. In her autobiography published decades later, Reiss's widow wrote that she had concluded that her onetime friend Zborowski had helped finger her husband to the KGB.

Finally, Zborowski personally met Kravchenko in the Dallins' apartment in late June 1944. Employing all of his considerable charm, Zborowski began their conversation at 9 P.M. and ended it at 4 A.M. in his own nearby flat. One of Zborowski's tasks was to discover who had assisted Kravchenko in his defection. He was able to tell his KGB superiors that Kravchenko had told him the story of a Russian friend he identified only as Konstantin Mikhajlovich, a winner of a Stalin Prize in metallurgy, who had been arrested in 1936 on orders of the Chelyabinsk Directorate of the KGB. Set free in 1938, he had met Kravchenko in Moscow and told him of the moral duty to work against the Stalin regime. The KGB would have had little trouble identifying the person in question as Konstantin Mikhajlovich Kolpovsky. Zborowski also provided the KGB with the name of a Russian woman who worked for the Soviet Government Purchasing Commission in Washington who had first introduced Kravchenko to the Dallins on the evening of March 30, 1944. She was Sara-Sonja Judey. Born Sara Veksler, she had known Mrs. Dallin in Berlin in the 1920s. Her punishment for this offense is not known, but any Soviet citizen meeting with refugee Soviet dissidents and Trotskyists in the United States or introducing them to someone who would defect a week later would likely face sanctions.

Zborowski and several other KGB agents among the anti-Stalinist refugees assiduously cultivated Kravchenko's friendship while reporting to the KGB on ways to discredit him. One Kravchenko project they followed very closely was his preparation of an autobiographical account of his life under Stalinism and his decision to defect. So closely did the KGB worm its way into Kravchenko's circle that one of the typists of his manuscript was a KGB agent, as was one of the translators preparing the English-language version. Consequently, the KGB received a copy of Kravchenko's manuscript as soon as it was typed. It was published in 1946 under the title *I Chose Freedom: The Personal and Political Life of a Soviet Official*. The book, an immediate best seller, described in detail the fear and horror of Soviet society in the 1930s during Stalin's Great Terror and assisted in reviving the American distaste for Soviet communism that had been in temporary remission during the wartime alliance. Forewarned by the KGB about the nature of the book, the Soviet Union, Communist parties throughout the world, and pro-Soviet sympathizers undertook a massive campaign to discredit both it and its author. Late in 1947 a French Communist weekly, *Les Lettres Françaises*, published an article by "Siam Thomas," identified as an American journalist, who claimed that Kravchenko had not written his own book but was a tool of American intelligence, which had invented tales of Gulag prison camps and political prisoners to defame the Soviet Union. Kravchenko responded aggressively and sued for libel in France.

Kravchenko's libel trial, in Paris in 1949, attracted worldwide attention. Huge crowds of both Communists and anti-Communists demonstrated in the streets as the trial began, and it was front-page news in France, where the Communist Party was a powerful political and trade-union presence. Hundreds of people attended every court session. Kravchenko, continuing his aggressive stance, called numerous witnesses, many of them Russian refugees from displaced-persons camps, who testified to the accuracy of his assertions about the brutal collectivization campaigns, purges, and concentration camps of the 1930s. The intense press coverage carried these stories of the brutal nature of the Stalin regime to a worldwide audience.

The powerful statements of ordinary refugees who had been victimized by Soviet oppression contrasted with the testimony of French Communist witnesses who insisted that on their visits to Russia they had seen no violence or starvation or repression. Maurice Thorez, head of the French Communist Party, appeared as a witness for the defendants and called Kravchenko a traitor. On cross-examination Kravchenko skewered him by pointing out that Thorez had been drafted into the French Army in 1939 to fight Nazi Germany, but since the Nazi-Soviet Pact was in effect, Thorez had deserted the French army and fled to Moscow. Some defense witnesses justified Stalin's purges; others insisted they did not occur. Soviet officials, appearing as witnesses for the defendants, refused to speak about Stalin's Terror or denied knowing prominent Soviet officials who had been executed, even though they had worked with them. The Soviet witnesses were carefully chaperoned around Paris and followed a clear script in denouncing Kravchenko as an ingrate, liar, and malcontent. One witness, his ex-wife, whom he had divorced seventeen years before, excoriated him as a tyrant and liar and denied that her own parents had been arrested and deported to Siberia. Kravchenko located and called as a witness one of her former lovers who testified that she had lied on the witness stand. Particularly damaging to the defendants was the fact that there was no American journalist named Siam Thomas. The inability of *Les Lettres Françaises* to produce the alleged author of the article seriously hurt its defense.

On April 4, 1949, the French court rendered its verdict, finding that Kravchenko had proved his case and that those who had accused him of being a front for American intelligence had not. His accusers were found guilty of libel. The trial had been a public relations disaster for the Soviet Union in Western Europe, and particularly in France. In 1950 Kravchenko published a second book, *I Chose Justice*, a story of the French libel trial. Thereafter he avoided the public limelight and faded into private life and obscurity. But he was haunted by knowledge of the terrible vengeance the Stalin regime had inflicted on his family and friends in the USSR and in 1966 committed suicide.

By that time, his supposed friend, Mark Zborowski, had achieved distinction as an anthropologist but had also been disgraced as a Soviet spy. In 1946 Zborowski got a job as a librarian at the YIVO Institute, a center for research on the history and culture of East European Jews, where he met and impressed the well-known anthropologist Ruth Benedict. With her assistance, he became a consultant to Columbia University's Institute on Contemporary Culture. He wrote a path-breaking study of Jewish shtetls in Eastern Europe, *Life Is with People;* became research director of the American Jewish Committee; and did a three-year study of "the reaction of various races of people to pain," which turned into *Cultural Components in Responses to Pain*, published in 1953. As this project was ending, Zborowski was hired by the Russell Sage Foundation to do research at a veterans' hospital on reaction to pain among disabled veterans.

Just as he was earning a scholarly reputation, however, Zborowski's long career of spying on Trotskyists, Russian émigrés, and his friends began to catch up with him. Numerous Venona decryptions about an agent with the cover name Tulip who had provided information on anti-Stalinist Russian refugees led the FBI to suspect him. They questioned his old friend, Elizabeth Poretsky, whose husband, Ignace Reiss, had been assassinated in Switzerland after defecting from the KGB. Still not suspecting that Zborowski had been reporting on her to Soviet intelligence, she promptly informed him that he was under suspicion.

Zborowski's Trials

Meanwhile, a new source whose evidence could be used in court – Alexander Orlov, a senior KGB officer who had defected in 1937 and tried to warn Trotsky about Zborowski – emerged from more than a decade in hiding. Orlov had dropped out of sight after arriving in the United States, living quietly to avoid Soviet reprisals. After Stalin died in 1953, he published *The Secret History of Stalin's Crimes,* in which he carefully hid his own extensive involvement with Soviet intelligence and his knowledge of scores of Soviet agents still active but laid out a detailed recital of Stalin's brutality. After meeting with David and Lola Dallin, however, he confirmed that Zborowski was the agent about whom he had anonymously warned Trotsky in 1938, shortly after his own defection. Orlov also gave Zborowski's name to the government when the FBI questioned him.

When he was questioned by the FBI, Zborowski admitted working for the Soviets in Europe but denied any spying in the United States. Both Orlov and Zborowski testified before the Senate Internal Security Subcommittee in 1955–1956, at which time Zborowski claimed that he had only intended to help the KGB kidnap Trotsky's son, not kill him, but once again denied without qualification any work for the KGB in the United States. Based on decoded Venona messages, the FBI knew this to be a lie, but Venona could not be made public.

Zborowski had reported his FBI interview to his KGB controller, Jack Soble. When Zborowski was called before the Senate Internal Security Subcommittee, Soble, frightened that he would be exposed, wrote a letter to the KGB headquarters in Moscow discussing the situation and entrusted it to one of his agents, Boris Morros, for delivery. Morros, however, was working as a double agent for the FBI and gave a copy to the bureau. Early in 1957, the FBI arrested the members of the Soble ring. Jack Soble confessed and agreed to testify against the others, including Zborowski. Called before a grand jury, Zborowski, then an anthropologist with the Harvard School of Public Health, denied knowing Soble. In April 1958 the grand jury indicted him for perjury for this statement.

Zborowski's trial began on November 5, 1958, in New York City. Federal prosecutors called Jack Soble as their chief witness, and he testified in detail regarding his role as Zborowski's espionage supervisor. Prosecutors also introduced a statement Zborowski had made after the FBI had arranged a confrontation with Soble at which Zborowski admitted knowing him. Zborowski's defense repeated his earlier admission that he had worked for Soviet intelligence in the 1930s in France but had not done so after he came to the United States. His lawyers argued that his testimony to the grand jury had been misunderstood: he had known Soble, but only under a cover name. But the defense also maintained that Soble was lying about Zborowski's espionage, which raised the question of why Zborowski only knew Soble under a cover name if no espionage was involved. The jury was unimpressed and on November 20, 1958, convicted him of perjury after three hours of deliberation. The conviction was overturned a year later on a technicality – some of Soble's pretrial statements had been withheld from the defense.

The government retried Zborowski in 1962, and Jack Soble again testified in detail about his relationship with Zborowski and their work for the KGB. Testifying in his own defense, Zborowski attempted to minimize the importance of his grand jury testimony in which he denied "knowing" Soble. Zborowski stated "Well, I was asked about my contact with the Russians. He [Soble] was not a Russian. He was a kind of messenger to whom I gave material for transfer to the Russians. This man did not represent authority to me. He was not, to my mind, an actual contact. The Russians were people of significance. Soble was not." Prosecutors responded by introducing a contradictory statement Zborowski signed after an FBI interview in 1957, "I do not recall Jack Soble as anyone ever known to me. Since I never met Soble, it follows that I could not know his code name or that of his brother [Dr. Robert A. Soblen]. I cannot understand why this man, a total stranger to me, should torture me in any way. I deny any knowledge of Jack Soble. I do not recall every having met him. To the best of my recollection I have never transmitted any message through Jack Soble." On November 29, 1962, the jury convicted Zborowski once again, and on December 13 he was sentenced to three years and eleven months in prison. Upon his release he resumed his career as an anthropologist of pain, working at universities and hospitals in the San Francisco area.

Zborowski was never prosecuted for his espionage activities in Europe that had led directly to the murders of several Trotskyists because these were not offenses against the United States or under American jurisdiction. In America he never worked for the government or tried to elicit secrets from government employees. He spied on private persons, refugees, and exiles largely, whose activities the Soviet Union wanted to monitor and disrupt, but this was not illegal under American espionage statutes. His mistake was lying about his activities to a grand jury.

Boris Morros: Double Agent

While Zborowski's section of Jack Soble and Robert Soblen's apparatus concentrated on spying on Trotskyists and other political opponents, a second part ranged more widely. This group of agents infiltrated the OSS and created business covers for Soviet intelligence. The FBI learned a good deal about the latter aspect of the Soble-Soblen network through Boris Morros. Born in Russia in 1895, Morros made his way to the United States in the early 1920s. For sixteen years he was a music director at Paramount Studios in Hollywood and worked on a number of successful films. Morros claimed that he first agreed to help the KGB to ensure delivery of parcels of food he sent to his brothers in the Soviet Union and because the KGB arranged for his father to immigrate to the United States. His chief duty was to provide business cover for KGB agents by giving them credentials as Paramount talent scouts looking for new performers in Europe.

There were, however, limits to the number of Paramount credentials that Morros could obtain, and in 1943 the chief of KGB operations in the United States, Vasily Zubilin, attempted to set up a better business cover using Morros. Zubilin, who nominally was a senior diplomat at the Soviet embassy, informed him he had found a wealthy couple willing to invest in a sheet music company that would serve as cover for Soviet espionage. Alfred and Martha Dodd Stern invested $130,000 in the Boris Morros Music Company.

Alfred Stern, born in 1897, was educated at elite Phillips Exeter Academy and Harvard. In 1921 he married Marion Rosenwald, wealthy daughter of the head of the Sears Roebuck mail-order firm, and directed the Rosenwald Foundation for a decade. After divorcing his wife in 1936 and obtaining a $1 million settlement (an enormous fortune at the time), Stern met and married Martha Dodd, socialite daughter of America's ambassador to Nazi Germany from 1933 to 1937.

Born in 1908, Martha Dodd was an attractive, vivacious, and aggressively liberated young woman in the 1930s. Her list of lovers included the poet Carl Sandburg and the novelist Thomas Wolfe. She shocked the diplomatic community in Germany with her torrid love affairs with, first, Rudolf Dies, a senior official in the Nazi Gestapo, and then Boris Vinogradov, first secretary of the Soviet embassy. Vinogradov, however, was actually a KGB field officer working under diplomatic cover. Jack Soble later testified that Martha Dodd had told him that she had worked as a Soviet spy while at the U.S. embassy in Berlin and during her relationship with Vinogradov. The KGB withdrew Vinogradov from Berlin in 1935, and he went on to other diplomatic assignments in Central Europe. He and Dodd kept in contact, however, and even met on occasion, and in early 1937 Dodd formally asked the Soviet government for permission to marry him. Vinogradov, meanwhile, was recalled to Moscow, and his correspondence with Dodd ended later that year. Decades after, she learned from Soviet contacts that he had been executed in 1938. Vinogradov's execution, though, had nothing to do with his relationship with Dodd and was simply a coincidental part of Stalin's late-1930s purge of his intelligence agencies.

Giving up on her relationship with Vinogradov, Martha Dodd returned to the United States and met and married Alfred Stern in 1938. In 1939 she published a well-received book, *Through Embassy Eyes*, on her observations of Nazi Germany during her father's ambassadorship and in 1941 published an edited version of his embassy diary, *Ambassador Dodd's Diary, 1933–1938*, which emphasized the vicious nature of the Nazi regime. The Sterns devoted themselves to promoting a variety of far-left causes, including investing in Morros's music company at the request of the KGB. Early in 1944 Jack Soble replaced Zubilin as Morros's KGB contact. Several Venona messages detail the fractious business relationship between Morros and the Sterns, who were increasingly concerned that Morros was a poor manager of their KGB-inspired investment. Jack Soble, unable to get Alfred Stern and Morros to agree on how the business should be conducted, arranged for Morros to repay the Sterns $100,000 in 1945 for their one-quarter interest in Morros's music company.

The Sterns were more than just a source of investment funds for the KGB, however. Martha Stern was also a recruiter who brought Jane Foster and, through her, Jane's husband George Zlatowski into the Soble apparatus. Jane Foster graduated from Mills College in 1935, toured Europe, met and married a Dutch government official in 1936, and moved with him to the Dutch East Indies (Indonesia). On a visit to her parents in California in 1938, she joined the American Communist Party and soon after divorced her Dutch husband. In 1941 she married George Zlatowski, a young Communist who had fought with the International Brigades in the Spanish Civil War. Jane Foster also met Alfred and Martha Stern as well as William Browder, the brother of the head of the CPUSA. She later wrote that both he and Martha told her "not to be so open in my Party work, as I could be more helpful to the Party if I were more discreet." After her husband was drafted, Jane moved to Washington in 1942 and, with her Indonesian experience and Malay language skills, found work with the Netherlands Study Unit, a wartime agency (later absorbed by the Board of Economic Warfare) set up to coordinate intelligence on the Dutch East Indies. She then transferred to the chief American intelligence agency, the Office of Strategic Services, in the fall of 1943. Deciphered Venona cables show that Martha Stern recruited Jane Foster into KGB service in 1942 and that she provided the Soviets with information on the work of the Board of Economic Warfare and OSS throughout 1943 and 1944.

The Soble Ring Trials

The FBI had tabbed Morros as early as 1944 as an espionage suspect and had had him under surveillance from time to time. FBI agents approached him in 1947, and he quickly agreed to cooperate, provided a (partial) confession of his activities, and began working as a double agent. With an informant on the inside, the FBI was able to monitor the work of Soble and his network and often insure that it was only minimally effective. By 1957, however, the FBI concluded that the usefulness of the arrangement was over and indicted Jack and Myra Soble, Jacob Albam (Soble's assistant), Alfred and Martha Stern, and George and Jane Zlatowski on espionage-related charges.

Jack Soble initially claimed complete innocence and prepared a vigorous legal defense. When he realized that Boris Morros had been an FBI double agent for a decade, he reconsidered. With the assistance provided by Morros, and FBI surveillance that had gone on for a decade, the government had ample evidence against Jack Soble and others in the apparatus. Further, government prosecutors talked about asking for the death penalty, and in 1957 that was not an idle threat. Soble abruptly dropped his defense, pled guilty, made a detailed statement of his past activities, and agreed to testify against his confederates. His wife also pled guilty, as did Jacob Albam, who also agreed to cooperate. In return for their cooperation, Jack Soble received only a seven-year prison sentence, Myra Soble got four years, while Albam was sentenced to five years.

Alfred and Martha Dodd Stern were in Mexico at the time of their 1957 indictment. They had fled the United States in 1953 when subpoenaed by the House Committee on Un-American Activities to answer questions about their promotion of pro-Soviet causes. Fearing extradition for the much more serious charges of espionage, the Sterns moved first to Moscow and then to Communist Czechoslovakia. In the 1960s they lived for a time in Castro's Cuba but found life there uncomfortable and returned to Prague, where Alfred advised the Communist government on urban planning and Martha wrote numerous denunciations of American society and government. They were disconcerted by the Soviet Union's suppression of Czechoslovakia's "socialism with a human face" in 1968 but quickly reconciled to Communist orthodoxy in the wake of the Soviet invasion. Although their indictments were dismissed in 1979 as too old to be prosecutable, they remained in Prague and both died in Czechoslovakia. Jane Foster and her husband George Zlatowski had been living in France for years at the time of their indictment in 1957. They refused to return to the United States to face trial, and the French government declined to extradite them, likely because in return the two provided French authorities information on Soviet espionage in France. Jane Foster later published an autobiography, *An Unamerican Lady*, in which she admitted to being a secret Communist but denied participation in espionage.

The grand jury in the Soble case also listed a number of other persons as co-conspirators in the espionage network but did not indict them because they were noncitizens no longer in the United States, dead, cooperated with the prosecution, or had spied on Trotskyists or Zionist Jewish organizations and not the United States government. Spying on Trotskyists and Zionists on behalf of the USSR was reprehensible but not a criminal violation of federal law. Three of those named were Germans: Johanna Koenen Beker, Hans Hirschfeld (a consultant for OSS during World War II), and Horst Baerensprung (another OSS consultant). After the Nazi seizure of power in Germany, Johanna Beker, whose father had held high positions in the Communist International, moved to Moscow where she worked as a translator. She testified that she was recruited by the KGB in 1937 to spy on Americans visiting Moscow and then was sent to the United States in 1939 and for a time worked for Robert Soblen as a courier.

She also testified at the Soblen trial that Hirschfeld and Baerensprung had passed information to her for transmittal to Soblen. Baerensprung, she said, had supplied information on German émigré groups and material from OSS files. After the war ended Baerensprung returned to the Soviet occupation zone, became a police official in the new East German

Communist regime, but died before the Soble case broke in the United States. Beker said Hirschfeld also had given her material on other German émigrés, including their fields of interest and their political views. He had also passed on information he had heard about the development of new American weapons. After the war Hirschfeld moved to West Berlin and in 1960 became press chief for West Berlin's Social Democratic (and anti-Communist) mayor Willy Brandt. Hirschfeld met with American government agents in West Berlin and admitted "extended illegal activity and contacts with Communist agents in Europe prior to 1940" but denied Beker's statements about his activities in the United States. The U.S. government offered him limited immunity to return and testify in the Robert Soblen case. This limited immunity provided that his actions prior to coming to the United States would not be prosecuted and that his testimony about his activity in the United States would not be used as evidence against him but that he would be liable to perjury charges if it could be shown that he testified falsely. He refused to return unless given total immunity, including exemption from prosecution for lying under oath. This was refused, and he did not testify in the Soblen case. He also resigned his position with the West Berlin government.

Two mysterious figures listed in the Soble network indictment were Dr. Henry Spitz and his wife, Dr. Beatrice Spitz. Both physicians and naturalized citizens, they had lived in Albuquerque, New Mexico, in 1950, where they took photographs of a military base where atomic weapons research was done and passed it to Dr. Soblen. In 1950 they left for their native Austria. Following Soblen's arrest in 1960, they renounced their American citizenship to lessen the chance of their being extradited.

Ilya Wolston, the son of one of Jack Soble's and Robert Soblen's sisters, also served as a member of their espionage ring. Wolston entered the U.S. Army in World War II and became a U.S. Army military intelligence officer. He promptly began reporting to the KGB on the organization, curriculum, and personnel of the U.S. Army's intelligence school at Fort Ritchie, Maryland. The KGB valued his position inside American military intelligence, and in one of the deciphered Venona messages the New York KGB station assured Moscow that "Slava [Wolston] was warned about appropriate secrecy and caution." Wolston was posted to Alaska with an assignment to army counterintelligence dealing with Soviet matters. At the time considerable American Lend-Lease aid and accompanying Soviet personnel went to the Soviet Union through Alaska. From the point of view of the KGB, Wolston had received the perfect assignment: protecting the United States from Soviet spies. After the war Wolston worked for the KGB network run by his uncle Jack. By the 1950s, however, he developed mental health problems and became a rural recluse. He ignored multiple subpoenas to testify to the U.S. grand jury. Tried for contempt, he pled guilty but claimed mental illness as a mitigating circumstance. He was given a one-year suspended sentence in 1958.

The Robert Soblen Trial

The government did not formally indict Robert Soblen until 1960 because the evidence it had earlier largely related to Soblen's activities as a Soviet agent working against exiled Russian dissidents, Trotskyists, and Jews, which was not illegal under American espionage law. Once federal prosecutors had gathered evidence they thought sufficient to convince a jury that Soblen's espionage included U.S. government targets, however, they sought indictments. In November 1960 a U.S. grand jury indicted Soblen for his role in transmitting stolen information from the World War II U.S. intelligence agency, the Office of Strategic Services, to the Soviets, and in transmitting photographs of U.S. atomic testing sites to the Soviets in the post–World War II period.

Soblen's trial began on June 20, 1961. His lawyer, Joseph Brill, immediately attempted to blackmail the government into dropping the prosecution by demanding access to 1,600 pages of confidential material, chiefly grand jury records and FBI files, related to the Soble case. Brill claimed that access to the files was necessary for Soblen's defense. He hoped that Judge William Herlands would order the files made public, the FBI would balk at allowing public disclosure of confidential counterintelligence files, and prosecutors would be forced to drop the case.

Judge Herlands, however, took a different view of his responsibilities than had Judge Reeves in the earlier case of Judith Coplon. Judge Reeves had required the Justice Department to release sensitive FBI data demanded by Coplon's lawyers or drop the case. After agonizing internal debate and over FBI protests, the Justice Department made the data public and continued the Coplon prosecution, but at the cost of revealing sensitive counterintelligence information. Judge Herlands, however, said that as a federal judge he had a responsibility to reconcile protecting American security with the need for Soblen to present an adequate defense. He personally reviewed the 1,600 pages and ruled that only selected passages from about one hundred items were relevant to the Soblen case and needed to be made public as part of the trial record. Justice Department prosecutors, David Hyde and Richard Casey, agreed to the release of those passages.

Having lost that gambit (which was, however, pursued on appeal), Soblen's defense faced a difficult task in the face of the testimony of Soblen's former colleagues in espionage. Jack Soble, serving his own sentence for espionage, testified in detail about how he and his brother had worked for the KGB since their arrival in the United States in 1941. He detailed Robert's role as link between the KGB and a Soviet source inside the Office of Strategic Services. Soblen's lawyer alternated between depicting Soble's testimony about his brother as fiction and attempting to get him to narrow his description of his brother's spying to involve only American Trotskyists and exiled Russians.

Floyd Cleveland Miller, an unindicted co-conspirator in the case, testified about his infiltration of the Trotskyist movement first under Soble's direction and then in 1945 under Soblen's. Johanna Koenen Beker, another unindicted co-conspirator, stated that one of her KGB controllers, Elizabeth Zubilin (wife of Vasily Zubilin, chief of the KGB American station), turned her over to Soblen for courier work, and she continued in contact with him until 1947. Beker testified that during her work with Soblen she had carried OSS information to him from Horst Baerensprung and Hans Hirschfeld, German exiles who worked for the American OSS. Soblen himself declined to testify in his own defense, claiming that his medical condition (he suffered from leukemia) left him too weak. Throughout the trial he lay curled up in a large contour chair the court provided for him, frequently took pills, coughed, kept his eyes closed, and appeared to breathe with difficulty. The jury, however, was unimpressed and on July 13, 1961, convicted him on two counts of espionage after less than an hour and a half of deliberation.

Judge Herlands deferred sentencing until August, stating that the severity of the sentence would in part hinge on Soblen's willingness to provide the government with a full account of his espionage. He remained defiant, however, and refused any cooperation. Consequently, Judge Herlands sentenced him to life in prison on August 7, 1961. Soblen dramatically collapsed when the sentence was announced, and the defense responded with accusations that it was cruel because Soblen was not expected to live another year due to his leukemia. In deference to his medical condition,

Judge Herlands agreed that Soblen could remain free on bail during his appeal of his conviction.

On March 13, 1962, the U.S. Court of Appeals unanimously upheld the conviction, and in June the Supreme Court denied Soblen's appeal. But he failed to report to begin his prison term on June 28, 1962. His lawyer, Ephraim London, immediately denied he had jumped bail and fled, claiming instead that he was dying and likely was physically unable to appear. In fact, after liquidating investments to gather cash and using the Canadian passport of a deceased brother, Soblen took an Air France flight to Israel, checked into a hotel, and immediately hired legal assistance, claiming that, under Israel's "Law of Return" that provided that any Jew could claim Israeli citizenship, he was now an Israeli citizen and could not be returned to the United States. Meanwhile, in the United States his $100,000 bail was forfeited, and his attorney quit. Helen Lehman Buttenwieser, a prominent left-wing lawyer (a member of Alger Hiss's defense team) who had put up $60,000 of Soblen's bail denounced his act as "very dishonorable."

The Israeli government, anxious to remain on good terms with its chief ally, stated that the "Law of Return" was not an open invitation for Jewish lawbreakers. It arrested Soblen for use of a false passport. Quickly disposing of his legal appeals, Israel deported him for illegal entry, placing him on a flight to the United States via London on July 1. During the flight Soblen used a dinner knife to slash his wrists and stomach and was taken off the plane and hospitalized in London. Once in Britain, he hired lawyers and demanded political asylum or the right to go to any country other than the United States. He asserted that his actions had not been a suicide attempt but merely a ruse to gain admittance to England. British doctors examined him in a prison hospital and determined that Soblen did not face imminent death from leukemia. While he had the disease, it was dormant and he had a life expectancy of several years rather than several months. British courts turned down a complex series of legal appeals, and in September ordered him deported to the United States. On the day of departure, however, Soblen took an overdose of barbiturates, fell unconscious while being escorted to the airport, and was immediately rehospitalized. He never regained consciousness and died on September 11, 1962. It was not clear whether Soblen's overdose was suicide or only an attempt to delay deportation that went too far.

With Robert Soblen's death, the last of the early Cold War spy cases came to an end.

FURTHER READINGS

Fox, John Francis, Jr. "'In Passion and in Hope': The Pilgrimage of an American Radical, Martha Dodd Stern and Family, 1933–1990." Ph.D. diss., University of New Hampshire, 2001.

Excellent scholarly study of Martha Dodd Stern and her role in Soviet espionage and as a Communist fellow traveler.

Foster, Jane. *An Unamerican Lady*. London: Sidgwick and Jackson, 1980.

Autobiography in which Jane Foster Zlatowski admits to being a secret Communist but denies participation in espionage.

Kern, Gary. *A Death in Washington: Walter G. Krivitsky and the Stalin Terror*. New York: Enigma Books, 2003.

Thorough and comprehensive biography of Krivitsky and his career in Soviet intelligence and his activities in the United States after breaking with Stalin and the USSR.

Krivitsky, Walter G. *In Stalin's Secret Service: An Exposé of Russia's Secret Policies by the Former Chief of the Soviet Intelligence in Western Europe*. New York: Harper & Brothers, 1939.

Account by a senior Soviet intelligence agent, who defected in the late 1930s.

Levine, Isaac Don. *The Mind of an Assassin*. New York: Farrar, Straus, and Cudahy, 1959.

Study of Trotsky's murderer and his accomplices. Discusses the involvement of American Communists in the murder.

Morros, Boris. *My Ten Years as a Counterspy: As Told to Charles Samuels*. Assisted by Charles Samuels. New York: Viking Press, 1959.

A melodramatic and self-justifying autobiography by a Soviet spy turned FBI double agent.

Poretsky, Elisabeth K. *Our Own People: A Memoir of "Ignace Reiss" and His Friends*. Ann Arbor: University of Michigan Press, 1970.

Memoir about Ignace Reiss [Poretsky], a senior Soviet intelligence officer who broke with Stalin in the late 1930s and was murdered by KGB agents in Switzerland, written by his widow. Discusses Mark Zborowski.

Schwartz, Stephen. "Intellectuals and Assassins: Annals of Stalin's Killerati" (chapter 1). In *Intellectuals and Assassins: Writings at the End of Soviet Communism*, by Stephen Schwartz. London: Anthem Press, 2000.

Discusses the history of Mark Zborowski.

vanden Heuvel, Katrina. "Grand Illusions." *Vanity Fair* 54, no. 9 (September 1991): 220–256.

> *Written before the appearance of Venona, this lengthy biographical essay assumes that Martha Dodd Stern was innocent of espionage.*

Weissman, Susan. *Victor Serge: The Course Is Set on Hope*. New York: Verso, 2001.

> *Biography of a Russian émigré intellectual that discusses his relationship with American anti-Stalinist leftists and efforts to disrupt the anti-Stalinist left in the United States by KGB agent provocateur Mark Zborowski.*

8

Conclusion

THE DECLINE OF THE IDEOLOGICAL SPY

A LTHOUGH ESPIONAGE TRIALS CONTINUED TO FASCINATE Americans well into the twenty-first century, by the 1960s the nature of the defendants had changed considerably. The spy trials of the early Cold War had featured defendants motivated by some animus against capitalism or loyalty to communism. By the 1960s the day of the ideological spy was gone, replaced by the greedy or disgruntled or blackmailed malcontent, whose betrayal of his country had its origins in personal crises or anger. Aldrich Ames, Robert Hansen, John Walker, and many others did enormous damage to American security but not because of their adherence to some abstract set of beliefs.

There were occasional exceptions. Larry Wu-tai Chin, a Chinese-born naturalized American citizen, worked for decades as a translator for the CIA's Foreign Broadcast Information Service. At some point, however, he became a spy for the Chinese Communist government, apparently motivated by ethnic loyalty. A defecting Chinese intelligence officer identified Chin as a Chinese agent in 1985. He confessed and was convicted of espionage in 1986 but committed suicide before his sentencing. Kurt Stand and Theresa Squillacote, former college New Left radicals motivated by revolutionary Marxist beliefs, were identified as spies for Communist East Germany when the CIA obtained records of that regime's intelligence service, the "Stasi," after the collapse of the German Democratic Republic. A handful of Cuban spies motivated by a combination of Cuban nationalism and Castroist ideology have been arrested in recent years. But in general Communist ideology lost its attractive power as a motive for espionage. Few Americans after the 1960s could have been very confident that the Soviet Union was the wave of the future or that its cause was mankind's.

The millennial hopes that thousands of people had invested in the Soviet Union began to wither as the Cold War developed and suffered a crushing blow in 1956 when Soviet leader Nikita Khrushchev made a secret speech to a Soviet Communist Party Congress admitting and detailing Stalin's crimes that was soon published in the *New York Times*. The speech, in fact, had reached the West through intelligence channels. Israeli intelligence gained access to a translation of the speech circulating in Communist Poland and passed it to the CIA. The CIA shared it with the State Department from which it reached the *New York Times* and other Western media. The Khrushchev speech confirmed many of the charges about the Soviet Union so long denied by American Communists, but because it came from an authoritative Soviet source, this time it could not be denied. Combined with the revelations about extensive Soviet anti-Semitism and the crushing of the Hungarian Revolution by Soviet troops, the Khrushchev speech psychologically devastated American Communists, and within two years the party lost three-quarters of its already small membership. The beliefs that had motivated the espionage of the Rosenbergs, Coplon, Bentley's recruits, and others were torn apart. The myth of the Soviet Union was shattered and never again totally glued back together. What was left of the American Communist Party was a tiny, ineffectual, and isolated shell. The demise of the ideological spy reflected the demise of the ideology.

Even those few who continued to cling to Communist ideology, however, were usually in no position to assist its implementation by spying. The federal government's assault on the CPUSA during the 1940s and 1950s had deeply wounded it and destroyed the party's ability to serve as a recruiting ground for espionage. The loyalty-security program, sometimes applied in a heavy-handed manner, had resulted in the firing or resignations of almost everyone with Communist ties from federal employment. Not only were there fewer people with the ideological motive to spy, there were far fewer of them with either the means or the opportunity. And even those spies who were motivated by residual Communist sympathies, such as Stand and Squillacote, did so individually and not as part of a political organization that encouraged and supported espionage. By the 1950s FBI penetration of the American Communist Party made its continuing function as an auxiliary to Soviet intelligence too risky. The KGB continued contact with the top leadership of the CPUSA, but chiefly as a communications channel for sensitive political information and for delivery of secret Soviet subsidies for the party's political work.

That is not to say, of course, that espionage became a trivial problem. Nonideological spies present their own difficulties for counterespionage investigations. They may well be harder to keep out of sensitive positions precisely because their decision to spy stems from the opportunity to benefit themselves, and their pasts may lack any obvious markers or signals to alert authorities. Even in the 1930s and 1940s, a relatively small number of Communists worked for the government in sensitive positions, but there will always be individuals in financial difficulty or disgruntled about their careers or with some deep secret or shameful blemish that can subject them to blackmail.

Although such spies can do enormous damage to American interests, there is something particularly jarring to most Americans about ideological spies. The person who betrays his country for money or has a personal grievance against his superiors may be despicable, but he is, in a way, easy to understand. Aldrich Ames, a veteran CIA officer who betrayed scores of American agents to the Soviet Union, wanted fancy cars and a nice house and had no compunction about betraying anyone and anything to obtain them. Ames's motivation was neither complicated nor difficult to understand. The Americans who betrayed secrets because they admired Joseph Stalin's Russia or believed that the United States was fascist, however, were more puzzling and more frightening because they rejected the very political and social system under which so many of them flourished.

Spy Trials and Understanding Soviet Espionage

The spy trials of the 1940s and 1950s were only partially successful in helping Americans understand the nature of Soviet espionage, the motivations of the Americans who engaged in it, its extent, and the amount of damage it caused. In part, that was a consequence of the need to protect secrets, to cloak counterintelligence methods and techniques, to develop and present cases as streamlined as possible, and to accommodate restrictions on legally admissible evidence. That is to say, trials can rarely expose everything about a particular issue or case and even less when the underlying crime is as sensitive as espionage.

That said, there was tremendous variation among the trials. Alger Hiss and the Rosenbergs received intense media scrutiny and significantly affected public attitudes. Judith Coplon's trials were scenes of farce and melodrama. The *Amerasia* case was so plagued by evidentiary problems and political interference that its quick resolution through plea bargains created a festering sore that helped to ignite the McCarthy era.

Through defectors, confessions, decoded KGB cables, or other sources, the FBI identified several hundred Americans as having consciously assisted and cooperated with Soviet espionage against the United States in 1930s and 1940s. Fewer than two dozen were ever prosecuted. Counterintelligence, however, is not primarily about putting spies in jail, as satisfying as that may be. The chief priority of counterintelligence is denying foreign powers and, sometimes, domestic subversives access to information that might threaten American national security. Counterintelligence is principally concerned with disrupting foreign espionage networks, identifying and neutralizing those cooperating with them, and preventing the loss of government secrets. Sending spies to prison is a lesser concern and may actually get in the way of the chief priorities if sensitive information or informants have to be disclosed in open court.

The outcome of the Bentley case is a perfect example of how trials, or their absence, can distort perspectives. Given that she first went to the FBI with her story in 1945 and accused dozens of government employees of espionage in public testimony in 1948, it is striking that only two ever served any prison time and both of them for offenses far less serious than espionage. For decades historians used the paucity of successful prosecutions as prima facie evidence that her story was more fiction than fact and as a weapon with which to pummel the FBI for orchestrating a witch-hunt of innocent people.

While successful prosecutions in which the irrefutable evidence from decrypted Venona cables punctured the self-serving denials and the bland refusals to testify would undoubtedly have been both morally satisfying and just, the decision to forgo justice in the interest of counterintelligence was more bureaucratically compelling. No one can know the effect of spies like Ted Hall being confronted with the Venona cables and threatened with convictions. Would they have broken down and confessed? Would Venona cables have been accepted in court as legally admissible evidence? Since the Soviets were partially aware of the Venona project's cryptanalytic breakthrough, was keeping the deciphered cables secret worth allowing numerous spies to avoid legal punishment for their betrayal of their country?

Although many of the guilty escaped punishment, the FBI did accomplish many of its primary counterintelligence goals. Those people Bentley identified were put under surveillance and isolated from sensitive information. By 1947 most were no longer employed by the federal government and were neutralized as security threats. The KGB understood that her defection had precipitated an intelligence disaster for the USSR. Anatoly Gorsky, head of the KGB station in the United States at the time of her defection, prepared a memo entitled "Collapses in the United States" in 1948 to catalog the damage done to the KGB operation by five defectors. He listed forty-three Soviet sources and KGB field officers identified to American authorities by Bentley. Only two of them went to prison, but the memo makes clear that a significant portion of the Soviet espionage network in the United States was exposed and rendered useless.

Counterespionage and the American Criminal Justice System

The very tools of counterintelligence endangered criminal prosecutions. Telephone wiretaps and electronic surveillance are and were essential in most counterintelligence operations. After a 1937 Supreme Court decision prohibited the introduction of wiretap evidence in court, Congress took thirty years to enact a remedy. Meanwhile, American presidents and their attorney generals administratively authorized the FBI and other security officials to use secret wiretaps in national security investigations. Although this allowed investigations to go forward, it complicated and often blocked successful prosecutions because of the need to keep such activities secret. Even more problematically, judges disallowed other evidence if it appeared that a wiretap had led to its discovery, invoking the legal concept of "fruit of a poisoned tree" – namely, that valid evidence became tainted if obtained improperly and should not be admitted at trial.

In 1968 Congress statutorily legalized wiretaps when authorized by judicial warrant and permitted warrantless wiretaps in national security cases. After another adverse Supreme Court case, Congress enacted a more comprehensive solution in 1978, the Foreign Intelligence Surveillance Act (FISA). FISA created a secure forum, the Foreign Intelligence Surveillance Court, to provide timely and secret approval of government requests for national security wiretaps and other electronic surveillance. The special court consisted of seven federal district court judges designated by the chief justice of the United States. It also created a special three-member court of review to hear appeals of denials of government applications. FISA required that the government's applications for electronic surveillance include detailed information about the targets, what facts justify the belief that the targets are agents of foreign powers, and the means of conducting the surveillance. In the wake of the September 11, 2001, terrorism attacks, Congress expanded FISA to include authorization of secret physical searches and certain other methods of gathering evidence. However, FISA's standards were premised on rapidly obsolescing telephone technology, and the rapid advance of newer communications technology, particularly the Internet, has outpaced much of FISA's structure. Consequently, presidents both in the 1990s and after 2001 have used their constitutional authority as commander in chief to authorize some types of electronic intelligence activities outside FISA. Critics have objected to these presidential actions and are attempting to contest them in federal courts.

One of the most effective defense strategies in espionage prosecutions has long been to threaten the counterintelligence function of the government by demanding access to a wide range of government investigatory records under "discovery" procedures in a criminal trial, a defense technique sometimes termed "graymail." The actual secrets the government was seeking to protect or sensitive FBI records of its counterintelligence sources and methods could be put at risk. Often the government would forgo prosecution rather than disclose sensitive information in open court, where it would immediately be known to America's foreign enemies. The failure of the Rosenberg defense team to employ this tactic may not have cost their clients their freedom, but it certainly made the prosecution's task easier.

When faced with the graymail tactic, different judges created different balances between protecting national security and protecting defendants' rights, forcing prosecutors to craft strategies for particular trials on an ad hoc basis. In a very belated response to this confusion, in 1980 the Congress passed the Classified Information Procedures Act (CIPA) establishing detailed procedures for handling such classified information in criminal trials. CIPA provided that government prosecutors could request that a judge review classified information demanded by a defense attorney under discovery procedures both *in camera* (nonpublicly, in judicial chambers) and *ex parte* (presented by only one side, the government, without the presence of defense attorneys). The judge would then rule on what classified information necessarily had to be disclosed in order for the defendant to present an adequate defense and included an option of substituting unclassified summaries for the sensitive materials. CIPA called upon judges to balance the need of the government to protect intelligence information and the right of a defendant to a fair trial. CIPA reduced but did not eliminate the graymail problem in espionage and terrorism cases because a large element of individual judicial discretion (arbitrariness) remained.

The question of justice does not relate only to the successful prosecution of people for crimes they did commit. There was wide variation and inconsistency in sentences handed down to those who were convicted. Ethel Rosenberg received a death sentence even though the government knew that she was a minor participant in her husband's espionage ring; her trial and conviction was largely a lever, an unsuccessful one, to get him to talk. William Perl provided the Soviets with very significant military aviation technology, but he was convicted only of perjury and received five years in prison because Venona could not be used in court. Robert Soblen directed his espionage largely against political opponents of Stalin's regime, not the American government, yet he received a sentence of life in prison.

The Elusive Balance between Security and Liberty

The trade-offs between protecting the United States and its people from foreign espionage (or contemporary Jihadist terrorism) and the usual practices of the American criminal justice system are not easy to make. Most Americans regard the elaborate protections of the right of the accused afforded in the American criminal justice system as highly valued and precious protections of personal liberty against arbitrary government power and are willing to accept the trade-off that, in order to reduce the chances of convicting an innocent person, these procedures allow a guilty party to go free in some criminal cases. In theory, most Americans would like to have matters of espionage (or ideological terrorism) dealt with in the same way. In the real world, however, Americans have reacted differently when the threat of espionage or terrorism became serious.

During the American Civil War President Lincoln not only imposed military rule over the rebelling southern states but also suspended the right of habeas corpus and gave military courts jurisdiction over civilians in sections of loyal states that harbored large numbers of southern sympathizers (known as "copperheads"). In answer to complaints that he had suspended a precious liberty, Lincoln tartly remarked, "Are all the laws, but one, to go unexecuted, and the government go to pieces, lest that one be violated?" While the Civil War raged, federal courts avoided interfering with Lincoln's wartime action. But in 1866 in *Ex Parte Milligan*, the Supreme Court found that the U.S. military officers had exceeded their authority by trying a civilian Confederate sympathizer in Indiana – a state where the normal functioning of the court system had not been interrupted by the war. It was, however, only an after-the-fact objection to Lincoln's wartime action. By 1866 southern secession had been defeated, and with that defeat the subversive threat of southern sympathizers that had prompted Lincoln's suspension of habeas corpus and authorization of military tribunals to try civilians had vanished as well.

Through much of the 1930s most Americans shrugged off warnings about the potential threat of the pro-Nazi German-American Bund and native movements such as the Silver Shirts that emulated the practices and doctrines of European fascism. There were some congressional investigations, and President Roosevelt ordered the FBI to watch these organizations, but otherwise the federal government did not launch any prosecutorial actions against them. But as tensions in Europe grew in the late 1930s and war approached, Americans became more alarmed about reports of Nazi use of pro-fascist sympathizers, the "fifth column," to prepare the way for German aggression, a tactic used with particular success in 1940 to assist the German conquest of Norway, the Netherlands, and Belgium. Congress passed the Foreign Agents Registration Act in 1938 requiring those promoting the interests or disseminating the propaganda of a foreign power to register with the Justice Department and in 1939 denied federal jobs to members of organizations advocating overthrow of the government. The Smith Act of 1940 made it a federal crime to urge military insubordination or advocate the violent overthrow of the government, and the Voorhis Act of 1941 required the registration of organizations having foreign ties and advocating the violent overthrow of the government.

In 1942, after America had entered the war, Nazi submarines landed eight spies on the Atlantic coast, four on a Long Island beach and four in Florida. Two of the spies were naturalized Americans, one a German immigrant who had gained citizenship by service in the U.S. Army. All had been trained for a variety of sabotage missions. All were also quickly captured when one of the team turned himself in to the FBI. President Roosevelt immediately decided that they would not be tried in an ordinary American civilian court. The spies had been caught before carrying out a single act of sabotage or even undertaking any direct preparation for an act of sabotage. And the American criminal justice system is geared to trying someone for an overt act that was carried out, not an act that was merely contemplated or intended. A civilian court proceeding could have turned into a circus with defense lawyers seeking endless delays and might have resulted in a judge's decision to reduce the charges to a lesser crime because no actual sabotage had taken place or even to dismiss charges altogether. Instead, Roosevelt ordered the creation of a special military commission that would try the captured Nazi agents as enemy combatants found behind American lines in civilian clothing, a violation of the laws of war that would subject them to the death penalty. At the trial, appointed military lawyers represented them. The accused admitted they had been trained as saboteurs but claimed they had had no choice but to go along and never intended to carry out their mission once they reached America. All were found guilty and sentenced to death. President Roosevelt reviewed the decision and reduced the sentences of two who had cooperated fully with American authorities: one to thirty years and another to life in prison. The other six spies were executed.

During the trial, one of the military lawyers appointed to represent the defendants appealed to the Supreme Court, arguing that the president had no authority to appoint the military tribunal and that the accused should be tried in a civilian court under the usual rules of the American criminal justice system. The Supreme Court rejected the petition in *Ex Parte Quirin* (1942), holding that the president had acted within his authority as commander in chief in wartime. Decades later legal purists looked back at Roosevelt's military tribunal and *Ex Parte Quirin* with horror as departures from their theoretical ideal that even in wartime spies, saboteurs, terrorists, and other irregular combatants should be treated in accordance with the practices of the ordinary criminal law and tried in civilian courts with civilian judges and juries. During World War II, however, few Americans thought that enemy combatants should be given the rights of defendants in ordinary American courts.

In the Cold War the balance between security and accustomed American liberty also became a question, but a more difficult one. World War II had been an open, armed conflict with officially designated enemy nations. The Cold War, in contrast, was a twilight struggle waged covertly over many decades and often through proxies, although a number of regional "hot" wars were fought on the periphery of the main struggle.

There were those who refused any trade-off, demanding that security must always give way to accustomed freedoms and liberties. Supreme Court Justice Robert H. Jackson responded to the absolutist position in his dissenting opinion in *Terminiello v. Chicago* (1949). The majority overturned the disorderly conduct conviction of an anti-Semite whose pro-Nazi rantings at a rally had incited a riot. The court held that Chicago's breach-of-the-peace ordinance violated the free speech rights guaranteed by the First Amendment. Jackson in his dissent wrote, "The choice is not between order and liberty. It is between liberty with order and anarchy without either. There is danger that, if the court does not temper its doctrinaire logic with a little practical wisdom, it will convert the constitutional Bill of Rights into a suicide pact." Jackson's view paralleled that of Lincoln – that in the midst of a desperate civil war he was not going to privilege one right, habeas corpus, at the cost of the survival of the American union.

Jackson's view was a minority one in *Terminiello v. Chicago*, but the majority of the court just a year later cited Jackson's position in *Communications Assn. v. Douds* (1950) when it upheld a provision of the National Labor Relations Act requiring officials of unions making use of its protections to file declarations that they were not members of the CPUSA. The plaintiffs had argued that these declarations were violations of First Amendment free speech rights. Chief Justice Vincent for the majority noted one of the purposes of the Labor Management Relations Act was to remove the obstructions to the free flow of commerce resulting from political strikes instigated by Communists who had infiltrated labor organizations and subordinated legitimate trade-union objectives to obstructive strikes when dictated by Communist Party leaders, often in support of the policies of a foreign government. He wrote that in light of the law's goal, the anti-Communist affidavit was reasonable and to take the opposite view "hardly commends itself to reason unless, indeed, the Bill of Rights has been converted into a 'suicide pact.'" It is, however, a measure of the difficulty of judging an appropriate balance between security and liberty that Justice Jackson dissented in *Communications Assn. v. Douds*, arguing that in this particular case the balance between liberty and order should be decided for the former.

In the late 1940s and early 1950s, the internal threat posed by the American Communist Party, both as a subversive political force and an auxiliary to Soviet espionage, loomed large. But by the late 1950s that threat had vanished. The CPUSA had become politically isolated by 1950 and imploded in 1956 under the impact of Khrushchev's speech on Stalin's crimes and the Soviet suppression of the Hungarian Revolution. While it experienced a minor revival in the heyday of the New Left in the 1970s, the CPUSA remained on the margins of politics. Absent a real internal Communist threat, the need for trade-offs between security and liberty became unnecessary, and federal courts invalidated or Congress repealed many of the internal security laws of the 1940s and early 1950s.

But balancing accustomed liberties with security needs always reoccurs when a significant threat to national security emerges. In the wake of the September 11, 2001, Jihadist terrorist attacks on the United States, the Congress significantly expanded the government's internal security authority in the Patriot Act. The president, the federal courts, and the Congress are also engaged in an as yet unresolved debate over the appropriateness of military tribunals or ordinary federal courts for the trials of enemy combatants and terrorists. And those cases that have gone to ordinary federal courts have confronted the same dilemmas faced in several of the early Cold War spy trials where defense lawyers demanded disclosure of counterintelligence information that the government insists would seriously harm its efforts to protect the public against terrorist attacks. In light of real threats to national security, doctrinaire logic must be tempered with practical wisdom, or one does risk converting the "Bill of Rights into a suicide pact." The difficulty, an inherent one, is in determining how serious the threat is and, in light of that threat, what is the proper balance between security and liberty.

FURTHER READINGS

Belknap, Michael R. *Cold War Political Justice: The Smith Act, the Communist Party, and American Civil Liberties.* Westport, Conn.: Greenwood Press, 1977.

Chase, Harold William. *Security and Liberty: The Problem of Native Communists, 1947–1955.* Garden City, N.Y.: Doubleday, 1955.

Fisher, Louis. *Nazi Saboteurs on Trial: A Military Tribunal and American Law.* Lawrence: University Press of Kansas, 2003.

Guttmann, Allen, and Benjamin Munn Ziegler. *Communism, the Courts, and the Constitution.* Boston: D. C. Heath, 1964.

Hook, Sidney. *Heresy, Yes – Conspiracy, No!* New York: J. Day, 1953.

Hook, Sidney. *Political Power and Personal Freedom: Critical Studies in Democracy, Communism, and Civil Rights.* New York: Criterion Books, 1959.

Rehnquist, William H. *All the Laws but One: Civil Liberties in Wartime.* New York: Knopf, 1998.

Sabin, Arthur J. *In Calmer Times: The Supreme Court and Red Monday.* Philadelphia: University of Pennsylvania Press, 1999.

Whitfield, Stephen J. "Civil Liberties and the Culture of the Cold War, 1945–1965" (chapter 5). In *Crucible of Liberty: 200 Years of the Bill of Rights*, edited by Raymond Arsenault. New York: Free Press, 1991.

Index